The Hyperkinetic Child

To Philip

THE HYPERKINETIC CHILD

A Bibliography of Medical, Educational, and Behavioral Studies

CAROL ANN WINCHELL

Greenwood Press

WESTPORT, CONNECTICUT • LONDON, ENGLAND

Library of Congress Cataloging in Publication Data

Winchell, Carol Ann.
  The hyperkinetic child.

  Includes indexes.
  1. Hyperactive children—Bibliography. I. Title.
[DNLM: 1. Hyperkinesis—In infancy and childhood—
Bibliography. ZWS350 W759h 1950-74]
Z5814.C52W53   016.6189'28'5   74-28527
ISBN 0-8371-7813-4

Library of Congress Catalog Card Number: 74-28527
ISBN: 0-8371-7813-4

First published in 1975

Greenwood Press, a division of Williamhouse-Regency Inc.
51 Riverside Avenue, Westport, Connecticut 06880

Manufactured in the United States of America

TABLE OF CONTENTS

PREFACE

PURPOSE

During the last decade the syndrome of hyperkinesis in children has received a tremendous amount of attention from physicians, educators, parents, legislators, and the general community. This overwhelming interest is reflected in the accelerated rate of publication in both popular and professional literature. The present bibliography has been prepared to facilitate the search for current and retrospective sources of information, and to help provide a much needed measure of bibliographic control to a rapidly expanding body of literature.

During an initial search of the literature a researcher quickly discovers that little standardization appears in terminology from one source to another. A U.S. Department of Health, Education, and Welfare report of 1966 (Item number thirty-nine in text) lists thirty-eight different terms used to describe the conditions generally designated as "minimal brain dysfunction." During an extensive search of the literature in various disciplines, seventy-five research terms were located concerning the hyperkinetic phenomenon and related topics (Appendix A). Research, then, is extremely difficult when there are numerous interchangeably used subject headings, and frequently it is impossible to separate discussions of the hyperkinetic child from those of larger entities. The individual descriptors alone have been defined differently by various interest specialists at differing points in time. This bibliography does not attempt to standardize the terminology of this ill-defined syndrome, but merely to collect references on the recently recognized disease manifestation commonly referred to as hyperkinesis or hyperactivity, and to treat this syndrome as the most obvious item in a symptom complex.

COVERAGE

The bibliography primarily covers the period from the 1950s through June 1974, with emphasis on the 1960s. In an effort to be complete and to give a historical perspective to the work, the "classic" studies of the early twentieth century are included.

SCOPE

Since the subject is broad and interdisciplinary, an attempt has been made to be comprehensive rather than selective. The hyperkinetic child is placed in his total environment; references cover the gifted, the "typical," the educable mentally retarded, and the institutionalized child. Topics include the syndrome and its characteristics, etiological studies, diagnostic procedures, management, the child in the classroom, and related research studies.

Nearly 1,900 citations have been culled from an extensive search of both manual and computerized information sources. Over 300 medical, educational, and psychological journals (popular and professional) were covered, as well as many abstracting and indexing sources. Also included are books, chapters in books, conference reports, proceedings of symposia, government documents, pamphlets, and theses and dissertations. Items excluded are (1) studies on animals, (2) unpublished papers, (3) foreign language references, (4) personal correspondence, (5) newspaper articles, and (6) speeches.

ARRANGEMENT

Entries are grouped according to the major categories listed in the Table of Contents. Arrangement of entries within each category is determined primarily by evaluative judgment. Each entry is cited only once under the most significant topic. When two or three broad categories are discussed together in an article, placement has been with the subject that is dealt with first or that was given the predominant focus in the article. Since there is much overlapping between subjects, the user should consult the Selective Key Word Subject Index for specific concepts.

Within each section, arrangement is alphabetical by author. Entry numbers preceding the authors' names run consecutively through the text.

THE ENTRIES

For monographs the complete citation includes author, title, edition used, place, publisher, date, pages, and inclusive pages of sections appearing as parts of larger works. Journal citations contain author (three are given; *et al.* is used to signify additional names), title of the article, journal abbreviation, volume number, issue number (in parentheses), month, year, and inclusive pages. Abstracts of doctoral dissertations can be found in *Dissertation Abstracts International,* with volume number, issue number, page, and date given. Books and conference proceedings have been verified and entered in the bibliography under the U.S. Library of Congress *National Union Catalog: Author List* entry to facilitate retrieval for the user. On those occasions when the main entry is the book title, cross references are used from the authors' or editors' names. EC and ED numbers (Eric Document numbers) have been included where available.

APPENDICES

Appendix A, Nomenclature, alphabetically lists the various research terms applied to the syndrome.

Appendix B, Drugs, alphabetically lists frequently mentioned medications used to treat hyperkinesis. The generic name, trade name, manufacturer, and date of issue are given.

Appendix C, List of Journal Abbreviations, alphabetically lists all journals cited in the text. Journal title abbreviations have been formulated according to the rules of the *American National Standard for the Abbreviation of Titles of Periodicals* (American

National Standards Institute, 1969), and the individual words of the title are abbreviated according to the forms given in the *International List of Periodical Title Word Abbreviations* (Paris: ICSU-AB Secretariat, 1970).

INDICES

The Author Index includes the personal names of all individuals in the text who are cited as author, joint author, editor, or compiler, including up to four names per citation. Forenames and surnames are given in most cases. Numbers following the names refer to item numbers in the text.

The Selective Key Word Subject Index alphabetically lists important words in entry titles. The user may find it desirable to use the browsing capabilities of the broad subject arrangement, or this index may be consulted for more specific aspects of the topic. In general, (1) only unique words are given—approximate synonyms for the syndrome and other high frequency terms are omitted; (2) phrases are used to put certain words in more meaningful contexts, with *see also* references between the phrases and the individual words; and (3) inclusive item numbers are given for terms synonymous with those used in the Table of Contents. Numbers following the words refer to item numbers in the text.

ACKNOWLEDGMENTS

Expressions of gratitude are in order for my husband, son, and parents, who have patiently coexisted in my "3 x 5" world for several years. I am also indebted to Professor Jo-Ann Suleiman, coordinator of Library Services, The Ohio State University Health Sciences Library, for indexing and editorial assistance; Dr. Irene Hoadley, assistant director of Administrative Services, The Ohio State University Libraries, for publication advice; and Mrs. Noelle P. Cooper, information specialist, Mechanized Information Center, The Ohio State University Libraries, for assistance with the subject index. Thanks also to Miss Robin Lamb, my typist, and Miss Eleanor Devlin, head, Reference Department, The Ohio State University Libraries, whose cooperation made this project easier.

INTRODUCTION

Hyperactivity is generally recognized as one aspect or one variant of the broad spectrum of abnormal behaviors in childhood that are now commonly linked together under the heading "minimal brain dysfunction syndrome." The phenomenological, etiological, and conceptual variability of this group of disorders of mental performance appears to be documented by the existence of some forty synonyms.[1] The one functional element that interconnects all of these children is a reduction of academic achievement— often selectively, at least at first, with regard to the acquisition of reading and writing skills—in the presence of cognitive abilities and a level of general intelligence that are higher than could be extrapolated from much of the performance in school.[2] I prefer this functional definition of the intelligence of these children over the widely used terms of *near average, average,* and *above average* because there are indeed (and it should be recognized) many scholastic underachievers throughout the whole range of intelligence from the superior to the retarded. By limiting the concept of learning disability, which is one of the synonyms of the disease, to the child with normal intelligence, we would exclude many on a generally lower level of cognitive functioning who are nevertheless in need of specific techniques of remedial reading.

The estimate of incidence has been given by Masland[3] as occurring in from 5 to 10 percent of the school population and in more than 15 percent of urban, nonwhite, bilingual, and disadvantaged populations.[4] This attests to a fact of utmost importance with regard to the pathogenesis of developmental disabilities such as developmental dyslexia (yet another synonym): that a wide range of environmental factors will contribute to compound a primary handicap once a child has become vulnerable.

In addition to learning difficulties, the core symptomatology of minimal brain dysfunction syndrome in populations of school age children includes hyperactivity, distractibility, un-coordination, short attention span, and "perceptual" difficulties. However, in the individual child, these behaviors have not been shown to intercorrelate, and the presence of one or more of them does not predict the others.[5, 6, 7]

Hyperactivity, together with poor attention span, is clearly among those clinical signs that are most frequently part of the syndrome. In fact, a significant degree of hyperactivity is practically always associated with at least some learning difficulties and with behavior that is at least in part at variance with environmental expectations. Yet, it is still largely a matter of conjecture whether these occur secondary to hyperactivity or whether some underlying cause may directly produce both an unusual pattern of motor behavior (hyperactivity, rarely hypoactivity) as well as abnormalities of more complex human performance (learning, emotionality, social behavior).

Whereas the term *minimal brain dysfunction* clearly implies some (poorly understood, by no means unitary, and never universally proven) organicity,[8] the pathogenesis of the hyperactivity could be interpreted in different ways in even those unequivocally brain-damaged children that were originally described by Strauss and Lehtinen.[9] Certainly, changes in the rate of motor behavior do represent an important means of expression in many psychiatric states in both children as well as adults.[10]

On the other hand, every clinician has observed clearly, and seemingly primarily, hyperactive infants and has seen in young children that excessive, empty, and purpose-less hyperactivity that gives an impression of the child being "driven" by a physiologic rather than a psychological force. In prospective studies Drillien has demonstrated a statistically significant relationship between hyperactivity and behavior problems and low birth weight.[11] Evidence in favor of a genetic component in hyperactivity has been advanced by Morrison and Stewart.[12]

The finding of so-called soft neurological signs, however, which is frequently used to support the concept of minimal brain dysfunction, appears to be quite variable, irregular, and unreliable.[13]

Following the discovery of the vigilance and arousal regulating functions of the mesencephalic reticular formation by Moruzzi and Magoun[14] and the demonstration of the beneficial effect of amphetamines in a considerable number of hyperactive and learning impaired children,[15] a more subtle organic etiological concept has been developed. The prevalent hypothesis is that hyperactive children are congenitally over-aroused and that amphetamines dampen this arousal.[16] However, the opposite has also been suggested: hyperactive children have a state of particularly low arousal[17] and therefore are in a constant "search for a stimulus."

A number of studies have implicated quite specific focal brain lesions in locations other than the reticular activating system.[18-22]

Recently, Paul H. Wender has undertaken the monumental task of integrating many of the various neuroanatomical, biochemical, pharmacological, neuropathological, genetic, epidemiological, and clinical aspects of this multifaceted syndrome into a comprehensive neuropsychological theory, based on a conditioning model.[8]

Personally, I would like to think that hyperactivity represents a specific response in childhood to a variety of repetitive, unpleasant but not overwhelming stimuli, both internal as well as external, primary as well as secondary, monofactorial as well as multi-factorial. Hyperactivity is probably the single most common disorder seen by child psychiatrists, particularly when it occurs as part of the minimal brain dysfunction syndrome.

Regardless of the underlying theory and, more often than not, even the detailed etiology, treatment nearly always calls for a combination of medical, psychological, and educational measures. If handled properly, the management of these children will be highly rewarding.

Gerhard E. Martin, M.D.   Assistant Professor in   The Division of Neurology
                             Medicine (Neurology)   Department of Medicine,
                             The Nisonger Center for   Ohio State University
                             Mental Retardation and   1580 Cannon Drive
                             Developmental Disabilities Columbus, Ohio 43210

                                                        April 1974

NOTES

1. U. S., Department of Health, Education and Welfare, Public Health Service, *Minimal Brain Dysfunction in Children; Terminology and Identification, Phase One of a Three-Phase Project* (Washington, D.C.: Government Printing Office, 1966).

2. U. S., Department of Health, Education and Welfare, Public Health Service, *Central Processsing Dysfunctions in Children; a Review of Research, Phase Three of a Three-Phase Project* (Washington, D.C.: Government Printing Office, 1969), p. 147.

3. U. S., Congress, House, Committee on Appropriations, *Testimony by R. Masland,* before a subcommittee of the Committee on Appropriations, House of Representatives, 89th Congress, 1st session, part 3 (Washington, D.C.: Government Printing Office, 1965).

4. Leon Eisenberg, "The Epidemiology of Reading Retardation and a Program for Preventive Intervention," *The Disabled Reader,* edited by J. Money (Baltimore: The Johns Hopkins Press, 1966).

5. L. A. Sroufe, "Drug Treatment of Children with Behavior Problems. Review of Child Development Research, vol. 4," *Society for Research in Child Development Research,* edited by F. Horowitz, in press.

6. H. Palkes and M. A. Stewart, "Intellectual Ability and Performance of Hyperactive Children," *American Journal of Orthopsychiatry* 42 (1972), p. 35.

7. L. A. Sroufe and M. A. Stewart, "Treating Problem Children with Stimulant Drugs," *New England Journal of Medicine* 289, no. 8 (1973), p. 407.

8. Paul H. Wender, *Minimal Brain Dysfunction in Children* (New York: Wiley and Sons, Inc., 1971).

9. A. A. Strauss and L. E. Lehtinen, *Psychopathology and Education of the Brain-Injured Child* (New York: Grune & Stratton, 1947).

10. W. Goldfarb, "The Effect of Early Institutional Care on Adolescent Personality," *Journal of Experimental Education* 12 (1943), p. 106.

11. C. M. Drillien, "Aetiology and Outcome in Low-Birthweight Infants," *Developmental Medicine and Child Neurology* 14 (1972), p. 563.

12. J. R. Morrison and M. A. Stewart, "A Family Study of the Hyperactive Child Syndrome," *Biological Psychiatry* 3 (1971), p. 189.

13. J. S. Werry, "Organic Factors in Childhood Pathology," in *The Psychopathological Disorders of Childhood,* edited by H. C. Quay and J. S. Werry (New York: Wiley and Sons, Inc., 1972).

14. G. Moruzzi and H. W. Magoun, "Brain Stem Reticular Formation and Activation of the EEG," *Electroencephalography and Clinical Neurophysiology* 1 (1949), p. 455.

15. C. Bradley, "The Behavior of Children Receiving Benzedrine," *American Journal of Psychiatry* 94 (1937), p. 577.

16. M. W. Laufer, E. Denhoff, and G. Solomons, "Hyperkinetic Impulse Disorder in Children's Behavior Problems," *Psychosomatic Medicine* 19 (1957), p. 38.

17. J. H. Satterfield and M. E. Dawson, "Electrodermal Correlates of Hyperactivity in Children," *Psychophysiology* 8 (1971), p. 191.

18. T. C. Ruch and J. F. Fulton (editors), *Medical Physiology and Biophysics,* 18th edition (Philadelphia: W. B. Saunders Co., 1960).

19. F. W. Maire and H. D. Patton, "Neural Structures Involved in the Genesis of 'Preoptic Pulmonary Edema,' Gastric Erosions and Behavior Changes," *American Journal of Physiology* 184 (1956), p. 345.

20. G. D. Davis, "Effects of Central Excitant and Depressant Drugs on Locomotor Activity in the Monkey," *American Journal of Physiology* 188 (1958), p. 619.

21. J. T. Coyle and S. H. Snyder, "Catecholamine Uptake by Synaptosomes in Homogenates of Rat Brain: Stereospecifity in Different Areas," *Journal of Pharmacology and Experimental Therapy* 170 (1969), p. 221.

22. A. Routtenberg, "The Two-Arousal Hypothesis: Reticular Formation and Limbic System," *Psychological Review* 75 (1968), p. 51.

The Hyperkinetic Child

If a man does not keep pace with his companions, perhaps it is because he hears a different drummer. Let him step to the music which he hears, however measured or far away.

—Thoreau

SECTION 1

INTRODUCTORY RESEARCH

A. The Syndrome: Descriptions and Symptomatology

1 Adler, Sidney J. Your overactive child: normal or not? New York: Medcom, 1972. 70p.

2 Anderson, Camilla M. Jan, my brain-damaged daughter. Portland, Oregon: Durham, 1963. 188p.

3 ———. "Minimal brain damage." Ment Hyg* 56(2): 62-66, Spring, 1972.

4 Anthony, E. James. "A psychodynamic model of minimal brain dysfunction." Ann NY Acad Sci 205: 52-60, February 28, 1973.

5 Arnold, L. Eugene, and Knopp, Walter. "The making of a myth." JAMA 223(11): 1273-74, March 12, 1973.

6 Aron, Alan M. "Minimal cerebral dysfunction in childhood." J Commun Disord 5(2): 142-53, July, 1972.

7 Baker, Harry J. Introduction to exceptional children. 3rd ed. New York: Macmillan, 1959. 523p.

8 Bakwin, Harry, ed. "Developmental disorders of motility and language." Pediatr Clin North Am 15(3): 565-67, August, 1968.

9 Bakwin, Harry, and Bakwin, Ruth M. Behavior disorders in children. 4th ed. Philadelphia: Saunders, 1972. 714p.

10 Battle, Esther S., and Lacey, Beth. "Context for hyperactivity in children, overtime." Child Dev 43(3): 757-73, September, 1972.

11 Bauman, S. S., and Greene, S. K. "Brain dysfunction in adolescence: II. Life Styles." Am J Orthopsychiatry 40(2): 334-35, March, 1970.

12 Bax, Martin O. "The active and over-active school child." Dev Med Child Neurol 14(1): 83-86, February, 1972.

13 ———. "The larger half." Dev Med Child Neurol 13(2): 135-36, April, 1971.

* Journal title abbreviations are given in Appendix C.

Becker, Wesley, ed.
see Conference on Children with Minimal Brain Impairment, University of Illinois, 1963. Proceedings. (Item No. 42).

14 Bender, Lauretta. "Psychological problems of children with organic brain disease." Am J Orthopsychiatry 19(3): 404-15, July, 1949.

15 ————. "The psychology of children suffering from organic disturbances of the cerebellum." Am J Orthopsychiatry 10(2): 287-93, April, 1940.

16 Bender, Lauretta, ed. Psychopathology of children with organic brain disorders. Springfield, Illinois: Thomas, 1956. 151p.

17 Benton, Arthur L. "Minimal brain dysfunction from a neuropsychological point of view." Ann NY Acad Sci 205: 29-37, February 28, 1973.

18 Bettelheim, Bruno. "Bringing up children: hyperkinetic children." Ladies Home J 90: 28-29, 130, February, 1973.

19 Birch, Herbert G. "Brain-injured children: a definition of the problem." Rehabil Lit 25(2): 34-39, February, 1964.

20 ————. "The problem of 'brain damage' in children." In: Birch, Herbert G., ed. Brain damage in children: the biological and social aspects. Baltimore: Williams & Wilkins, 1964. 3-12.

21 Birch, Herbert G., ed. Brain damage in children: the biological and social aspects. Baltimore: Williams & Wilkins, 1964. 199p.

22 Blackman, Bernice. "A comparison of hyperactive and non-hyperactive problem children." Smith Coll Stud Social Work 4: 54-66, 1933.

23 Bond, Earl D. "Postencephalitic, ordinary and extraordinary children." J Pediatr 1(3): 310-14, September, 1932.

Boshes, Benjamin.
see Minimal brain damage in children: final report. (Item No. 135).

24 Bradley, Charles. "Characteristics and management of children with behavior problems associated with organic brain damage." Pediatr Clin North Am 4: 1049-60, November, 1957.

25 Brain damage in school age children. H. Carl Haywood, editor. Washington, D. C.: Council for Exceptional Children, 1968. 273p.

26 Brandon, S. "Overactivity in childhood." J Psychosom Res 15(4): 411-15, December, 1971.

27 Brazelton, T. B. "Children who can't sit still." Redbook 139: 70-71ff., August, 1972.

28 Burks, Harold F. "The hyperkinetic child." Except Child 27(1): 18-26, September, 1960.

29 ————. "Research on pseudo-mental retardation." In: Rothstein, Jerome H., ed. Mental retardation: readings and resources. New York: Holt, Rinehart & Winston, 1961. 64-68.

30 Burr, C. W. "The nervous child." NY Med J 114: 205-10, 1921.

31 Burrows, W. G. "Minimal cerebral dysfunction." Nebr State Med J 56(11): 444-47, November, 1971.

32 Cameron, K.; Lewis, Melvin; Stone, Frederick H. "Is there a syndrome of brain damage in children?" Cereb Palsy Bull 3(1): 74-77, 1961.

33 Caplan, Gerald, ed. Emotional problems of early childhood. New York: Basic Books, 1955. 544p.

34 Chalfant, James C., and Scheffelin, Margaret. Central processing dysfunctions in children; a review of research: phase three of a three-phase project. Bethesda, Maryland: U. S. National Institutes of Health; for sale by the Superintendent of Documents, U. S. Government Printing Office, Washington, D. C., 1969. 148p. (NINDS Monograph, No. 9).

35 Chapple, P. A. "Hyperactive children." Br Med J 1: 616-17, March 10, 1973.

36 Charlton, Maurice H. "Minimal brain dysfunction and the hyperkinetic child." NY State J Med 72(16): 2058-60, August 15, 1972.

37 Childers, A. T. "Hyperactivity in children having behavior disorders." Am J Orthopsychiatry 5(2): 227-43, April, 1935.

38 CIBA Pharmaceutical Company. The child with hyperkinetic behavior problems and minimal brain dysfunction...a profile. Summit, New Jersey: CIBA Pharmaceutical Company, 1970.

39 Clements, Sam D. Minimal brain dysfunction in children; terminology and identification: phase one of a three-phase project. Washington, D. C.: U. S. Department of Health, Education and Welfare; for sale by the Superintendent of Documents, U. S. Government Printing Office, 1966. 18p. (NINDB Monograph, No. 3); (PHS Publication, No. 1415).

40 Clemmens, Raymond L. "Minimal brain damage in children—an interdisciplinary problem." Children 8(5): 179-83, September, 1961.

41 Clemmens, Raymond L., and Kenny, Thomas J. "Clinical correlates of learning disabilities, minimal brain dysfunction and hyperactivity." Clin Pediatr 11(6): 311-13, June, 1972.

42 Conference on Children with Minimal Brain Impairment, University of Illinois, 1963. Proceedings. Edited by Samuel A. Kirk and Wesley Becker. Chicago: National Society for Crippled Children and Adults, 1963. 85p.

43 Conners, C. Keith. "The syndrome of minimal brain dysfunction: psychological aspects." Pediatr Clin North Am 14(4): 749-66, November, 1967.

44 Consilia, Sister Mary. "USA in the '70's--a look at the learning-disabled child." Acad Ther 9(5): 301-8, Spring, 1974.

45 Copeland, LaVon. "Non-stop Timmy, our two-year-old terror." Redbook 137: 38-42, October, 1971.

46 Crawford, John E. Children with subtle perceptual-motor difficulties. Pittsburgh: Stanwix, 1966. 264p.

47 Cruickshank, William M. The brain-injured child in home, school and community. Syracuse, New York: Syracuse University Press, 1967. 294p.

48 Daryn, E. "Problems of children with 'diffuse brain damage.'" Arch Gen Psychiatry 4(3): 299-306, March, 1961.

49 Dekaban, Antole S. Neurology of early childhood. Baltimore: Williams & Wilkins, 1970. 488p.

50 De la Cruz, Felix; Fox, Bernard H.; Roberts, Richard H.; eds. "Minimal brain dysfunction." Ann NY Acad Sci 205: 1-396, February 28, 1973.

51 Denhoff, Eric. "Bridges to burn and to build: a presidential address." Dev Med Child Neurol 7(1): 3-8, February, 1965.

52 ———. "The hyperkinetic behavior syndrome: clinical reflections." Pediatr Ann 2(5): 15-28, May, 1973.

53 Denhoff, Eric, and Robinault, I. P. Cerebral palsy and related disorders: a developmental approach to dysfunction. New York: McGraw-Hill, 1960. 421p.

54 Derby, B. M. "Minimal brain dysfunction and the hyperkinetic child: a structural basis." NY State J Med 72: 2061-62, August 15, 1972.

55 Deutsch, Cynthia P., and Schumer, Florence. Brain-damaged children: a modality-oriented exploration of performance. New York: Brunner/Mazel, 1970. 162p.

56 DiLeo, Joseph H. "Brain damage and the 'brain-injured child.'" Young Child 20(3): 158-63, January, 1965.

57 Doyle, P. J. "Organic hyperkinetic syndrome." J Sch Health 32(8): 299-306, October, 1962.

58 Eisenberg, Leon. "Behavioral manifestations of cerebral damage in childhood." In: Birch, Herbert G., ed. Brain damage in children: the biological and social aspects. Baltimore: Williams & Wilkins, 1964. 61-77.

59 ————. "Psychiatric implications of brain damage in children." Psychiatr Q 31(1): 72-92, 1957.

60 ————. "Dynamic considerations underlying the management of the brain-damaged child." GP 14(4): 101-6, October, 1956.

61 Ellingson, Careth. "Children with no alternative." Saturday Rev 53: 67, November 21, 1970.

62 Ellis, Norman R., ed. Handbook of mental deficiency: psychological theory and research. New York: McGraw-Hill, 1963. 722p.

63 Ernhart, Claire B.; Graham, Frances K.; Eichman, P. L.; et. al. "Brain injury in the preschool child: some developmental considerations: II. Comparison of brain injured and normal children." Psychol Monogr 77(11, Whole No. 574): 17-33, 1963.

64 Ewalt, J. R. "Organic behavior problems." Tex Rep Biol Med 3: 247-52, 1945.

65 Faas, Larry A., compiler. The emotionally disturbed child: a book of readings. Springfield, Illinois: Thomas, 1970. 386p.

66 Ford, Frank R. Diseases of the nervous system in infancy, childhood and adolescence. 5th ed. Springfield, Illinois: Thomas, 1966. 1416p.

67 Freeman, Roger D. "Child psychiatry." Prog Neurol Psychiatry 23: 454-68, 1968.

68 Gamstorp, Ingrid. Pediatric neurology. New York: Appleton-Century-Crofts, 1970. 394p.

69 Gardner, Richard A. MBD; the family book about minimal brain dysfunction: I. For parents; II. For boys and girls. 2 pts. in 1. New York: Aronson, 1973. 185p.

70 Garrison, Karl C., and Force, Dewey G., Jr. "Brain-damaged children." In: Garrison, Karl C., and Force, Dewey G., Jr. The psychology of exceptional children. 4th ed. New York: Ronald, 1965. 343-59.

71 Gazzaniga, M. S. "Brain theory and minimal brain dysfunction." Ann NY Acad Sci 205: 89-92, February 28, 1973.

72 Goddard, G. F. J., and Payne, Rudolph. "Hyperactive children." Br Med J 1: 481, February 24, 1973.

73 Goering, Jacob D., and Waldrop, Mary F. "Hyperactivity and minor physical anomalies in elementary school children." Res J 1(1): 1-2, July, 1970.

74 Gofman, Helen F., and Allmond, Bayard W., Jr. Learning and language disorders in children: I. The preschool child." Curr Probl Pediatr 1(10): 1-45, August, 1971.

75 Goldstein, H., and Seigle, Dorothy M. "Characteristics of educable mentally handicapped children." In: Rothstein, Jerome H., ed. Mental retardation: readings and resources. New York: Holt, Rinehart & Winston, 1961. 204-30.

76 Gomez, Manuel R. "Minimal cerebral dysfunction." Clin Pediatr 6 (10): 589-91, October, 1967.

77 Gordon, Sol. The "brain injured" adolescent. East Orange, New Jersey: New Jersey Association for Brain-Injured Children, 1966. 12p.

78 ———. "The 'brain-injured' high school student." Acad Ther 4(2): 87-91, Winter, 1968-69.

79 Gorman, R. F. Letter: "Minimal brain dysfunction." Med J Aust 2: 908, November 10, 1973.

80 Graham, Philip, and Rutter, Michael. "Organic brain dysfunction and child psychiatric disorder." Br Med J 3: 695-700, September 21, 1968.

81 Greenberg, E. S. "Brain dysfunction in adolescence: I. Scope of the research." Am J Orthopsychiatry 40(2): 333-34, March, 1970.

82 Greenberg, Milton M.; Paine, Richmond S.; Eisenberg, Leon; et. al. "The hyperactive child." Clin Proc Child Hosp 19(9): 256-61, September, 1963.

83 Groover, Robert V. "The hyperkinetic child." Psychiatr Ann 2(1): 36-44, January, 1972.

84 Hamblin, Robert L., et. al. Humanization process: a social, behavioral analysis of children's problems. New York: Wiley, 1971. 305p.

85 Hamblin, Robert L., and Buckholdt, David. Structured exchanges and childhood learning: hyperaggressive children. St. Ann, Missouri: Central Midwestern Regional Educational Laboratory, 1967. 89p. (Program Activity, No. 12).

86 Harrison, Saul I., and McDermott, John F., compilers. Childhood psychopathology: an anthology of basic readings. New York: International Universities Press, 1972. 903p.

87 Harth, Robert, compiler. Issues in behavior disorders: a book of readings. Springfield, Illinois: Thomas, 1971. 674p.

88 Hartocollis, P. "The syndrome of minimal brain dysfunction in young adult patients." Bull Menninger Clin 32: 102-14, 1968.

89 Hatton, Daniel A. "The child with minimal cerebral dysfunction." Dev Med Child Neurol 8(1): 71-77, February, 1966.

Haywood, H. Carl, ed.
   see Brain damage in school age children. (Item No. 25).

Hellmuth, Jerome, ed.
see National Northwest Conference on the Special Child. 2nd, Seattle, 1962. The special child in century 21. (Item No. 140).

90 Howell, Mary C.; Rever, George W.; Scholl, Mary L.; et. al. "Hyper-activity in children: types, diagnosis, drug therapy, approaches to management." Clin Pediatr 11(1): 30-39, January, 1972.

91 Hughes, James G., ed. "Brain damage in children." Pediatr Clin North Am 4: 981-1092, November, 1957.

92 Hutt, Corinne; Hutt, Sidney J.; Lee, Douglas; et. al. "Arousal and childhood autism." Nature 204: 908-9, November 28, 1964.

93 Hutt, Corinne; Hutt, Sidney J.; Ounsted, Christopher. "Behavior of children with and without upper CNS lesions." Behaviour 24: 246-68, 1965.

94 Hutt, Sidney J., and Hutt, Corinne. "Hyperactivity in a group of epileptic (and some non-epileptic) brain-damaged children." Epilepsia 5(4): 334-51, December, 1964.

95 "Hyperactive children." Br Med J 1: 305-6, February 10, 1973.

96 "Hyperactive children." Br Med J 1: 481, February 24, 1973.

97 Hyperactivity; exceptional child bibliography series. Arlington, Virginia: Council for Exceptional Children, Information Center on Exceptional Children, 1971. 6p. (ED 050 521).

98 "The hyperkinetic child." Newsweek 79: 56, April 3, 1972.

99 Ingram, T. T. S. "A characteristic form of overactive behavior in brain-damaged children." J Ment Sci 102: 550-58, July, 1956.

100 Jenkins, Richard L. "Behavior disorders of childhood." Am Fam Physician 1(5): 68-73, May, 1970.

101 Jenkins, Richard L., and Stable, Galen. "Special characteristics of retarded children rated as severely hyperactive." Child Psychi-atry Hum Dev 2(1): 26-31, Fall, 1971.

102 Johnson, K. "Hyperkinetic syndrome in children." Nurs Mirror Midwives J 128: 21ff., May 23, 1969.

103 Kahn, E., and Cohen, L. H. "Organic driveness: brain-stem syn-drome and an experience, with case reports." N Engl J Med 210: 748-56, April 5, 1934.

104 Kahn, J. P. "The emotional concomitants of the brain-damaged child." J Learn Disabil 2(12): 644-51, December, 1969.

105 Kennard, Margaret A. "Behavior problems and the brain-injured child." Northwest Med 58: 1535-41, November, 1959.

106 Kenny, Thomas J., and Clemmens, Raymond L. "Medical and psychological correlates in children with learning disabilities." J Pediatr 78(2): 273-77, February, 1971.

107 Kenny, Thomas J.; Clemmens, Raymond, L.; Hudson, B. W.; et. al. "Characteristics of children referred because of hyperactivity." J Pediatr 79(4): 618-22, October, 1971.

108 Kinsbourne, Marcel. "Minimal brain dysfunction as a neurodevelopmental lag." Ann NY Acad Sci 205: 268-73, February 28, 1973.

      Kirk, Samuel A., ed.
      see Conference on Children with Minimal Brain Impairment, University of Illinois, 1963. Proceedings. (Item No. 42).

109 Knobel, Mauricio; Wolman, Mary B.; Mason, Elizabeth. "Hyperkinesis and organicity in children." Arch Gen Psychiatry 1(3): 310-21, September, 1959.

110 Kurlander, L. F., and Colodny, Dorothy. "'Pseudoneurosis' in the neurologically handicapped child." Am J Orthopsychiatry 35(4): 733-38, July, 1965.

111 Laufer, Maurice W. "Cerebral dysfunction and behavior disorders in adolescents." Am J Orthopsychiatry 32(3): 501-6, April, 1962.

112 Laufer, Maurice W.; Denhoff, Eric; Riverside, R. I. "Hyperkinetic behavior syndrome in children." J Pediatr 50(4): 463-74, April, 1957.

113 Laufer, Maurice W.; Denhoff, Eric; Solomons, Gerald. "Hyperkinetic impulse disorder in children's behavior problems." Psychosom Med 19(1): 38-49, January/February, 1957.

114 Levin, P. M. "Restlessness in children." Arch Neurol Psychiatry 39: 764-70, April, 1938.

115 Levy, Sol. "The hyperkinetic child." GP 37(6): 112-16, June, 1968.

116 ———. "The hyperkinetic child--a forgotten entity: it's diagnosis and treatment." Int J Neuropsychiatry 2(4): 330-36, August, 1966.

117 Lewis, Richard S.; Strauss, Alfred A.; Lehtinen, Laura E. The other child; the brain-injured child: a book for parents and laymen. 2d rev. and enl. ed. New York: Grune & Stratton, 1960. 148p.

118 Lightfoot, O. B. "Hyperactivity in children." J Natl Med Assoc 65: 58-62, January, 1973.

119 Lindsay, Janet. "The difficult epileptic child." Br Med J 3: 283-85, July 29, 1972.

120 Lippman, H. S. "Restlessness in infancy." JAMA 91: 1848-52, December 15, 1928.

121 Littleton, Arthur C., and Davis, Frances. "The mystique of brain injury." Train Sch Bull 68(1): 15-22, May, 1971.

122 Livingston, S. "The hyperkinetic behavior syndrome." Med Insight 3: 22-23ff., November, 1971.

123 MacKeith, Ronald C., and Bax, Martin O. Minimal cerebral dysfunction: papers from the International Study Group held at Oxford, September, 1962. London: National Spastics Society, Medical Education and Information Unit, 1963. 104p. (Little Club clinics in developmental medicine, No. 10).

124 McMahon, Shirley A.; Deem, Michael A.; Greenberg, Lawrence M. "The hyperactive child." Clin Proc Child Hosp 26(10): 295-316, November, 1970.

125 McNamara, John J. "Hyperactivity in the apartment bound child." Clin Pediatr 11(7): 371-72, July, 1972.

126 Magary, James F., and Eichorn, John R., eds. The exceptional child: a book of readings. New York: Holt, Rinehart & Winston, 1960. 561p.

127 Malmquist, Carl. "Depressions in childhood and adolescence. II." N Engl J Med 284(17): 955-61, April 29, 1971.

128 Marwit, Samuel J., and Stenner, A. Jack. "Hyperkinesis: delineation of two patterns." Except Child 38(5): 401-6, January, 1972.

129 Masland, Richard L. "Children with minimal brain dysfunction--a national problem." In: Tarnopol, Lester, ed. Learning disabilities: introduction to educational and medical management. Springfield, Illinois: Thomas, 1969. 67-94.

130 Michael-Smith, Harold. "Reciprocal factors in the behavioral syndrome of the neurologically impaired child." In: Hellmuth, Jerome, ed. The special child in century 21. Seattle: Special Child Publications of the Seguin School, 1964. 57-67.

131 Miles, R. S. "Common nervous conditions of children." Arch Pediatr 38: 664, 1921.

132 Miller, B. J. A parent's view: the child with brain damage. New York: Association for the Aid of Crippled Children, 1959.

133 Millman, Howard L. "Minimal brain dysfunction in children: evaluation and treatment." J Learn Disabil 3(2): 89-99, February, 1970.

134 Milman, Doris H. "Organic behavior disorder: behavior characteristics of brain-damaged children." Am J Dis Child 91(6): 521-28, June, 1956.

135 Minimal brain damage in children: final report. Helmer R. Myklebust and Benjamin Boshes, co-directors. Washington, D. C.: U. S. Health Services and Mental Health Administration, 1970. 332p.

136 Minimal brain dysfunction; a new problem area for social work: a
symposium. Chicago: National Easter Seal Society for Crippled Children and Adults, 1968. 28p.

137 Minimal brain dysfunction in children; educational, medical, and
health related services: phase two of a three-phase project. Washington, D. C.: U. S. Public Health Service; for sale by the Superintendent of Documents, U. S. Government Printing Office, 1970. 81p.
(PHS Publication, No. 2015).

138 "Minimal brain dysfunction: the three million 'other children.'"
Med World News 11(21): 30-36, May 22, 1970.

139 Mordock, John B. "Behavioral problems of the child with minimal
cerebral dysfunction." Phys Ther 51(4): 398-404, April, 1971.

     Myklebust, Helmer R.
       see Minimal brain damage in children: final report. (Item No.
       135).

140 National Northwest Conference on the Special Child. 2nd, Seattle,
1962. The special child in century 21. Jerome Hellmuth, editor.
Seattle: Special Child Publications of the Seguin School, 1964. 370p.

141 National Society for Crippled Children and Adults. Library. Brain
injury and related disorders in children: selected references annotated. Chicago: The Society, 1965.

142 Neisworth, J. T., and Smith, R. M. "Analysis and redefinition of
developmental disabilities." Except Child 40(5): 345-47, February,
1974.

143 Nichamin, Samuel J., and Comly, Hunter M. "The hyperkinetic or
lethargic child with cerebral dysfunction." Mich Med 63(11): 790-
92, November, 1964.

144 North, H. M. "The nervous child." Med J Aust 1: 612-14, May 2,
1953.

145 O'Gara, Mary J. "The child in the middle." J Learn Disabil 7(6):
353-58, June/July, 1974.

146 Olds, Sally W. "Is there a tornado in the house?" Todays Health
47: 33-35ff., November, 1969.

147 O'Malley, John E., and Eisenberg, Leon. "The hyperkinetic syndrome." In: Walzer, Stanley, and Wolff, Peter H., eds. Minimal
cerebral dysfunction in children: seminars in psychiatry. New York:
Grune & Stratton, 1973. 95-103.

148 Ounstead, Christopher. "The hyperkinetic syndrome in epileptic
children." Lancet 2: 303-11, August 13, 1955.

149 Pacella, Bernard L. "Behavior problems in children." Med Clin
North Am 32: 655-67, May, 1948.

150 Paine, Richmond S. "Minimal chronic brain syndromes in children."
Dev Med Child Neurol 4(1): 21-27, February, 1962.

151 ————. "Syndromes of 'minimal cerebral' damage." Pediatr Clin
North Am 15(3): 779-801, August, 1968.

152 Paine, Richmond S.; Werry, John S.; Quay, Herbert C. "A study of
'minimal cerebral dysfunction.'" Dev Med Child Neurol 10(4): 505-
20, August, 1968.

153 Peterson, Donald R. "Behavior problems of middle childhood." J
Consult Psychol 25(3): 205-9, June, 1961.

154 Pincus, J. H., and Glaser, G. H. "The syndrome of 'minimal brain
damage' in childhood." N Engl J Med 275(1): 27-35, July 7, 1966.

155 Pond, D. A. "Is there a syndrome of 'brain damage' in children?"
Cereb Palsy Bull 2(4): 296-97, 1960.

156 ————. "Psychiatric aspects of epileptic and brain-damaged children." Br Med J 2: 1377-82, 1454-59, December, 1961.

157 Prechtl, H. F. R., and Stemmer, Ch. J. "The choreiform syndrome in
children." Dev Med Child Neurol 4(2): 119-27, April, 1962.

158 Prentky, Joseph. "Minimal brain dysfunction in children." J Spec
Educ Ment Retarded 9(1): 14-20, 37, Fall, 1972.

159 Quay, Herbert C., ed. Children's behavior disorders: an enduring
problem in psychology. Princeton, New Jersey: Van Nostrand, 1968.
186p.

160 Quay, Herbert C., and Werry, John S., eds. Psychopathological disorders in childhood. New York: Wiley-Interscience, 1972. 469p.
(Series in psychology).

161 Quinn, Patricia O., and Rapoport, Judith L. "Minor physical
anomalies and neurologic status in hyperactive boys." Pediatrics
53(5): 742-47, May, 1974.

162 Rapoport, Judith L.; Quinn, Patricia O.; Lamprecht, F. "Minor
physical anomalies and plasma dopamine B-hydroxylase activity in
hyperactive boys." Am J Psychiatry 131(4): 386-90, April, 1974.

163 Reece, R. M. "The hyperactive child syndrome." Am Fam Physician
8(3): 98-103, September, 1973.

164 Reed, James C. "Problems of adaptation to the effects of brain
damage." Nat Bus Educ Q 38(3): 28-30, Spring, 1970.

165 Reger, Roger. "Hyperactivity and exhilaration in children." Am J
Dis Child 107(6): 590-92, June, 1964.

166 Reistroffer, Mary, and Kuhn, Roy. The hyperactive child without
mental retardation. Madison, Wisconsin: University of Wisconsin
Press, 1970. 32p. (EC 042 769).

167 Reitan, Ralph M., and Boll, Thomas J. "Neuropsychological correlates of minimal brain dysfunction." Ann NY Acad Sci 205: 65-88,
February 28, 1973.

168 Renshaw, Domeena C. The hyperkinetic child. Chicago: Nelson-
Hall, 1974. 197p.

169 Rosen, E. J. "Behavioral and emotional disturbances associated
with cerebral dysfunction." Appl Ther 11: 531-43, 1969.

170 Rosenthal, Joseph H. "Neurophysiology of minimal cerebral dysfunctions." Acad Ther 8(3): 291-94, Spring, 1973.

171 Rourke, Philip G., and Quinlan, Donald M. "Psychological characteristics of problem children at the borderline of mental retardation." J Consult Clin Psychol 40(1): 59-68, February, 1973.

172 Routh, Donald K., and Roberts, Robert D. "Minimal brain dysfunction in children: failure to find evidence for a behavior syndrome."
Psychol Rep 31(1): 307-14, August, 1972.

173 Rubin, Eli Z. "Secondary emotional disorders in children with perceptual-motor dysfunction." Am J Orthopsychiatry 34(2): 296-97,
March, 1964. (Abstract of speech).

174 Russell, J. A. "The hyperactive child." Am J Dis Child 63(1):
94-101, January, 1942.

175 Rutter, Michael. "Emotional disorder and educational underachievement." Arch Dis Child 49(4): 249-56, April, 1974.

176 Rutter, Michael; Graham, Philip; Birch, Herbert G. "Interrelations
between the choreiform syndrome, reading disability and psychiatric
disorder in children of eight to eleven years." Dev Med Child Neurol
8(2): 149-59, April, 1966.

177 Sachs, Bernard, and Hausman, Louis. Nervous and mental disorders
from birth through adolescence. New York: Hoeber, 1926. 861p.

178 Schain, Richard J. "Minimal brain dysfunction in children: a
neurological viewpoint." Bull Los Angeles Neurol Soc 33: 145-55,
July, 1968.

179 Schmitt, Barton D.; Martin, Harold P.; Nellhaus, Gerhard; et. al.
"The hyperactive child." Clin Pediatr 12(3): 154-69, March, 1973.

180 Schrager, Jules M.; Lindy, Janet M.; Harrison, Saul I.; et. al.
"The hyperkinetic child: an overview of the issues." J Am Acad
Child Psychiatry 5(3): 526-33, July, 1966.

181 Schulman, Jerome L.; Kaspar, Joseph C.; Throne, Frances M. Brain
damage and behavior: a clinical-experimental study. Springfield,
Illinois: Thomas, 1965. 164p.

182 Schulman, Jerome L.; Throne, Frances M.; Kaspar, Joseph C.; et. al. "Studies on the behavior correlates of organic brain damage." In: International Congress on Mental Retardation, 2nd, Vienna, 1962. Proceedings. Part II. Edited by O. Star. Basel: Karger, 1963. 76-82.

183 Schwalb, Eugene; Blau, Harold; Blau, Harriet. "The child with brain dysfunction." J Learn Disabil 2(4): 182-88, April, 1969.

184 Schwalb, Eugene, and Schwalb, Rita B. "Minimal brain damage, congenital dyslexia and developmental aphasia." In: International Association for the Scientific Study of Mental Deficiency, 1st, Montpellier, France, 1967. Proceedings. Edited by B. W. Richards. Surrey, England: Michael Jackson, 1968. 358-67.

185 Schwartz, Louis. "The myth of the brain-injured child." NJ Educ Rev 36: 284-85, 310-13, January, 1963.

186 Scott, W. C. "Hyperactive children." Br Med J 2: 113-14, April 14, 1973.

   Segal, Julius, ed.
   see U. S. National Institute of Mental Health. The mental health of the child...(Item No. 209).

187 Shaffer, David. "Psychiatric aspects of brain injury in childhood: a review." Dev Med Child Neurol 15(2): 211-20, April, 1973.

188 Shaw, Charles R., and Lucas, Alexander R. The psychiatric disorders of childhood. 2nd ed. New York: Appleton-Century-Crofts, 1970. 499p.

189 Signor, Roger. "Hyperactive children." Wash Univ Mag 37: 2, Winter, 1967.

190 Silver, Archie A. "A behavioral syndrome associated with brain damage in children." Pediatr Clin North Am 5(3): 687-98, August, 1958.

191 Silverman, Jerome S. "Obsessional disorders in childhood and adolescence: developmental, therapeutic and nosologic aspects." Am J Psychother 26(3): 362-77, July, 1972.

192 Small, B. J. "Hyperactive children." Todays Educ 63: 34-36, January, 1974.

193 Smith, Aaron. "Ambiguities in concepts and studies of 'brain damage' and 'organicity.'" J Nerv Ment Dis 135(4): 311-26, October, 1962.

194 Solomons, Gerald. "The hyperactive child." J Iowa Med Soc 55(8): 464-69, August, 1965.

195 Stewart, Mark A. "Hyperactive child syndrome recognized 100 years ago." JAMA 202(13): 28-29, December 25, 1967.

196 Still, George F. "The Coulstonia lectures on some abnormal physical conditions in children." Lancet 1: 1008-12, April 12, 1901; 1: 1077-82, April 19, 1901; 1: 1163-68, April 26, 1901.

197 Stock, Claudette. The minimal brain dysfunction child: some clinical manifestations, definitions, descriptions and remediation approaches. Boulder, Colorado: Pruett, 1969. 64p. (ED 038 818).

198 Stone, Frederick H. "Psychodynamics of brain-damaged children: a preliminary report." J Child Psychol Psychiatry 1(3): 203-14, October, 1960.

199 Strauss, Alfred A., and Werner, Heinz. "Comparative psychopathology of the brain-injured child and traumatic brain-injured adult." Am J Psychiatry 99: 835-40, May, 1943.

200 Strother, Charles R. "Minimal cerebral dysfunction: a historical overview." Ann NY Acad Sci 205: 6-17, February 28, 1973.

201 Sylvester, Doris M. "A descriptive definition of hyperactivity." Smith Coll Stud Social Work 4: 2-27, 1933.

202 Tec, Leon. "Hyperkinetic children and the staccato syndrome." Am J Psychiatry 130(3): 330, March, 1973.

203 ————. "The staccato syndrome: a new clinical entity in search of recognition." Am J Psychiatry 128(5): 647-48, November, 1971.

204 Thomas, Alexander, et. al. Behavioral individuality in early childhood. New York: New York University Press, 1963. 135p.

205 Thomas, Alexander; Chess, Stella; Birch, Herbert G. Temperament and behavior disorders in children. New York: New York University Press, 1968. 309p.

206 Timme, A. R. "The choreiform syndrome: its significance in children's behavior problems." Calif Med 68: 154-58, March, 1948.

207 Trapp, E. Philip, and Himelstein, Philip, eds. Readings on the exceptional child: research and theory. 2nd ed. New York: Appleton-Century-Crofts, 1972. 714p.

208 Tymchuk, Alexander J., and Knights, Robert M. A two-thousand item bibliography: the description, etiology, diagnosis, and treatment of children with learning disabilities or brain damage. London, Ontario, Canada: Children's Psychiatric Research Institute, 1969. 186p.

209 U. S. National Institute of Mental Health. The mental health of the child: program reports. Julius Segal, editor. Rockville, Maryland: Program Planning and Evaluation, 1971. 588p. (PHS Publication, No. 2168).

210 Van Osdol, Bob M., and Carlson, Larry. "A study of developmental hyperactivity." Ment Retard 10(3): 18-24, June, 1972.

211 Vernallis, Francis F. Teeth-grinding: some relationships to anxiety, hostility and hyperactivity. Unpublished doctoral dissertation. Penn State University: Penn State University Abstract Series 16: 590.

212 Voller, George. "Is the brain-injured child something new?" Acad Ther 5(4): 267-69, Summer, 1970.

213 Waldrop, Mary F., and Goering, Jacob D. "Hyperactivity and minor physical anomalies in elementary school children." Am J Orthopsychiatry 41(4): 602-7, July, 1971.

214 Waldrop, Mary F., and Halverson, Charles F., Jr. "Minor physical anomalies and hyperactive behavior in young children." In: Hellmuth, Jerome, ed. The exceptional infant. Vol. 2. New York: Brunner/Mazel, 1971. 343-80.

215 Waldrop, Mary F.; Pedersen, Frank; Bell, Richard Q. "Minor physical anomalies and behavior in preschool children." Child Dev 39(2): 391-400, June, 1968.

216 Walzer, Stanley, and Wolff, Peter H., eds. Minimal cerebral dysfunction in children: seminars in psychiatry. New York: Grune & Stratton, 1973. 117p.

217 Weiss, Jules M., and Kaufman, Herbert S. "A subtle organic component in some cases of mental illness: a preliminary report of cases." Arch Gen Psychiatry 25(1): 74-78, July, 1971.

218 Welsbacher, B. T. "More than a package of bizarre behaviors: neurologically handicapped child." Music Educ J 58(8): 26-28, April, 1972.

219 Wender, Paul H. Minimal brain dysfunction in children. New York: Wiley-Interscience, 1971. 242p. (Wiley series on psychological disorders).

220 ———. "Minimal brain dysfunction: some recent advances." Pediatr Ann 2(5): 42-54, May, 1973.

221 Werry, John S. "Developmental hyperactivity." Pediatr Clin North Am 15(3): 581-99, August, 1968.

222 ———. "Developmental hyperactivity." In: Chess, Stella E., and Thomas, Alexander B., eds. Annual progress in child psychiatry and child development. New York: Brunner/Mazel, 1969. 485-505.

223 ———. "Studies on the hyperactive child: IV. An empirical analysis of the minimal brain dysfunction syndrome." Arch Gen Psychiatry 19(1): 9-16, July, 1968.

224 Werry, John S.; Minde, Klaus; Guzman, Anthony; et. al. "Studies on the hyperactive child: VII. Neurological status compared with neurotic and normal children." Am J Orthopsychiatry 42(3): 441-51, April, 1972.

225 Werry, John S., and Sprague, Robert. "Hyperactivity." In: Costello, Charles G., ed. Symptoms of psychopathology: a handbook. New York: Wiley, 1970. 397-417.

226 Werry, John S.; Weiss, G.; Douglas, Virginia I. "Studies on the hyperactive child: I. Some preliminary findings." Can Psychiatr Assoc J 9: 120-30, 1964.

227 Wilcox, John C., and Wilcox, Evangeline. "A neurophysiologic view of the neurologically handicapped adolescent." Acad Ther 5(4): 271-75, Summer, 1970.

228 Williams, Cyril E. "Some psychiatric observations on a group of maladjusted deaf children." J Child Psychol Psychiatry 11(1): 1-18, May, 1970.

229 Wilson, Ruth. "A future for Jimmy." Volta Rev 75(1): 47-53, January, 1973.

230 Wolff, Sula. "Behavioural characteristics of primary school children referred to a psychiatric department." Br J Psychiatry 113: 885-93, August, 1967.

231 Wolski, William, and Light, Gerald S. "Cerebral dysfunction in children: do not procrastinate!" Clin Pediatr 8(1): 5, January, 1969.

232 Woodburne, Lloyd S. The neural basis of behavior. Columbus, Ohio: Merrill, 1967. 378p.

233 Woods School for Exceptional Children. A selective bibliography on brain-damaged children. Langhorne, Pennsylvania: Woods Schools, 1964. 69p. (ED 014 181).

234 Work, Henry H., and Haldane, Jane E. "Cerebral dysfunction in children." Am J Dis Child 111(6): 573-80, June, 1966.

235 Work, Henry H., and Haldane, Jane E. "Something wrong with his brain." Am J Dis Child 108(3): 219-20, September, 1964.

236 Wortis, Joseph. "A note on the concept of the 'brain-injured child.'" Am J Ment Defic 61(1): 204-6, July, 1956.

237 Wunderlich, Ray C. "Hyperkinetic disease." Acad Ther 5(2): 99-108, Winter, 1969-70.

238 ———. Kids, brains, and learning: what goes wrong--prevention and treatment. St. Petersburg, Florida: Johnny Reads, 1970. 534p.

239 Wyllie, W. C. "Behavior problems and the backward child." Lancet 1: 1247-48, June 10, 1933.

240 Zrull, Joel P.; McDermott, John F.; Poznanski, Elva. "Hyperkinetic syndrome: the role of depression." Child Psychiatry Hum Dev 1(1): 33-40, Fall, 1970.

B. Classification and Nomenclature

241 Achenbach, Thomas M. "The classification of children's psychiatric symptoms: a factor analytic study." Psychol Monogr 80(7, Whole No. 615): 1-37, 1966.

242 American Psychiatric Association. Committee on Nomenclature and Statistics. Diagnostic and statistical manual of mental disorders (DSM-II). 2nd ed. Washington, D. C.: American Psychiatric Association, 1968. 134p.

243 Calobrisi, Dominick. "Classification of children's mental disorders." Am J Psychiatry 125(10): 1457-58, April, 1969.

244 Dreger, R. M. "The establishment of diagnostic categories for the evaluation of specific therapies for children's emotional disorders." Ala J Med Sci 7(1): 55-60, January, 1970.

245 Dreger, R. M.; Lewis, P. M.; Rich, T. A.; et. al. "Behavioral classification project." J Consult Psychol 28(1): 1-13, February, 1964.

246 Eron, Leonard D., ed. The classification of behavior disorders. Chicago: Aldine, 1966. 180p. (ED 023 224).

247 Finch, Stuart M. "Nomenclature for children's mental disorders need improvement." Int J Psychiatry 7(6): 414, June, 1969.

248 Fish, Barbara. "Limitations of the new nomenclature for children's disorders." Int J Psychiatry 7(6): 393-98, June, 1969.

249 Fish, Barbara, and Shapiro, Theodore. "A typology of children's psychiatric disorders: I. Its application to a controlled evaluation of treatment." J Am Acad Child Psychiatry 4(1): 32-52, January, 1965.

250 Fish, Barbara; Shapiro, Theodore; Campbell, Magda; et. al. "A classification of schizophrenic children under five years." Am J Psychiatry 124(10): 1415-23, April, 1968.

251 Frosch, John, and Wortes, S. Bernard. "Contribution to the nosology of the impulse disorders." Am J Psychiatry 111: 132-38, August, 1954.

252 Group for the Advancement of Psychiatry. Committee on Child Psychiatry. Psychopathological disorders in childhood: theoretical considerations and a proposed classification. New York: 1966. 173-343. (Group for the Advancement of Psychiatry, Vol. 6, Report No. 62).

253 Jenkins, Richard L. "Classification of behavior problems of children." Am J Psychiatry 125(8): 1032-39, February, 1969.

254 Jenkins, Richard L., and Cole, Jonathan O., eds. Diagnostic classification in child psychiatry. Washington, D. C.: American Psychiatric Association, 1964. 152p. (Psychiatric Research Report, No. 18).

255 Kobayashi, Shigefumi; Mizushima, Keiichi; Shinohara, Mutsuharu. "Clinical groupings of problem children based on symptoms and behavior." Int J Soc Psychiatry 13(3): 206-15, Summer, 1967.

256 Lorr, M. "Classification of the behavior disorders." Annu Rev Psychol 12: 195-216, 1961.

257 Patterson, Gerald Roy. "An empirical approach to the classification of disturbed children." J Clin Psychol 20(3): 326-37, July, 1964.

258 ———. "A tentative approach to the classification of children's behavior problems." Diss Abstr 16(6): 1175, 1956.

259 Rodin, E. A.; Beckett, P.; Sokolov, S. "A coding system for patients with convulsive disorders and children with behavior disturbances." IRE Trans Bio-Med Electron 9: 61, 1962.

260 Ross, Donald C. "Poor school achievement: a psychiatric study and classification: II. Case management and follow up." Clin Pediatr 7(1): 43-54, January, 1968.

261 Rutter, Michael. "Classification and categorization in child psychiatry." J Child Psychol Psychiatry 6(2): 71-83, November, 1965.

262 Rutter, Michael; Lebovici, S.; Eisenberg, Leon; et. al. "A triaxial classification of mental disorders in childhood: an international study." J Child Psychol Psychiatry 10(1): 41-61, September, 1969.

263 Silver, Larry B. "DSM-II and child and adolescent psychopathology." Am J Psychiatry 125(9): 1267-69, March, 1969.

264 Stengel, E. "Classification of mental disorders." Bull WHO 21: 601-63, 1959.

265 Stephens, Thomas M.; Braun, Benjamin L.; Mazzoli, Louis A. "Certification requirements for teachers of emotionally disturbed children and nomenclature used to describe the handicap, reported by states." Except Child 34(9): 707, May, 1968.

266 Stevens, Godfrey D., and Birch, Jack W. "Proposal for clarification of the terminology used to describe brain-injured children." Except Child 23(7): 346-49, May, 1957.

267 Wolff, Sula. "Dimensions and clusters of symptoms in disturbed children." Br J Psychiatry 118: 421-27, April, 1971.

268 Wysocki, Boleslaw A., and Wysocki, Aydin C. "Behavior symptoms as a basis for a new diagnostic classification of problem children." J Clin Psychol 26(1): 41-45, January, 1970.

C. Epidemiology

269 Alley, Gordon R.; Solomons, Gerald; Opitz, Erica. "Minimal cerebral dysfunction as it relates to social class." J Learn Disabil 4 (5): 246-49, May, 1971.

270 Baldwin, J. A. "The incidence of reported deviant behavior in children." Int Psychiatry Clin 8: 161-75, 1971.

271 Buchmueller, A. D.; Porter, F.; Gildea, Margaret. "A comparative study of behavior problems occurring in two school districts." Nerv Child 10: 415-24, 1953.

272 Commission on Emotional and Learning Disorders in Children. One million children. Toronto: Leonard Crainford, 1970. 521p.

273 Drillien, Cecil M. "The incidence of mental and physical handicaps in school age children of very low birth weight: II." Pediatrics 39(2): 238-47, February, 1967.

274 Egdell, H. G., and Stanfield, J. P. "Paediatric neurology in Africa: a Ugandan report." Br Med J 1: 548-52, February 26, 1972.

275 Gochman, Stanley I., and Grubler, Eva R. "A study of brain damage in a suburban population." Psychol Rep 10(3): 828, June, 1962.

276 Gorin, Thomas, and Kramer, Robert A. "The hyperkinetic behavior syndrome." Conn Med 37: 559-63, November, 1973.

277 Huessy, Hans R. "Study of the prevalence and therapy of the choreatiform syndrome or hyperkinesis in rural Vermont." Acta Paedopsychiatr 34(4/5): 130-35, April/May, 1967.

278 Huessy, Hans R., and Gendron, Richard M. "Prevalence of the so-called hyperkinetic syndrome in public school children of Vermont." Acta Paedopsychiatr 37(9/10): 243-48, September/October, 1970.

279 Lapouse, Rema, and Monk, Mary A. "Behavior deviations in a representative sample of children: variation by sex, age, race, social class, and family size." Am J Orthopsychiatry 34(3): 436-46, April, 1964.

280 Lapouse, Rema, and Monk, Mary A. "An epidemiologic study of behavior characteristics in children." Am J Public Health 48(9): 1134-44, September, 1958.

281 Levy, Sol. "Post-encephalitic behavior disorder--a forgotten entity: a report of 100 cases." Am J Psychiatry 115(2): 1062-67, June, 1959.

282 Lewis, Margaret A. "Hyperactivity and variations in prevalence rates for assignment to special classes among black, white and Spanish surnamed students in twenty-five urban and suburban school districts in New Jersey." Diss Abstr Int 34(7-A): 4040, January, 1974.

283 Lindy, Janet M. "Hyperkinetic behavior among kindergarten children." Diss Abstr 28(1-B): 341, July, 1967.

284 Michaels, Joseph J., and Secunda, Lazarus. "Relationship of neurotic traits to the electroencephalogram in children with behavior disorders." Am J Psychiatry 101: 407-9, November, 1944.

285 Miller, Lovick C.; Hampe, Edward; Barrett, Curtis; et. al. "Children's deviant behavior within the general population." J Consult Clin Psychol 37(1): 16-22, August, 1971.

286 Miller, Ray G., Jr. "Hyperactivity, self-concept, and achievement." Diss Abstr Int 31(5-A): 2014-15, November, 1970.

287 Miller, Ray G.; Palkes, Helen S.; Stewart, Mark A. "Hyperactive children in suburban elementary schools." Child Psychiatry Hum Dev 4(2): 121-27, Winter, 1973.

288 Minskoff, J. Gerald. "Differential approaches to prevalence estimates of learning disabilities." Ann NY Acad Sci 205: 139-45, February 28, 1973.

289 Richardson, Sylvia O., and Normanly, Jerrod. "Incidence of pseudo-retardation in clinic population." Am J Dis Child 109(5): 432-35, May, 1965.

290 Richmond, Julius B. "Epidemiology of learning disorders." In: Ross Conference on Pediatric Research, 61st, Columbus, Ohio, 1971. Report. Edited by John H. Menkes, and Richard J. Schain. Columbus, Ohio: Ross Laboratories, 1971. 14-20.

291 Rutter, Michael. "Psychiatric disorder in ten and eleven year old children." Proc R Soc Med 59: 382-87, 1966.

292 Shepherd, M.; Oppenheim, A. N.; Mitchell, S. "Childhood behavior disorders and the child-guidance clinic: an epidemiological study." J Child Psychol Psychiatry 7(1): 39-52, June, 1966.

293 Silverman, Leslie J., and Metz, A. Stafford. "Numbers of pupils with specific learning disabilities in local public schools in the United States: Spring, 1970." Ann NY Acad Sci 205: 146-57, February 28, 1973.

294 Solomons, Gerald. "Prevalence of speech and hearing problems in a child development clinic population." Clin Pediatr 9(7): 384-89, July, 1970.

295 Stennett, R. G. "Emotional handicap in the elementary years: phase or disease?" Am J Orthopsychiatry 36(3): 444-49, April, 1966.

296 Swift, Marshall S.; Spivack, George; Delisser, O.; et. al. "Children's disturbing classroom behavior: a cross-cultural investigation; DESB used with American and French children." Except Child 38(6): 492-93, February, 1972.

297 Ullmann, Charles A. "Prevalence of reading disability as a function of the measure used." J Learn Disabil 2(11): 556-58, November, 1968.

298 Wehrle, P. F.; Day, P. A.; Whalen, J. P.; et. al. "The epidemiology of accidental poisoning in an urban population: II. Prevalence and distribution of poisoning." Am J Public Health 50(12): 1925-33, December, 1960.

299 Wehrle, P. F.; Defreest, L.; Penhollow, J.; et. al. "The epidemiology of accidental poisoning in an urban population: III. The repeater problem in accidental poisoning." Pediatrics 27(4): 614-20, April, 1961.

300 Werry, John S., and Quay, Herbert C. "The prevalence of behavior symptoms in younger elementary school children." Am J Orthopsychiatry 41(1): 136-43, January, 1971.

301 Wolff, Peter H., and Hurwitz, Irving. "The choreiform syndrome." Dev Med Child Neurol 8(2): 160-65, April, 1966.

302 Yule, William, and Rutter, Michael. "Educational aspects of childhood maladjustment: some epidemiological findings." Br J Educ Psychol 38(1): 7-9, February, 1968.

SECTION II

ETIOLOGY

A. General Etiological Aspects

303 Adams, Elizabeth. "The mother is the first to know." <u>Acad Ther</u>
9(5): 373-76, Spring, 1974.

304 Anderson, Camilla M., and Plymate, H. B. "Management of the brain-
damaged adolescent." <u>Am J Orthopsychiatry</u> 32(3): 492-500, April,
1962.

305 Bakwin, Harry. "Cerebral damage and behavior disorders in children." <u>J Pediatr</u> 34(3): 371-81, March, 1949.

306 Bell, Richard Q. "Retrospective and prospective views of early
personality development." <u>Merrill-Palmer Q</u> 6(3): 131-44, April,
1960.

307 Bender, Lauretta. "Genesis of hostility in children." <u>Am J Psy-
chiatry</u> 105: 241-45, October, 1948.

308 ———. "Organic brain conditions producing behavior disorders."
In: Lewis, Nolen D., and Pacella, Bernard L., eds. <u>Modern trends in
child psychiatry.</u> New York: International Universities Press, 1945.
157-92.

309 Blau, Abram. "Psychiatric approach to post-traumatic, traumatic
and post-encephalitic syndromes." In: Association for Research in
Nervous and Mental Disease. <u>Neurology and psychiatry in childhood,
proceedings of the association, New York, 1954.</u> Baltimore: Williams
& Wilkins, 1954. 404ff. (Its Research Publications, Vol. 34).

310 Bradley, Charles. "Organic factors in psychopathology of childhood." In: Hoch, Paul H., and Zubin, Joseph, eds. <u>Psychopathology
of childhood.</u> New York: Grune & Stratton, 1955. 82-104.

311 Buddenhagen, R. G., and Sickler, Patricia. "Hyperactivity: a
forty-eight hour sample plus a note on etiology." <u>Am J Ment Defic</u> 73
(4): 580-89, January, 1969.

312 Burks, Harold F. <u>A study of the organic basis for behavior deviations in school children.</u> Unpublished doctoral dissertation. Los
Angeles: University of Southern California, 1955.

313 Chess, Stella. "Neurological dysfunction and childhood behavioral pathology." J Autism Child Schizophr 2(3): 299-311, July/September, 1972.

314 Denhoff, Eric. "Emotional and psychological background of the neurologically handicapped child." Except Child 27: 347-49, March, 1961.

315 Douglas, Virginia I.; Werry, John S.; Weiss, G. "Hyperactive behavior in children: some findings regarding aetiology and treatment." Can Psychol 6: 219, 1965. (Abstract).

316 Friedland, Seymour J., and Shilkret, Robert B. "Alternative explanations of learning disabilities: defensive hyperactivity." Except Child 40(3): 213-15, November, 1973.

317 Greenacre, Phyllis. Trauma, growth and personality. New York: International Universities Press, 1952. 328p.

318 "Hyperactivity is not necessarily a symptom of brain dysfunction." Pediatr News 8(6): 43ff., June, 1974.

319 Lambert, Nadine M., and Grossman, Herbert. Problems in determining the etiology of learning and behavior handicaps: report of a study. Sacramento, California: State Department of Education, 1964. 156p.

320 Paine, Richmond S. "The contribution of neurology to the pathogenesis of hyperactivity in children." Clin Proc Child Hosp 19(9): 235-45, September, 1963.

321 ———. "Organic neurological factors related to learning disorders." In: Hellmuth, Jerome, ed. Learning disorders. Vol. 1. Seattle: Special Child Publications, 1965. 1-29.

322 Prechtl, H. F. R. "The mother-child interaction in babies with minimal brain damage: a follow-up study." In: Foss, B. M. Determinants of infant behavior. Vol. 2. London: Methuen, 1963. 53-66.

323 Roswell, Florence G. "Observations on causation and treatment of learning disabilities." Am J Orthopsychiatry 24(4): 784-88, October, 1954.

324 Rutter, Michael. "The influence of organic and emotional factors on the origins, nature and outcome of childhood psychosis." Dev Med Child Neurol 7(5): 518-28, October, 1965.

325 Rutter, Michael; Birch, Herbert G.; Thomas, Alexander; et. al. "Temperamental characteristics in infancy and later development of behavioral disorders." Br J Psychiatry 110: 651-61, September, 1964.

326 Silver, Larry B. "A proposed view on the etiology of the neurological learning disability syndrome." J Learn Disabil 4(3): 123-33, March, 1971.

327 Weithorn, Corinne J. "Hyperactivity and the CNS: an etiological and diagnostic dilemma." J Learn Disabil 6(1): 41-45, January, 1973.

328 Wender, Paul H. "Some speculations concerning a possible biochemical basis of minimal brain dysfunction." Ann NY Acad Sci 205: 18-28, February 28, 1973.

329 Werry, John S. "Organic factors in childhood psychopathology." In: Quay, Herbert C., and Werry, John S., eds. Psychopathological disorders of childhood. New York: Wiley-Interscience, 1972. 83-121. (Series in psychology).

B. Genetic Factors

330 Bentzen, Frances. "Sex ratios in learning and behavior disorders." Am J Orthopsychiatry 33(1): 92-98, January, 1963.

331 Black, F. William. "Season of birth and intelligence in a sample of learning-disabled children." J Genet Psychol 123(1st half): 31-34, September, 1973.

332 Bogart, K. C., and Froozan, H. "Excessive high voltage fast activity in familial mental retardation, hyperkinesis and macrocephaly." Electroencephalogr Clin Neurophysiol 28: 419-20, April, 1970.

333 Cantwell, Dennis P. "Psychiatric illness in the families of hyperactive children." Arch Gen Psychiatry 27(9): 414-17, September, 1972.

334 Crichton, J. U. "The evaluation of minimal cerebral dysfunction in children of low birth weight." In: International Congress of Pediatrics, 13th, Vienna, 1971. Proceedings. 111-29, 135-40.

335 Culver, Charles M., and Dunham, Frances. "Birth order and spatial-perceptual ability: negative note." Percept Mot Skills 28(1): 301-2, February, 1969.

336 Eysenck, H. J., and Prell, D. B. "The inheritance of neuroticism: an experimental study." J Ment Sci 97: 441-65, 1951.

337 Freedman, D. G., and Keller, Barbara. "Inheritance of behavior in infants." Science 140: 196-98, April 12, 1963.

338 Fries, M. E., and Wolff, Paul J. "Some hypotheses on the role of the congenital activity type in personality development." Psychoanal Study Child 8: 48-62, 1953.

339 Gottesman, Irving I. "Heritability of personality: a demonstration." Psychol Monogr 77(9, Whole No. 572): 1-21, 1963.

340 Greer, Bobby G., and Whitley, Carolyn. "The relationship between birth order and learning disabilities." Except Child 37(8): 608, April, 1971.

341 Hallgren, Bertil. "Specific dyslexia (congenital word-blindness): a clinical and genetic study." Acta Psychiatr Neurol Scand (Suppl. 65): 1-287, 1950.

342 Lindenbaum, R. H.; Borrow, M.; Barber, L. "Monozygotic twins with ring chromosome 22." J Med Genet 10(1): 85-89, March, 1973.

343 Lopez, Rafael E. "Hyperactivity in twins." Can Psychiatr Assoc J 10(5): 421-26, October, 1965.

344 Morrison, James R. Letter: "Hereditary factors in hyperkinesis." Am J Psychiatry 131: 472, April, 1974.

345 Morrison, James R., and Stewart, Mark A. "Bilateral inheritance as evidence for polygenicity in the hyperactive child syndrome." J Nerv Ment Dis 158(3): 226-28, March, 1974.

346 Morrison, James R., and Stewart, Mark A. "Evidence for polygenetic inheritance in the hyperactive child syndrome." Am J Psychiatry 130 (7): 791-92, July, 1973.

347 Morrison, James R., and Stewart, Mark A. "A family study of the hyperactive child syndrome." Biol Psychiatry 3(3): 189-95, 1971.

348 Omenn, Gilbert S. "Genetic approaches to the syndrome of minimal brain dysfunction." Ann NY Acad Sci 205: 212-22, February 28, 1973.

349 Owen, F. W.; Adams, P. A.; Forrest, T.; et. al. "Learning disabilities in children: sibling studies." Bull Orton Soc 18: 33-62, 1968.

350 Pratt, R. T. C. The genetics of neurological disorders. London: Oxford University Press, 1967. 310p.

351 Rutter, Michael; Korn, Sam; Birch, Herbert G. "Genetic and environmental factors in the development of 'primary reaction patterns.'" Br J Soc Clin Psychol 2(pt. 3): 161-73, October, 1963.

352 Scarr, Sandra. "Genetic factors in activity motivation." Child Dev 37(3): 663-73, September, 1966.

353 Shrader, William K., and Leventhal, Theodore. "Birth order of children and parental report of problems." Child Dev 39(4): 1165-75, December, 1968.

354 Silver, Larry B. "Familial patterns in children with neurologically-based learning disabilities." J Learn Disabil 4(7): 349-58, August/ September, 1971.

355 Stewart, Mark A., and Morrison, James R. "Affective disorder among the relatives of hyperactive children." J Child Psychol Psychiatry 14(3): 209-12, September, 1973.

356 Vandenberg, S. G. "The hereditary abilities study: hereditary components in a psychological test battery." Am J Hum Genet 14(2): 220-37, 1962.

357 ————. "Possible hereditary factors in minimal brain dysfunction." Ann NY Acad Sci 205: 223-30, February 28, 1973.

358 Vockell, Edward L., and Bennett, Blair. "Birth order, sex of siblings, and incidence of learning disabilities." Except Child 39(2):
162-64, October, 1972.

359 Warren, R. J.; Karduck, W. A.; Bussaratid, S.; et. al. "The hyperactive child syndrome: normal chromosome findings." Arch Gen Psychiatry 24(2): 161-62, February, 1971.

360 Willerman, Lee, and Plomin, Robert. "Activity level in children
and their parents." Child Dev 44(4): 854-58, December, 1973.

C. Pre- and Perinatal Complications

361 Anderson, Camilla M. "Early brain injury and behavior." J Am Med
Womens Assoc 11(4): 113-19, April, 1956.

362 Campbell, W. A. B.; Cheeseman, E. A.; Kilpatrick, W. W. "The
effects of neonatal asphyxia on physical and mental development."
Arch Dis Child 25: 351-59, 1950.

363 Colligan, Robert C. "Psychometric deficits related to perinatal
stress." J Learn Disabil 7(3): 154-60, March, 1974.

364 Corah, Norman L.; Anthony, E. James; Painter, Paul; et. al.
"Effects of perinatal anoxia after seven years." Psychol Monogr 79
(3, Whole No. 596): 1-34, 1965.

365 Drillien, Cecil M. "Obstetric hazard, mental retardation and behaviour disturbance in primary school." Dev Med Child Neurol 5(1):
3-13, February, 1963.

366 Fraser, M. S. and Wilks, J. "Residual effects of neonatal
asphyxia." J Obstet Gynaecol Br Emp 66(5): 748-52, October, 1959.

367 Graham, Frances K.; Ernhart, Claire B.; Thurston, Don L.; et. al.
"Organic development three years after pre-natal anoxia and other
potentially damaging newborn experience." Psychol Monogr 76(3, Whole
No. 522): 1-53, 1962.

368 Kawi, Ali A. "Prenatal and paranatal factors in the development of
childhood reading disorders." Monogr Soc Res Child Dev 24(4, Whole
No. 73): 1-80, 1959.

369 Kawi, Ali A., and Pasamanick, Benjamin. "Association of factors of
pregnancy with reading disorders in childhood." JAMA 166(12): 1420-
23, March 22, 1958.

370 Keith, Haddow M.; Norval, Mildred A.; Hunt, Arthur B. "Neurologic
lesions in relation to the sequelae of birth injury." Neurology 3:
139-47, 1953.

371 Knobloch, Hilda, and Pasamanick, Benjamin. "Prospective studies on
the epidemiology of reproductive casualty: methods, findings, and
some implications." Merrill-Palmer Q 12(1): 27-43, January, 1966.

372 "Link trauma in first trimester to hyperactivity." Pediatr News 8 (4): 1, 67, April, 1974.

373 Lyle, J. G. "Certain antenatal, perinatal, and developmental variables and reading retardation in middle-class boys." Child Dev 41 (2): 481-91, June, 1970.

374 McNeil, T. F. "Pregnancy and birth complications in the births of seriously, moderately, and mildly behaviorally disturbed children." J Nerv Ment Dis 151(1): 24-34, July, 1970.

375 Masland, Richard L. "Researches into the prenatal factors that lead to neuropsychiatric sequelae in childhood." In: Caplan, Gerald, ed. Prevention of mental disorders in children: initial exploration. New York: Basic Books, 1961. 52-73.

376 Millsom, Carol A. "Prenatal environment and classroom performance." Educ Leadership 27(4): 421-25, January, 1970.

377 Minde, Klaus; Webb, G.; Sykes, D. "Studies on the hyperactive child: VI. Prenatal and paranatal factors associated with hyperactivity." Dev Med Child Neurol 10(3): 355-63, June, 1968.

378 Moya, F., and Thorndike, V. "The effects of drugs used in labor on the fetus and newborn." Clin Pharmacol Ther 4: 628-53, 1963.

379 Natelson, Stephen E., and Sayers, Martin P. "Fate of children sustaining severe head trauma during birth." Pediatrics 51(2): 169-74, February, 1973.

380 Nichols, M. M. "Acute alcohol withdrawal syndrome in a newborn." Am J Dis Child 113(6): 714-15, June, 1967.

381 Pasamanick, Benjamin, and Knobloch, Hilda. "Brain and behavior; Symposium, 1959: II. Brain damage and reproductive casualty." Am J Orthopsychiatry 30(2): 298-305, April, 1960.

382 Pasamanick, Benjamin, and Knobloch, Hilda. "Complications of pregnancy and neuropsychiatric disorder." J Obstet Gynaecol Br Emp 66 (5): 753-55, October, 1959.

383 Pasamanick, Benjamin, and Knobloch, Hilda. "Epidemiologic studies on the complications of pregnancy and the birth process." In: Caplan, Gerald, ed. Prevention of mental disorders in children: initial exploration. New York: Basic Books, 1961. 74-94.

384 Pasamanick, Benjamin, and Knobloch, Hilda. "Retrospective studies on the epidemiology of reproductive casualty: old and new." Merrill-Palmer Q 12(1): 7-26, January, 1966.

385 Pasamanick, Benjamin, and Knobloch, Hilda. "Syndrome of minimal cerebral damage in infancy." JAMA 170(12): 1384-87, July 18. 1959.

386   Pasamanick, Benjamin, and Lilienfeld, Abraham M.   "Association of
maternal and fetal factors with development of mental deficiency:
abnormalities in prenatal and paranatal periods." JAMA   159(3):
155-60, September 17, 1955.

387   Pasamanick, Benjamin; Rogers, Martha E.; Lilienfeld, A. M.   "Pregnancy experience and the development of behavior disorder in children."
Am J Psychiatry   112(8):   613-18, February, 1956.

388   Preston, Mary I.   "Late behavioral aspects found in cases of prenatal, natal, and postnatal anoxia."   J Pediatr   26(4):   353-66, April,
1945.

389   Rogers, Martha E.; Lilienfeld, Abraham M.; Pasamanick, Benjamin.
Prenatal and paranatal factors in the development of childhood behav-
ior disorders.   Baltimore: Johns Hopkins University, School of
Hygiene and Public Health, 1955.   157p.

390   Rogers, Martha E.; Lilienfeld, Abraham M.; Pasamanick, Benjamin.
"Prenatal and paranatal factors in the development of childhood behavior disorders."   Acta Psychiatr Neurol Scand   (Suppl. 102):   1-
157, 1955.

391   Rosenfeld, George B., and Bradley, Charles.   "Childhood behavior
sequelae of asphyxia in infancy, with special reference to pertussis
and asphyxia neonatorum."   Pediatrics   2(1):   74-84, July, 1948.

392   Schachter, Frances F., and Apgar, Virginia.   "Perinatal asphxia
and psychological signs of brain damage in childhood."   Pediatrics
24(6):   1016-25, December, 1959.

393   Schroeder, Paul L.   "Behavior difficulties in children associated
with the results of birth trauma."   JAMA   92(2):   100-104, January 12,
1929.

394   Schwartz, Philip.   Birth injuries of the newborn: morphology,
pathogenesis, clinical pathology and prevention.   New York: Hafner,
1961.   384p.

395   Singer, Judith E.; Westphal, Milton W.; Niswander, Kenneth R.   "Sex
differences in the incidence of neonatal abnormalities and abnormal
performance in early childhood."   Child Dev   39(1):   103-12, March,
1968.

396   Stechler, Gerald.   "Newborn attention as affected by medication
during labor."   Science   144:   315-17, April 17, 1964.

397   Touwen, B. C. L.   "Neurological follow-up of infants born after
obstetrical complications."   In: Stoelinga, G. B. A. and Van der
Werff ten Bosch, J. J., eds.   Normal and abnormal development of brain
and behaviour.   Baltimore: Williams & Wilkins, 1971.   179-87.
(Boerhaave series for postgraduate medical education).

398   Towbin, Abraham.   "Neonatal damage to the central nervous system."
In: Tedeschi, C. G., ed.   Neuropathology: methods and diagnosis.
Boston: Little, Brown, 1970.   609-54.

399 ⎯⎯⎯. "Organic causes of minimal brain dysfunction: perinatal origin of minimal cerebral lesions." JAMA 217(9): 1207-14, August 30, 1971.

400 Ucko, L. E. "A comparative study of asphyxiated and non-asphyxiated boys from birth to five years." Dev Med Child Neurol 7(6): 643-57, December, 1965.

401 Werner, Emmy; Bierman, J. M.; French, Fern E.; et. al. "Reproductive and environmental casualties: a report of a ten year follow-up of the children of the Kauai pregnancy study." Pediatrics 42(1): 112-27, July, 1968.

402 Werner, Emmy; Simonian, K.; Bierman, J. M.; et. al. "Cummulative effect of perinatal complications and deprived environment on physical, intellectual and social development of preschool children." Pediatrics 39(4): 490-505, April, 1967.

403 Windle, William F. "An experimental approach to the prevention or reduction of the brain damage of birth asphyxia." Dev Med Child Neurol 8(2): 129-40, April, 1966.

404 ⎯⎯⎯. "Role of respiratoid distress in asphyxial brain damage of the newborn." Cereb Palsy J 27: 3-6, 1966.

D. Sequelae: Relation to Disease

405 Bender, Lauretta. "Post-encephalitic behavior disorders in childhood." In: Neal, Josephine B. Encephalitis: a clinical study. New York: Grune & Stratton, 1942. 361-84.

406 Ebaugh, F. "Neuropsychiatric sequelae of acute epidemic encephalitis in children." Am J Dis Child 25: 89-97, 1923.

407 Fishman, Marvin A., and Peake, Glenn T. "Paradoxical growth in a patient with diencephalic syndrome." Pediatrics 45(6): 973-82, June, 1970.

408 Gatfield, P. D.; Haust, H. L.; Durrant, D. "Porphyria in childhood following transient neonatal quadriplegia." Dev Med Child Neurol 14 (4): 495-501, August, 1972.

409 Geist, R. W., and Antolak, S. J., Jr. "Interstitial cystitis in children." J Urol 104(6): 922-25, December, 1970.

410 Gibbs, Frederic A.; Gibbs, Eerna L.; Spies, H. W.; et. al. "Common types of childhood encephalitis: electroencephalographic and clinical relationships." Arch Neurol 10(1): 1-11, January, 1964.

411 Girdwood, T. G., and Ross, E. M. "The diencephalic syndrome of early infancy." Brit J Radiol 42(503): 847-50, November, 1969.

412 Grunberg, F., and Pond, D. A. "Conduct disorders in epileptic children." J Neurol Neurosurg Psychiat 20(1): 65-68, February, 1957.

413 Gunderman, J. Richard, and Stamler, Richard. "Neuropsychological residuals seven years after acute encephalitis." Clin Pediatr 12(4): 228-30, April, 1973.

414 Havard, Janice. "School problems and allergies." J Learn Disabil 6(8): 492-94, October, 1973.

415 Hohman, Leslie B. "Post-encephalitic behavior disorders in children." Johns Hopkins Hosp Bull 33(380): 372-75, October, 1922.

416 Kalyanaraman, K.; Chamukuttan, S.; Arjundas, G.; et. al. "Maple syrup urine disease (branched-chain keto-aciduria) variant type manifesting as hyperkinetic behavior and mental retardation: report of two cases." J Neurol Sci 15(2): 209-17, February, 1972.

417 Kappelman, Murray M.; Thomas, George H.; Howell, Rodney R. "Histidinemia in a Negro child." Am J Dis Child 122(3): 212-14, September, 1971.

418 Kennedy, R. "Prognosis of sequelae of epidemic encephalitis in children." Am J Dis Child 28: 158-72, 1924.

419 Lurie, Louis A., and Levy, Sol. "Personality changes and behavior disorders of children following pertussis--report based on study of 500 problem children." JAMA 120(12): 890-94, November 21, 1942.

420 Matoth, Yehuda; Zaizov, Rina; Frankel, Jacob J. "Minimal cerebral dysfunction in children with chronic thrombocytopenia." Pediatrics 47(4): 698-706, April, 1971.

421 Meyerhoff, James L. "Gilles de la Tourette's disease and minimal brain dysfunction: amphetamine isomers reveal catecholamine correlates in an affected patient." Psychopharmacologia 29: 211-20, 1973.

422 Pitt, D. "The natural history of untreated phenylketonuria." Med J Aust 1: 378-83, February 13, 1971.

423 Sabatino, David A., and Cramblett, Henry G. "Behavioral sequelae of California encephalitis virus infection in children." Dev Med Child Neurol 10(3): 331-37, June, 1968.

424 Schulman, Jerome L.; Ford, Robin C.; Kaspar, Joseph C.; et. al. "Brain-damage syndrome in phenylketonuria." Percept Mot Skills 33 (2): 367-72, October, 1971.

425 Sherman, M., and Beverly, B. "The factor of deterioration in children showing behavior and difficulties after epidemic encephalitis." Arch Neurol Psychiatry 10: 329-43, 1923.

426 Sproles, E. T.; Azerrad, J.; Williamson, C.; et. al. "Meningitis due to hemophilus influenzae: long-term sequelae." J Pediatr 75(5): 782-88, November, 1969.

427 Strecker, E. "Behavior problems in encephalitis." Arch Neurol Psychiatry 21: 137-44, 1929.

428 Teuber, Hans L., and Rudel, Rita G. "Behavior after cerebral lesions in children and adults." Dev Med Child Neurol 4(1): 3-20,
February, 1962.

429 Towbin, Abraham. The pathology of cerebral palsy: the causes underlying the nature of the disorder. Springfield, Illinois: Thomas,
1960. 206p.

430 Wagenheim, Lillian. "Learning problems associated with childhood
diseases contracted at age two." Am J Orthopsychiatry 29(1): 102-9,
January, 1959.

      E. Environmental Influence: Trauma, Poisoning, Family

431 Angle, C. R.; McIntire, M. S.; Meile, R. L. "Neurologic sequelae
of poisoning in children." J Pediatr 73(4): 531-39, October, 1968.

432 Baltimore, C. L., and Meyer, R. J. "A study of storage, child and
behavior traits, and mother's knowledge of toxicology in fifty-two
poisoned families and fifty-two comparison families." Pediatrics 42
(2): 312-17, August, 1968.

433 Barltrop, D. "Chronic neurological sequelae of lead poisoning."
Dev Med Child Neurol 15(3): 365-66, June, 1973.

434 Blau, Abram. "Mental changes following head trauma in children."
Arch Neurol Psychiatry 35: 723-69, 1937.

435 Byers, R. K., and Lord, M. E. "Late effects of lead poisoning on
mental development." Am J Dis Child 66: 471-94, 1943.

436 Chess, Stella; Thomas, Alexander; Rutter, Michael; et. al. "Interaction of temperament and environment on the production of behavioral
disturbances in children." Am J Psychiatry 120(2): 142-48, August,
1963.

437 Clarkson, Frank E., and Hayden, Benjamin S. "The relationship of
hyperactivity in a normal class setting with family background factors
and neurological status." In: American Psychological Association,
80th, Honolulu, 1972. Proceedings. 7(pt. 2): 559-60, 1972.

438 Cooke, T. J. "Dapsone poisoning." Med J Aust 1: 1158-59, June
6, 1970.

439 David, Oliver; Clark, Julian; Voeller, Kytja. "Lead and hyperactivity." Lancet 2: 900-903, October 28, 1972.

440 Dennis, Wayne, and Najarian, Pergrouhi. "Infant development under
environmental handicap." Psychol Monogr 71(7, Whole No. 436): 1-13,
1957.

441 Escalona, Sibylle K. "Patterns of infantile experience and the
developmental process." Psychoanal Study Child 18: 197-244, 1963.

442   Fabian, A. A., and Bender, Lauretta. "Head injury in children: predisposing factors." Am J Orthopsychiatry 17(1): 68-79, January, 1947.

443   Frank, George H. "The role of the family in the development of psychopathology." Psychol Bull 64(3): 191-205, September, 1965.

444   Goldfarb, William. "Effects and psychological deprivation in infancy and subsequent stimulation." Am J Psychiatry 102: 18-33, 1945.

445   Harrington, J. A., and Letemendia, F. J. "Persistent psychiatric disorder after head injury in children." J Ment Sci 104: 1205-18, 1958.

446   "Hot dogs and hyperkinesis." Newsweek 82: 57, July 9, 1973.

447   Hutt, Corinne, and Hutt, Sidney J. "Effects of environmental complexity on stereotyped behaviors of children." Anim Behav 13: 1-4, 1965.

448   Ianzito, Benjamin M.; Liskow, Barry; Stewart, Mark A. "Reaction to LSD in a two-year-old child." J Pediatr 80(4): 643-47, April, 1972.

449   Jenkins, Richard L. "Psychiatric syndromes in children and their relation to family background." Am J Orthopsychiatry 36(3): 450-57, April, 1966.

450   Kittler, F. J. "The role of allergic factors in the child with minimal brain dysfunction." Ann Allergy 28: 203-6, May, 1970.

451   Langford, William S. "Accident-prone children." Feelings Their Med Significance 5(2): 1-4, February, 1963.

452   "Lead and hyperactive children." Chemistry 46: 15, February, 1973.

453   Malone, Charles A. "Some observations on children of disorganized families and problems of acting out." J Am Acad Child Psychiatry 2(1): 22-49, January, 1963.

454   Margolis, James A. "Psychosocial study of childhood poisoning: a five-year follow-up." Pediatrics 47(2): 439-44, February, 1971.

455   Matheny, Adam P., Jr.; Brown, Ann M.; Wilson, Ronald S. "Behavioral antecedents of accidental injuries in early childhood: a study of twins." J Pediatr 79(1): 122-24, July, 1971.

456   Munro, Nancy. A study of food and poverty among 113 Head Start children in Missoula, Montana. Montana University, Missoula Foundation, 1968. 113p. (ED 028 829).

457   Nichamin, Samuel J. "Battered child syndrome and brain dysfunction." JAMA 223(12): 1390, March 19, 1973.

458 Pasamanick, Benjamin; Knoblock, Hilda; Lilienfeld, Abraham M. "Socioeconomic status and some precursors of neuropsychiatric disorder." Am J Orthopsychiatry 26(3): 594-601, July, 1956.

459 Rexford, Eveoleen N., and Taets van Amerongen, Suzanne. "The influence of unsolved maternal oral conflicts upon impulsive acting out in young children." Am J Orthopsychiatry 27(1): 75-87, January, 1957.

460 Schaefer, E. S., and Bayley, Nancy. "Maternal behavior, child behavior, and their intercorrelations from infancy through adolescence." Monogr Soc Res Child Dev 28(3, Whole No. 87): 1-127, 1963.

461 Sears, R. R.; Whiting, J. W. M.; Nowlis, V.; et. al. "Some child rearing antecedents of aggression and dependency in young children." Genet Psychol Monogr 47(2): 135-236, May, 1963.

462 Sieben, R. L.; Leavitt, J. D.; French, J. H. "Falls as childhood accidents: an increasing urban risk." Pediatrics 47(5): 886-92, May, 1971.

463 Sobel, Raymond. "The psychiatric implications of accidental poisoning in childhood." Pediatr Clin North Am 17(3): 653-85, August, 1970.

464 ———. "Traditional safety measures and accidental poisoning in childhood." Pediatrics 44(5): 811-16, November, 1969.

465 Sobel, Raymond, and Margolis, James A. "Repetitive poisoning in children: a psychosocial study." Pediatrics 35(4): 641-51, April, 1965.

466 Stewart, Mark A.; Thach, Bradley T.; Freidin, Miriam R. "Accidental poisoning and the hyperactive child syndrome: a psychiatric follow-up study of accidentally poisoned children." Dis Nerv Syst 31(6): 403-7, June, 1970.

467 Thomas, Alexander; et. al. "Neurological symptoms can be an allergic reaction." Pediatr News p. 2, February, 1968.

468 Thurston, Don L.; Middelkamp, J. Neal; Mason, Elizabeth. "The late effects of lead poisoning." J Pediatr 47(4): 413-23, October, 1955.

469 Yarrow, Leon J. "Maternal deprivation: toward an empirical and conceptual re-evaluation." Psychol Bull 58(6): 459-90, November, 1961.

SECTION III

DIAGNOSIS

A. Identification Techniques

470 Abrams, Alfred L. "A delayed and irregular maturation versus minimal brain injury." Clin Pediatr 7(6): 344-49, June, 1968.

471 Anderson, David O. "Computer assistance for the diagnosis of learning disabilities." Diss Abstr Int 34(6-A): 3185-86, December, 1973.

472 Anderson, Scott, and Anderson, Lauriel E. "Identification of the neurologically handicapped--the parents' viewpoints." Acad Ther 1 (2): 54-63, Winter, 1965-66.

473 Arnold, L. Eugene. "Detection and management of hyperkinetic children in school." Sch Couns 18(3): 177-84, January, 1971.

474 ———. "Is this label necessary? identifying hyperkinetic children." J Sch Health 43(8): 510-14, October, 1973.

475 Baldwin, Ruth W.; et. al. The doctor looks at the NH child: diagnosis and treatment. Toronto, Ontario: Ontario Association for Children with Learning Disabilities, 1967. 37p.

476 Barnard, Kathryn, and Collar, Bernice S. "Early diagnosis, interpretation, and intervention: a commentary on the nurse's role." Ann NY Acad Sci 205: 373-82, February 28, 1973.

477 Bateman, Barbara D. "An educator's view of a diagnostic approach to learning disorders." In: Hellmuth, Jerome, ed. Learning disorders. Vol. 1. Seattle: Special Child Publications, 1965. 219-39.

478 ———. "Three approaches to diagnosis and educational planning for children with learning disabilities." In: International Convocation on Children and Young Adults with Learning Disabilities. Proceedings. Pittsburgh: Home for Crippled Children, 1967.

479 Beck, Harry S. "Detecting psychological symptoms of brain injury." Except Child 28(1): 57-62, September, 1961.

480 Bennett, Chester C., and Rogers, Carl R. "The clinical significance of problem syndromes." Am J Orthopsychiatry 11(2): 222-30, April, 1941.

481 Boag, Audrey K. "Teachers can screen behavior problems." Instructor 77(2): 158, October, 1967.

482 Boder, Elena. "Developmental dyslexia: a diagnostic approach based on patterns of reading and spelling." In: International Congress of Pediatrics, 12th, Mexico, 1968. Proceedings. 1: 529, 1968.

483 Bower, Eli M. Early identification of emotionally handicapped children in school. Springfield, Illinois: Thomas, 1960. 120p.

484 Brueckner, Leo J., and Bond, Guy L. The diagnosis and treatment of learning difficulties. New York: Appleton-Century-Crofts, 1955. 424p.

485 Bryan, G. Elizabeth, and Brown, Moroni H. "A method for differential diagnosis of brain damage in adolescents." J Nerv Ment Dis 125 (1): 69-72, January/March, 1957.

486 Burks, Harold F. "The effects of learning on brain pathology." Except Child 24(3): 169-72, December, 1957.

487 California. Bureau of Special Education. The development and validation of a process for screening emotionally handicapped children in school. Nadine M. Lambert, education research project consultant. Sacramento, California: California State Department of Education, 1963. 1v.

488 Capobianco, R. J. "Diagnostic methods used with learning disability cases." Except Child 31(4): 187-94, December, 1964.

489 Chess, Stella. "Categories of hyperactivity in children." Feelings Their Med Significance 3(4): 1-4, April, 1961.

490 ———. "Childhood psychopathologies: the search for differentiation." J Autism Child Schizophr 2(2): 111-13, April/June, 1972.

491 ———. "Diagnosis and treatment of the hyperactive child." NY State J Med 60: 2379-85, August 1, 1960.

492 Clark, R. M. "Language and behavior of children with unsuspected brain injury." Logos 5: 22-24, 1962.

493 Clements, Sam D., and Peters, John E. "Minimal brain dysfunction in the school-age child: diagnosis and treatment." Arch Gen Psychiatry 6(3): 185-97, March, 1962.

494 Cochran, A. "Recognizing MBD in the problem child." RN 35: 35-39, May, 1972.

495 Colin, M. E. "The assessment of the child with minimal cerebral dysfunction." S Afr Med J 47: 1956-57, October 20, 1973.

496 Conners, C. Keith. "Psychological assessment of children with minimal brain dysfunction." Ann NY Acad Sci 205: 283-302, February 28, 1973.

497 ———. "Symptom patterns in hyperkinetic, neurotic, and normal children." Child Dev 41(3): 667-82, September, 1970.

498 Copel, Sidney L. Psychodiagnostic study of children with adolescents. Springfield, Illinois: Thomas, 1967. 201p.

499 Copple, Peggy J., and Isom, J. B. "Soft signs and scholastic success." Neurology 18(3): 304, March, 1968.

500 Denhoff, Eric. "Detecting potential learning problems of preschool medical examinations." Tex Med 65(3): 56-59, March, 1969.

501 ———. "Medical responsibilities in learning disorders." In: Tarnopol, Lester, ed. Learning disorders in children: diagnosis, medication, education. Boston: Little, Brown, 1971. 65-118.

502 Denhoff, Eric; Hainesworth, P. K.; Hainesworth, M. L. "The child at risk for learning disorder: can he be identified during the first year of life?" Clin Pediatr 11(3): 164-70, March, 1972.

503 DiLeo, Joseph H. "Early identification of minimal cerebral dysfunction." Acad Ther 5(3): 187-203, Spring, 1970.

504 Diller, Leonard, and Birch, Herbert G. "Psychological evaluation of children with cerebral damage." In: Birch, Herbert G., ed. Brain damage in children: the biological and social aspects. Baltimore: Williams & Wilkins, 1964. 27-43.

505 Eaves, L. C.; Kendall, D. C.; Crichton, J. U. "The early detection of minimal brain dysfunction." J Learn Disabil 5(8): 454-62, October, 1972.

506 Fish, Barbara. "Problems of diagnosis and the definition of comparable groups: a neglected issue in drug research with children." Am J Psychiatry 125(7): 900-908, January, 1969.

507 Freeman, Stephen. "Learning disabilities and the school health worker." J Sch Health 43(8): 521-22, October, 1973.

508 Gallagher, James J., and Bradley, R. "Early identification of developmental difficulties." In: Gordon, Ira J., ed. Early childhood education. Chicago: National Society for the Study of Education, 1972. 87-122. (Yearbook of the National Society for the Study of Education, 71st, pt. 2).

509 Gerard, Margaret E. The emotionally disturbed child: papers on diagnosis, treatment, and care. New York: Child Welfare League of America, 1956. 168p.

510 Glidewell, John C.; Mensh, Ivan N.; Gildea, Margaret. "Behavior symptoms in children and degree of sickness." Am J Psychiatry 114: 47-53, July, 1957.

511 Gofman, Helen F. "The physician's role in early diagnosis and management of learning disabilities." In: Tarnopol, Lester, ed. Learning disabilities: introduction to educational and medical management. Springfield, Illinois: Thomas, 1969. 95-127.

512 Goldenberg, Samuel. "Some aspects of diagnosis of cerebral damage in children." Diss Abstr 13: 1259, 1953.

513 Graham, Philip, and Rutter, Michael. "The reliability and validity of the psychiatric assessment of the child: II. Interview with the parent." Br J Psychiatry 114: 581-92, May, 1968.

514 Graham, Philip; Rutter, Michael; George, Sandra. "Temperamental characteristics as predictors of behavior disorders in children." Am J Orthopsychiatry 43(3): 328-39, April, 1973.

515 Gratton, L., and Pope, L. "Group diagnosis and therapy for young school children." Hosp Community Psychiatry 23(6): 188-90, June, 1972.

516 Grubler, Eva R., and Gochman, Stanley I. "Statistical observations regarding the clinical diagnosis of brain damage." Psychol Rep 11(1): 221-22, August, 1962.

517 Hanvik, Leo J.; Nelson, S. E.; Hanson, H. B.; et. al. "Diagnosis of cerebral dysfunction in children." Am J Dis Child 101(3): 364-75, March, 1961.

518 Hobhouse, E. W. N. "Differentiation of hyperkinesia in children." Lancet 1: 1112-17, June 2, 1928.

519 Hoffman, M. S. "Early indications of learning problems: developmental histories of failing and passing students." Acad Ther 7(1): 23-35, Fall, 1971.

520 Hogg, William F. "The case-filtering of children's behaviour problems by public health nurses." Can J Public Health 62(3): 239-42, May/June, 1971.

521 Hunt, J. V. "Early detection of potential learning disorders." Educ Dig 35(2): 12-15, October, 1969.

522 Hurowitz, Linda. A synthesis of the differential diagnostic signs of brain-injured children. Unpublished master's thesis. University of Chicago, 1961.

523 Hutt, Sidney J., and Hutt, Corinne. Direct observation and measurement of behavior. Springfield, Illinois: Thomas, 1970. 224p.

524 Jenkins, Richard L. "Diagnosis, dynamics and treatment in child psychiatry." In: Jenkins, Richard L., and Cole, Jonathan O., eds. Diagnostic classification in child psychiatry. Washington, D. C.: American Psychiatric Association, 1964. 91-120. (Psychiatric Research Reports, No. 18).

525 Keogh, Barbara K. "Psychological evaluation of exceptional children: old hangups and new directions." J Sch Psychol 10(2): 49-53, June, 1972.

526 Kernberg, P. F. "The problem of organicity in the child: notes on some diagnostic techniques in the evaluation of children." J Am Acad Child Psychiatry 8(3): 517-41, July, 1969.

527 Khanna, J. L., ed. Brain damage and mental retardation: a psychological evaluation. Springfield, Illinois: Thomas, 1973. 227p.

528 Kinsbourne, Marcel. "Neuropsychological and neurophysiological aspects of learning disorders." In: Ross Conference on Pediatric Research, 61st, Columbus, Ohio, 1971. Report. Edited by John H. Menkes, and Richard J. Schain. Columbus, Ohio: Ross Laboratories, 1971. 29-32.

529 Knights, Robert M. "Problems of criteria in diagnosis: a profile similarity approach." Ann NY Acad Sci 205: 124-31, February 28, 1973.

530 Knobel, Mauricio. "Diagnosis and treatment of psychiatric problems in children." J Neuropsychiatry 1: 82-91, 1959.

531 L'Abate, L. "Screening children with cerebral dysfunction through the laboratory method." In: Haywood, H. Carl, ed. Brain damage in school age children. Washington, D. C.: Council for Exceptional Children, 1968. 128-60.

532 Lacey, Harvey M. "Minimal brain damage: a meaningful diagnosis or an irrelevant label?" Child Welfare 49(4): 205-11, April, 1970.

533 Lagos, Jorge C. Differential diagnosis in pediatric neurology. Boston: Little, Brown, 1971. 346p.

534 Laufer, Maurice W. "Psychiatric diagnosis and treatment of children with minimal brain dysfunction." Ann NY Acad Sci 205: 303-9, February 28, 1973.

535 Lawrence, Margaret M. "Minimal brain injury in child psychiatry." Compr Psychiatry 1(6): 360-69, December, 1960.

536 Lovitt, Thomas C. "Assessment of children with learning disabilities." Except Child 34(4): 233-39, December, 1967.

537 Lytton, George J., and Knobel, Mauricio. "Diagnosis and treatment of behavior disorders in children." Dis Nerv Syst 20(8): 334-45, August, 1959.

538 Merifield, David O. "The otolaryngologist and learning disabilities." Arch Otolaryngol 91(5): 470-73, May, 1970.

539 Meyer, Edith, and Simmel, Marianne. "Psychological appraisal of children with neurological defects." J Abnorm Soc Psychol 42(2): 193-205, April, 1947.

540 Mofenson, H. C.; Greensher, J.; Horowitz, R. "Detection of the hyperactive child." J Pediatr 80(4): 687, April, 1972.

541 Nichamin, Samuel J. "Recognizing minimal cerebral dysfunction in the infant and toddler: some clinical clues and thoughts on management." Clin Pediatr 11(5): 255-57, May, 1972.

542 Paine, Richmond S. "Symptomatology of unrecognized chronic brain syndromes of children." J Maine Med Assoc 53: 84-88, April, 1962.

543 "The pediatrician is the one to identify the slow learner." Pediatr News 8(6): 1, 34, June, 1974.

544 Peters, John E., and Clements, Sam D. "Diagnosis and treatment of minimal brain dysfunction in the school-age child." Feelings Their Med Significance 8(8): 1-4, September, 1966.

545 "The problem child: spotting and helping the one with a behavior/ learning disorder." Nurs Update 3: 1-12, September, 1972.

546 Raskin, Larry M., and Taylor, William J. "Problem identification through observation." Acad Ther 9(1): 85-89, Fall, 1973.

547 Reitan, Ralph M., and Heineman, Charles E. "Interactions of neurological deficits and emotional disturbances in children with learning disorders: methods for their differential assessments." In: Hellmuth, Jerome, ed. Learning disorders. Vol. 3. Seattle: Special Child Publications, 1967. 93-135.

548 Rodin, E. A.; Lucas, Alexander R.; Simson, Clyde B. "A study of behavior disorders in children by means of general purpose computers." In: Rochester Conference on Data Acquisition and Processing in Biology and Medicine, 1963. Proceedings. Vol. 3. Edited by Kurt Enslein. London: Pergamon, 1964. 115-23.

549 Rogolsky, Maryrose M. "Screening kindergarten children: a review and recommendations." J Sch Psychol 7(2): 18-25, 1968.

550 Ross, Donald C. "Emotional disorder underlying poor school achievement." Feelings Their Med Significance 8(2): 1-4, February, 1966.

551 ———. "Poor school achievement: a psychiatric study and classification." Clin Pediatr 5(2): 109-17, February, 1966.

552 Rutter, Michael, and Graham, Philip. "The reliability and validity of the psychiatric assessment of the child: I. Interview with the child." Br J Psychiatry 114: 563-79, May, 1968.

553 Sainz, A. "Hyperkinetic disease of children: diagnosis and therapy." Dis Nerv Syst 27(7): 48-50, July, 1966.

554 Saunders, R. V. "The assessment and education of brain-damaged children." In: Brown, Roy I., ed. The assessment and education of slow-learning children. London: University of London Press, 1967. 44-48.

555 Schain, Richard J. "Differential diagnosis in children with learning disorders." <u>Trans Am Neurol Assoc</u> 94: 341-43, 1969.

556 Schneider, Wilmot F. "Psychiatric evaluation of the hyperkinetic child." <u>J Pediatr</u> 26(6): 559-70, June, 1945.

557 Schrager, Jules M.; Harrison, Saul I.; McDermott, John F.; et. al. "The hyperkinetic child: some early indicators of potential school problems." <u>Am J Orthopsychiatry</u> 37(2): 378-79, March, 1967.

558 Schrager, Jules M., and Lindy, Janet M. "Hyperkinetic children: early indicators of potential school failure." <u>Community Ment Health J</u> 6(6): 447-54, December, 1970.

559 Silver, A. "Diagnosis and prognosis of behavior disorder associated with organic brain disease in children." <u>J Insur Med</u> 6: 38-42, 1951.

560 Smith, Stanley A., and Solanto, J. R. "An approach to preschool evaluations." <u>Psychol Sch</u> 8(2): 142-47, April, 1971.

561 Solomons, Gerald. "Child hyperactivity: diagnosis and treatment." <u>Tex Med</u> 63: 52-57, 1967.

562 Stone, F. Beth. "Assessment of children's activity level." <u>Am J Orthopsychiatry</u> 44(2): 250, March, 1974. (Abstract of paper).

563 Strother, Charles R. <u>Discovering, evaluating, programming for the neurologically handicapped child, with special attention to the child with minimal brain damage.</u> Chicago: National Society for Crippled Children and Adults, 1963. 14p.

564 Sulzbacher, S. I. <u>Diagnosis and treatment with medication of learning and behavior problems in the school-age child.</u> Seattle: University of Washington, Child Development and Mental Retardation Center, 1971. (Working Paper, No. 5).

565 Taylor, Edith M. <u>Psychological appraisal of children with cerebral defects.</u> Cambridge, Massachusetts: Harvard University Press, 1959. 499p.

566 Thomas, James D. "An assessment of some psychological factors involved in brain injury." <u>Diss Abstr</u> 22(9): 3269-70, March, 1962.

567 Tuddenham, Read D. "Studies in reputation: I. Sex and grade difference in school children's evaluation of their peers. II. The diagnosis of social maladjustment." <u>Psychol Monogr</u> 66(1, Whole No. 333): 1-58, 1951.

568 Van Ophuijsen, J. H. W. "Primary conduct disturbances: their diagnosis and treatment." In: Lewis, Nolan D., and Pacella, Bernard L., eds. <u>Modern trends in child psychiatry.</u> New York: International Universities Press, 1945. 35-42.

569 Wedell, K. "Early identification of children with potential learning problems: perceptuo-motor factors." J Spec Educ 4(3): 323-31, Fall, 1970.

570 Werry, John S. "The diagnosis, etiology, and treatment of hyperactivity." In: Hellmuth, Jerome, ed. Learning disorders. Vol. 3. Seattle: Special Child Publications, 1968. 171-90.

571 Wilson, R. G. "The clumsy child." Midwife Health Visit 10: 53-55, February/March, 1974.

  B. Neurological Evaluation: Emphasis on the EEG

572 Anderson, William W. "The hyperkinetic child: a neurological appraisal." Neurology 13(11): 968-73, November, 1963.

573 Beintema, David J. A neurological study of newborn infants. London: Spastics International Medical Publications, 1968. 178p.

574 Black, F. William. "Neurogenic findings in reading-retarded children as a function of visual perceptual ability." Percept Mot Skills 36(2): 359-62, April, 1973.

575 Bortner, Morton; Hertzig, Margaret E.; Birch, Herbert G. "Neurological signs and intelligence in brain-damaged children." J Spec Educ 6(4): 325-33, Winter, 1972.

576 Boshes, Benjamin, and Myklebust, Helmer R. "A neurological and behavioral study of children with learning disorders." Neurology 14 (1): 7-12, January, 1964.

577 Boyle, Ronald H.; Dykman, Roscoe A.; Ackerman, Peggy T. "Relationships of resting autonomic activity, motor impulsivity, and EEG tracings in children." Arch Gen Psychiatry 12(3): 314-23, March, 1965.

578 Bray, Patrick F. Neurology in pediatrics. Chicago: Year Book Medical Publishers, 1969. 514p.

579 Brown, Warren T., and Solomon, Charles I. "Delinquency and the electroencephalograph." Am J Psychiatry 98: 499-503, January, 1942.

580 Capute, A. J.; Niedermeyer, E. F. L.; Richardson, F. "The electroencephalogram in children with minimal cerebral dysfunction." Pediatrics 41(6): 1104-14, June, 1968.

581 Cohn, Robert. "Delayed acquisition of reading and writing abilities in children: neurological study." Arch Neurol 4(2): 153-64, February, 1961.

582 ———. "The neurological study of children with learning disabilities." Except Child 31(4): 179-85, December, 1964.

583 Conners, C. Keith. "Neuro-physiological studies of learning disorders." Claremont Read Conf Yearb 35: 99-108, 1971.

584 Copple, Peggy J. "The electroencephalogram in minimal cerebral dysfunction." Pediatrics 42(5): 874-75, November, 1968.

585 Daveau, M. "EEG of 150 children with behavior disorders." Electroencephalogr Clin Neurophysiol 10: 198, 1958.

586 Davidson, N. "Alpha rhythms and hyperkinesis." Nature 238 (5358): 43, July 7, 1972.

587 Duenas, D. A.; Preissig, S.; Summitt, R. L.; et. al. "Neurologic manifestations of the noonan syndrome." South Med J 66(2): 193-96, February, 1973.

588 Dyment, Paul G.; Lattin, John E.; Herbertson, Leon M. "The value of the electroencephalogram in evaluating children with minimal cerebral dysfunction." J Sch Health 41(1): 9-11, January, 1971.

589 Ellingson, R. J. "The incidence of EEG abnormality among patients with mental disorders of apparently non-organic origin: a critical revue." Am J Psychiatry 111: 263-75, October, 1954.

590 Freeman, Roger D. "Special education and the electroencephalogram: marriage of convenience." J Spec Educ 2(1): 61-73, Fall, 1967.

591 Gallagher, J. Roswell; Gibbs, Eerna L.; Gibbs, Frederic A. "Relation between the electrical activity of the cortex and personality in adolescent boys." Psychosom Med 4(2): 134-39, April, 1942.

592 Gibbs, Frederic A.; Gibbs, Eerna L.; Carpenter, P. R.; et. al. "Electroencephalographic abnormality in 'uncomplicated' childhood diseases." JAMA 171(8): 1050-55, October 24, 1959.

593 Gottlieb, J. S.; Knott, John R.; Ashby, M. C. "Electroencephalographic evaluation of primary behavior disorders in children: correlations with age, sex, family history, and antecedent illness or injury." Arch Neurol Psychiatry 53: 138-43, 1945.

594 Green, J. B. "Association of behavior disorder with EEG focus in children without seizure." Neurology 11: 337-44, 1961.

595 Hertzig, Margaret E.; Bortner, Morton; Birch, Herbert G. "Neurologic findings in children educationally designated as 'brain-damage.'" Am J Orthopsychiatry 39(3): 437-46, April, 1969.

596 Hughes, John R. "Electroencephalography and learning." In: Myklebust, Helmer R., ed. Progress in learning disabilities. Vol. 1. New York: Grune & Stratton, 1968. 113-46.

597 ———. "Electroencephalography and learning disabilities." In: Myklebust, Helmer R., ed. Progress in learning disabilities. Vol. 2. New York: Grune & Stratton, 1971. 18-55.

598 Itil, T. M.; Stock, M. J.; Duffy, A. D.; et. al. "Therapeutic trials and EEG investigations with SCH-12, 679 in behaviorally disturbed adolescents." Curr Ther Res 14(3): 136-50, March, 1972.

599 Jasper, Herbert H.; Solomon, Philip; Bradley, Charles. "Electroencephalographic analyses of behavior problem children." Am J Psychiatry 95(3): 641-58, November, 1938.

600 Kalverboer, A. F. "Observations of free-field behavior in preschool boys and girls in relation to neurological findings." In: Stoelinga, G. B. A., and van der Werff ten Bosch, J. J., eds. Normal and abnormal development of brain and behaviour. Baltimore: Williams & Wilkins, 1971. 187-208. (Boerhaave series for postgraduate medical education).

601 Kellaway, Peter, ed. Neurological and electroencephalographic correlative studies in infancy. New York: Grune & Stratton, 1964. 364p.

602 Kennard, Margaret A. "The characteristics of thought disturbances as related to electroencephalographic findings in children and adolescents." Am J Psychiatry 115: 911-21, April, 1959.

603 ———. "The electroencephalogram and disorders of behavior: a review." J Nerv Ment Dis 124(2): 103-24, August, 1956.

604 ———. "Factors affecting the EEG of children in adolescence." Arch Neurol Psychiatry 63: 822-26, 1950.

605 ———. "Value of equivocal signs in neurologic diagnosis." Neurology 10(8): 753-64, August, 1960.

606 Kennard, Margaret A.; Rabinovitch, Ralph D.; Wexler, Donald. "The abnormal electroencephalogram as related to reading disability in children with disorders of behavior." Can Med Assoc J 67(4): 330-33, October, 1952.

607 Klinkerfuss, G. H.; Lange, P. H.; Weinberg, W. A.; et. al. "Electroencephalographic abnormalities of children with hyperkinetic behavior." Neurology 15(10): 883-91, October, 1965.

608 Knobloch, Hilda, and Pasamanick, Benjamin. "Developmental behavioral approach to neurologic examination in infancy." Child Dev 33 (1): 181-98, March, 1962.

609 Knott, John R. "EEG and behavior." Am J Orthopsychiatry 30(2): 292-98, April, 1960.

610 Lee, Douglas; Hutt, Sidney J.; Forrest, S.; et. al. "Concurrent EEG and behavioural observations on freely moving children." Dev Med Child Neurol 6(4): 362-65, August, 1964.

611 Lucas, Alexander R.; Rodin, E. A.; Simson, Clyde B. "Neurological assessment of children with early school problems." Dev Med Child Neurol 7(1): 145-56, February, 1965.

612 Luria, A. R. "Experimental study of the higher nervous activity of the abnormal child." In: Ellis, Norman R., ed. Handbook of mental deficiency: psychological theory and research. New York: McGraw-Hill, 1963. 353-87.

613 Michaels, Joseph J. "The relationship of anti-social traits to the electroencephalogram in children with behavior disorders." Psychosom Med 7: 41-44, January, 1945.

614 Mordock, John B., and DeHaven, George E. "Interrelations among indexes of neurological 'soft signs' in children with minimal cerebral dysfunction." In: American Psychological Association, 76th, San Francisco, 1968. Proceedings. 3: 471-72, 1968.

615 Nall, Angie. "Alpha training and the hyperkinetic child--is it effective?" Acad Ther 9(1): 5-20, Fall, 1973.

616 Ozer, Mark N. "The neurological evaluation of school-age children." J Learn Disabil 1(1): 84-87, January, 1968.

617 Pacella, Bernard L. "The electroencephalogram in behavior disorders." In: Lewis, Nolan D., and Pacella, Bernard L., eds. Modern trends in child psychiatry. New York: International Universities Press, 1945. 103-23.

618 Pond, D. A. "The EEG in pediatrics." In: Hill, Dennis and Parr, Geoffrey, eds. Electroencephalography: a symposium on its various aspects. 2nd ed. New York: Macmillan, 1963. 509p.

619 Prechtl, H. F. R. "The long term value of the neurological examination of the newborn infant." In: National Spastics Society. Child neurology and cerebral palsy: a report of an international study group, St. Edmund Hall, Oxford, 1960. London: 1961. 69-74. (Little Club clinics in developmental medicine, No. 2).

620 ———. "Prognostic value of neurological signs in the newborn infant." Proc R Soc Med 58(1): 3-4, January, 1965.

621 Prechtl, H. F. R., and Dijkstra, J. "Neurological diagnosis of cerebral injury in the new born." In: Symposium on prenatal care. The Netherlands: Noordhoff, 1960.

622 Reed, James C. "Brain pathology and behavioral deficits." Nat Bus Educ Q 38(2): 13-18, Winter, 1969.

623 Ritvo, E. R.; Ornitz, E. M.; Walter, R. D.; et. al. "Correlation of psychiatric diagnoses and EEG findings: a double-blind study of 184 hospitalized children." Am J Psychiatry 126(7): 988-96, January, 1970.

624 Ross, I. S. "Electroencephalography in behavior disorders of childhood." J Med Soc NJ 59: 460, 1962.

625 Rutter, Michael; Graham, Philip; Yule, William; eds. "A neuropsychiatric study in childhood." Clin Dev Med 35/36. London: Spastics International Medical Publications/Heinemann Medical Books, 1970. 272p.

626 Satterfield, James H.; Cantwell, Dennis P.; Saul, Ronald E.; et. al. "Intelligence, academic achievement, and EEG abnormalities in hyperactive children." Am J Psychiatry 141(4): 391-95, April, 1974.

627 Satterfield, James H., and Dawson, M. E. "Electrodermal correlates of hyperactivity in children." Psychophysiology 8(2): 191-97, March, 1971.

628 Satterfield, James H.; Lesser, Leonard I.; Saul, Ronald E.; et. al. "EEG aspects in the diagnosis and treatment of minimal brain dysfunction." Ann NY Acad Sci 205: 274-82, February 28, 1973.

629 Schain, Richard J. "Neurological diagnosis in children with learning disabilities." Acad Ther 7(2): 139-47, Winter, 1971-72.

630 ————. "Neurological evaluation of children with learning disorders." Neuropaediatrie 1: 307-17, February, 1970.

631 ————. Neurology of childhood learning disorders. Baltimore: Williams & Wilkins, 1972. 144p.

632 Schwade, Edward D., and Geiger, Sara G. "Abnormal electroencephalographic findings in severe behavior disorders." Dis Nerv Syst 17 (10): 307-17, October, 1956.

633 Secunda, Lazarus, and Finley, K. H. "Electroencephalographic studies in children presenting behavior disorders." N Engl J Med 226: 850-54, May 21, 1942.

634 Shetty, Taranth. "Alpha rhythms and hyperkinesis." Nature 241: 543, February 23, 1973.

635 ————. "Alpha rhythms in the hyperkinetic child." Nature 234: 476, December 24, 1971.

636 ————. "Alpha rhythms in the hyperkinetic child." Nature 238: 43-44, July 7, 1972.

637 ————. "Some neurologic, electrophysiologic, and biochemical correlates." Pediatr Ann 2(5): 29-40, May, 1973.

638 Solomons, Gerald; Holden, R. H.; Denhoff, Eric. "Changing picture of cerebral dysfunction." J Pediatr 63(1): 113-20, July, 1963.

639 Stevens, Janice R. "Clinical and electroencephalographic correlates in patients hospitalized with psychiatric disorders." Electroencephalogr Clin Neurophysiol 28(1): 90, January, 1970.

640 Stevens, Janice R., and Milstein, Victor. "Severe psychiatric disorders of childhood." Am J Dis Child 120(3): 182-92, September, 1970.

641 Stevens, Janice R.; Sachdev, Kuldip; Milstein, Victor. "Behavior disorders of childhood and the electroencephalogram." Arch Neurol 18(2): 160-77, February, 1968.

642 Strauss, H.; Rahm, W. E., Jr.; Barrera, S. E. "Studies on a group of children with psychiatric disorders: I. Electroencephalographic studies." Psychosom Med 2: 34-42, January, 1940.

643 Taterka, John H., and Katz, Joseph. "Study of correlations between electroencephalographic and psychological patterns in emotionally disturbed children." Psychosom Med 17: 62-72, 1955.

644 Toffler, Alvin E. "The effect of intervention on children classified as minimal brain damaged by psychological testing which has been confirmed or disconfirmed by EEG evaluation." Diss Abstr Int 32 (10-B): 6062-63, April, 1972.

645 Touwen, B. C. L., and Prechtl, H. F. R., eds. "The neurological examination of the child with minor nervous dysfunction." Clin Dev Med 38. London: Spastics International Medical Publications/Heinemann Medical Books, 1970. 105p.

646 VanPelt, John C. "Further doubts about the value of the EEG in minimal cerebral dysfunction." Pediatrics 43(3): 467-68, March, 1969.

647 White, Philip T.; DeMyer, William; DeMyer, Marian. "EEG abnormalities in early childhood schizophrenia: a double-blind study of psychiatrically disturbed and normal children during promazine sedation." Am J Psychiatry 120(10): 950-58, April, 1964.

648 Wikler, Abraham W.; Dixon, Joan F.; Parker, Joseph P. "Brain function in problem children and controls: psychometric, neurological and electroencephalographic comparisons." Am J Psychiatry 127(5): 634-45, November, 1970.

649 Winfield, D. L. "Emotional disturbances of the brain-damaged child with reference to the electroencephalogram." Memphis Mid-South Med J 36: 403-6, 1961.

650 Woody, Robert H. "Electroencephalography and minimal cerebral dysfunction: a research-based stance for school health personnel." J Sch Health 41(7): 351-54, September, 1971.

C. Psychological and Educational Testing

651 Ackerman, Peggy T.; Peters, John E.; Dykman, Roscoe A. "Children with learning disabilities: Bender-Gestalt findings and other signs." J Learn Disabil 4(8): 437-46, October, 1971.

652 Ackerman, Peggy T.; Peters, John E.; Dykman, Roscoe A. "Children with specific learning disabilities: WISC profiles." J Learn Disabil 4(3): 150-66, March, 1971.

653 Avakian, Sonia A. "The applicability of the Hunt-Minnesota Test for organic brain damage to children between the ages of ten and sixteen." J Clin Psychol 17(1): 45-49, January, 1961.

654 Baker, Rodney R. "The effects of psychotropic drugs on psychological testing." Psychol Bull 69(6): 377-87, June, 1968.

655 Beagley, H. A.; et. al. "Clinical experience of evoked response testing with sedation." Sound 6(1): 8-13, February, 1971.

656 Beck, Harry S., and Lam, Robert L. "Use of the WISC in predicting organicity." J Clin Psychol 11(2): 154-58, April, 1955.

657 Bender, Lauretta. "Use of the Visual Motor Gestalt Test in the diagnosis of learning disabilities." J Spec Educ 4(1): 29-39, Winter, 1970.

658 Berman, Allan, and McKinney, James D. "Factor structure of the WISC for hyperkinetic children." In: American Psychological Association, 81st, Montreal, 1973. Proceedings. 8: 513-14, 1973.

659 Birch, Herbert G., and Diller, Leonard. "Rorschach signs of 'organicity': a physiological basis for perceptual disturbances." J Proj Tech 23(2): 184-97, June, 1959.

660 Bortner, Morton, and Birch, Herbert G. "Patterns of intellectual ability in emotionally disturbed and brain-damaged children." J Spec Educ 3(4): 351-69, Winter, 1969.

661 Bradley, Charles, and Green, Emily. "Psychometric performance of children receiving amphetamine (benzedrine) sulfate." Am J Psychiatry 97: 388-94, September, 1940.

662 Burleigh, Allison C.; et. al. Development of a score that separates hyperkinetic and normal children and demonstrates drug effect. 1971. 9p. (ED 048 374).

663 Cattell, Psyche. The measurement of intelligence of infants and young children. New York: Psychological Corporation, 1940. 274p.

664 Clawson, Aileen. "Relationship of psychological tests to cerebral disorders in children: a pilot study." Psychol Rep 10(1): 187-90, February, 1962.

665 Corah, Norman L., and Powell, Barbara J. "A factor analytic study of the Frostig Development Test of Visual Perception." Percept Mot Skills 16(1): 59-63, February, 1963.

666 Crinella, Francis M. "An analysis of patterns of brain dysfunction in school-aged children." Diss Abstr Int 30(11-B): 5234-35, May, 1970.

667 Denhoff, Eric; Hainsworth, P. K.; Siqueland, M. L. "The measurement of psychoneurological factors contributing to learning efficiency." J Learn Disabil 1(12): 636-44, December, 1968.

668 Denhoff, Eric; Siqueland, Marian L.; Komich, M. Patricia; et. al. "Developmental and predictive characteristics of items from the Meeting Street School Screening Test." Dev Med Child Neurol 10(2): 220-32, April, 1968.

669 Doubros, Steve G., and Mascarennas, Juliet. "Relations among Wechsler Full-Scale Scores, Organicity-Sensitive Subtest Scores and Bender-Gestalt Errors Scores." Percept Mot Skills 29(3): 719-29, December, 1969.

670 Elizur, A. "A combined test used for the diagnosis of organic brain condition." Arch Neurol Psychiatry 81: 776-89, 1959.

671 Feinberg, Rosalind H. "The development of a screening device for the detection of minimal cerebral dysfunction in kindergarten children." Diss Abstr Int 33(7-A): 3376-77, January, 1973.

672 Fidel, Edward A., and Ray, Joseph B. "The validity of the Revised Objective Perceptual Test in differentiating among nonorganic, minimally organic and grossly organic children." J Spec Educ 6(3): 279-84, Fall, 1972.

673 Frostig, Marianne. Developmental Test of Visual Perception. Palo Alto, California: Consulting Psychologists Press, 1961.

674 ———. "Treatment of learning disorders." In: Ross Conference on Pediatric Research, 61st, Columbus, Ohio, 1971. Report. Edited by John H. Menkes, and Richard J. Schain. Columbus, Ohio: Ross Laboratories, 1971. 56-60.

675 Gallagher, James J.; Benoit, E. Paul; Boyd, Herbert F. "Measures of intelligence of brain-damaged children." J Clin Psychol 12(1): 69-71, January, 1956.

676 Glidewell, John C.; Domke, Herbert R.; Kantor, Mildred B. "Screening in schools for behavior disorders: use of mother's reports of symptoms." J Educ Res 56(10): 508-15, July/August, 1963.

677 Goldenberg, S. "Testing the brain-injured child with normal I. Q." In: Strauss, Alfred A., and Kephart, Newell C., Psychopathology and education of the brain-injured child. Vol. 2. New York: Grune & Stratton, 1955. 144-64.

678 Goodenough, Florence L. Measurement of intelligence by drawings. New York: World, 1926. 177p.

679 Graham, Frances K., and Berman, Phyllis W. "Current status of behavioral tests for brain damage in infants and preschool children." Am J Orthopsychiatry 31(4): 713-27, October, 1961.

680 Haines, Miriam S. "Test performance of preschool children with and without organic brain pathology." J Consult Psychol 18(5): 371-74, 1954.

681 Hainsworth, P. K., and Siqueland, M. L. Early identification of children with learning disabilities: the Meeting Street School Screening Test. Providence, Rhode Island: Crippled Children and Adults of Rhode Island, 1969.

682 Hanvik, Leo J. "A note on rotations in the Bender-Gestalt Test as predictors of EEG abnormalities in children." J Clin Psychol 9(4): 399, October, 1953.

683 Haring, Norris G., and Ridgway, Robert W. "Early identification of children with learning disabilities." Except Child 33(6): 387-95, February, 1967.

684 Harris, Dale B. Children's drawings as measures of intellectual maturity: a revision and extension of the Goodenough Draw-a-Man Test. New York: Harcourt, Brace & World, 1963. 367p.

685 Harth, Robert, and Glavin, John P. "Validity of teacher rating as a subtest for screening emotionally disturbed children." Except Child 37(8): 605-6, April, 1971.

686 Hartlage, L. "Common psychological tests applied to the assessment of brain damage." J Proj Tech 30: 319-38, 1966.

687 Hartman, Lenore D. "Psychological testing of children on and off medication." Am J Orthopsychiatry 43(2): 233-34, March, 1973.

688 Hayden, Benjamin S.; Talmadge, Max; Hall, Marjory; et. al. "Diagnosing minimal brain damage in children: a comparison of two Bender scoring systems." Merrill-Palmer Q 16(3): 278-85, July, 1970.

689 Haynes, Jack R., and Sells, S. B. "Assessment of organic brain damage by psychological tests." Psychol Bull 60(3): 316-25, May, 1963.

690 Herbert, M. "The concept and testing of brain-damage in children: a review." J Child Psychol Psychiatry 5(3/4): 197-216, December, 1964.

691 Holroyd, Jean, and Wright, Francis. "Neurological implications of WISC verbal performance discrepancies in a psychiatric setting." J Consult Psychol 29(3): 206-12, June, 1965.

692 Hopkins, Kenneth D. "An empirical analysis of the efficacy of the WISC in the diagnosis of organicity in children of normal intelligence." J Genet Psychol 105(1): 163-72, September, 1964.

693 Keller, James E. "The use of certain perceptual measures of brain injury with mentally retarded children." In: Trapp, E. Philip, and Himelstein, Philip, eds. Readings on the exceptional child. New York: Appleton-Century-Crofts, 1962. 485-91.

694 Keogh, Barbara K. "The Bender-Gestalt with children: research implications." J Spec Educ 3(1): 15-22, Winter/Spring, 1969.

695 Keogh, Barbara K.; Wetter, Jack; McGinty, Ann; et. al. "Functional analysis of WISC performance of learning-disordered, hyperactive, and mentally retarded boys." Psychol Sch 10(2): 178-81, April, 1973.

696 Klatskin, Ethelyn H.; McNamara, Nancy E.; Shaffer, David; et. al. "Mininal organicity in children of normal intelligence: correspondence between psychological test results and neurologic findings." J Learn Disabil 5(4): 213-18, April, 1972.

697 Knights, Robert M., and Hinton, George G. "Minimal brain dysfunction: clinical and psychological test characteristics." Acad Ther 4(4): 265-73, Summer, 1969.

698 Knights, Robert M., and Watson, Peter. "The use of computerized test profiles in neuropsychological assessment." J Learn Disabil 1 (12): 696-709, December, 1968.

699 Koppitz, Elizabeth M. The Bender-Gestalt Test for Young Children. New York: Grune & Stratton, 1964. 195p.

700 ———. "Diagnosing brain damage in young children with the Bender-Gestalt Test." J Consult Psychol 26: 541-46, December, 1962.

701 ———. Psychological evaluation of children's human figure drawings. New York: Grune & Stratton, 1968. 341p.

702 Koppitz, Elizabeth M.; Sullivan, John: Blyth, David D.; et. al. "Prediction of first grade school achievement with the Bender-Gestalt Test and human figure drawings." J Clin Psychol 15(2): 164-68, April, 1959.

703 Layman, Emma M. "Psychological testing of infants and preschool children." Clin Proc Child Hosp 11(6): 126-36, June, 1955.

704 Lesiak, Walter J. "Screening primary-grade children for educational handicaps: a teacher administered battery." Psychol Sch 10(1): 88-101, January, 1973.

705 Liem, G. Ramsey; Yellott, Ann W.; Cowen, Emory L.; et. al. "Some correlates of early-detected emotional dysfunction in the schools." Am J Orthopsychiatry 39(4): 619-26, July, 1969.

706 McConnell, Owen. "Koppitz's Bender-Gestalt scores in relation to organic and emotional problems in children." J Clin Psychol 23(3): 370-74, June, 1967.

707 Machover, Karen A. Personality projection in the drawing of the human figure: a method of personality investigation. New York: Thomas, 1949. 181p.

708 Maslow, Phyllis; Frostig, Marianne; Lefever, D. Welty; et. al. "The Marianne Frostig Developmental Test of Visual Perception, 1963 Standardization." Percept Mot Skills 19(2): 463-99, October, 1964.

709 Millichap, J. Gordon; Aymat, Fernando; Sturgis, Loretta H.; et. al. "Hyperkinetic behavior and learning disorders: III. Battery of neuropsychological tests in a controlled trial of methylphenidate." Am J Dis Child 116(3): 235-44, September, 1968.

710 Mordock, John B., and Bogan, Steve. "Wechsler patterns and symptomatic behaviors of children diagnosed as having minimal cerebral dysfunction." In: American Psychological Association, 76th, San Francisco, 1968. Proceedings. 3: 663-64, 1968.

711 Oliver, Ronald A., and Kronenberger, Earl J. "Testing the applicability of Koppitz's Bender-Gestalt scores to brain-damaged, emotionally disturbed and normal adolescents." Psychol Sch 8(3): 250-52, July, 1971.

712   Palkes, Helen S., and Stewart, Mark A. "Intellectual ability and performance of hyperactive children." Am J Orthopsychiatry 42(1): 35-39, January, 1972.

713   Palmer, James O. The psychological assessment of children. New York: Wiley, 1970. 475p.

714   Peabody Picture Vocabulary Test. Minneapolis, Minnesota: American Guidance Service, 1959.

715   Piotrowski, A. "The Rorschach ink-blot method in organic disturbances of the central nervous system." J Nerv Ment Dis 86: 525, 1937.

716   Porteus, Stanley D. "New applications of the Porteus Maze Test." Percept Mot Skills 26(1): 787-98, June, 1968.

717   _____. Porteus Maze Tests: fifty years application. Palo Alto, California: Pacific Books, 1965. 320p.

718   _____. Qualitative performance in the Maze Test. Vineland, New Jersey: Smith, 1942. 37p.

719   Reed, Homer B. C., Jr. "The use of psychological tests in diagnosing brain damage in school children." In: Haywood, H. Carl, ed. Brain damage in school age children. Washington, D. C.: Council for Exceptional Children, 1968. 109-27.

720   Reed, Homer B. C., Jr.; Reitan, Ralph M.; Klove, Hallgrim. "Influence of cerebral lesions on psychological test performances of older children." J Consult Psychol 29(3): 247-51, June, 1965.

721   Roach, Eugene G., and Kephart, Newell C. Purdue Perceptual-Motor Survey. Columbus, Ohio: Merrill, 1966. 82p.

722   Rosvold, H. E.; Mirsky, A. F.; Sarason, E.; et. al. "Continuous performance test of brain damage." J Consult Psychol 20(5): 343-50, 1956.

723   Rowley, Vinton. "Analysis of the WISC performance of brain-damaged and emotionally disturbed children." J Consult Psychol 25(6): 553, December, 1961.

724   Schafer, Roy. The clinical application of psychological tests: diagnostic summaries and case studies. New York: International Universities Press, 1948. 346p.

725   Sloan, William. "Lincoln-Oseretsky Motor Development Scale." Genet Psychol Monogr 51(pt. 2): 252, May, 1955.

726   Spivack, George, and Spotts, Jules. "Adolescence symptomatology." Am J Ment Defic 72(1): 74-95, July, 1967.

727   Spraings, V. Implications of psychologic testing for the detection and education of neurologically handicapped children. Los Angeles: Association for Neurologically Handicapped Children, 1963.

728 Spreen, Otfried, and Benton, Arthur L. "Comparative studies of
some psychologic tests for cerebral damage." J Nerv Ment Dis 140(5):
323-33, May, 1965.

729 Stevens, Douglas A.; Boydstun, James A.; Dykman, Roscoe A.; et. al.
"Presumed minimal brain dysfunction in children: relationship to performance on selected behavioral tests." Arch Gen Psychiatry 16(3):
281-85, March, 1967.

730 Swanson, M., and Jacobson, A. "Evaluation of the SIT for screening
children with learning disabilities." J Learn Disabil 3(1): 22-24,
January, 1970.

731 Tarnopol, Lester. "Testing children with learning disabilities."
In: Tarnopol, Lester, ed. Learning disabilities: introduction to
educational and medical management. Springfield, Illinois: Thomas,
1969. 180-91.

732 Twitchell, Thomas E.; Lecours, Andre-Roch; Rudel, Rita G.; et. al.
"Minimal cerebral dysfunction in children: motor tests." Trans Am
Neurol Assoc 91: 353-55, 1966.

733 Vacc, Nicholas A. "Study of emotionally disturbed children in regular and special classes." Except Child 35(3): 197-204, November,
1968.

734 Vinter, Robert D.; Sarri, R. C.; Vorwaller, D. J.; et. al. Pupil
behavior inventory: a manual for administration and scoring. Ann
Arbor, Michigan: Campus Publishers, 1966. 65p.

735 Wechsler, David. Wechsler Intelligence Scale for Children. New
York: Psychological Corporation, 1949. 113p.

736 Wittenborn, J. R. "Bellevue subtest scores as an aid in diagnosis."
J Consult Psychol 13(6): 433-39, December, 1949.

737 Wolfensberger, W.; Miller, M. B.; Cromwell, Rue L.; et. al. "Rorschach correlates of activity level in high school children." J
Consult Psychol 26(3): 269-72, June, 1962.

D. Behavioral Rating Scales: An Aid to Assessment

738 Alderton, H. R. "The children's pathology index as a predictor of
follow-up adjustment." Can Psychiatr Assoc J 15(3): 289-94, June,
1970.

739 Arnold, L. Eugene, and Smeltzer, Donald J. "Behavior checklist
factor analysis for children and adolescents." Arch Gen Psychiatry
30(6): 799-804, June, 1974.

740 Balint, M. "Activity level of retarded cerebral palsied children:
activity level rating scale for infants and preschool children."
Except Child 38(8): 641-42, April, 1972.

741 Bell, Richard Q.; Waldrop, Mary F.; Weller, George M. "Rating system for the assessment of hyperactive and withdrawn children in preschool samples." Am J Orthopsychiatry 42(1): 23-34, January, 1972.

742 Benton, Arthur L. "Behavioral indices of brain injury in school." Child Dev 33(1): 199-208, March, 1962.

743 Blunden, Dale; Spring, Carl; Greenberg, Lawrence M. "Validation of the classroom behavior inventory." J Consult Clin Psychol 42(1): 84-88, February, 1974.

744 Bryan, Tanis S., and McGrady, Harold J. "Use of a teacher rating scale." J Learn Disabil 5(4): 199-206, April, 1960.

745 Bullock, Lyndal M., and Brown, R. Keith. "Behavioral dimensions of emotionally disturbed children." Except Child 38(9): 740-41, May, 1972.

746 Burks, Harold F. "A behavior rating scale for screening brain impaired children." In: Regional Institute on Neurologically Handicapping Conditions in Children, University of California, Berkeley, 1961. Proceedings: Implications for maternal and child health and crippled children's programs...Edited by Eleanor H. Boydston. Berkeley, California, 1961. 89-98.

747 ————. Burks Behavior Rating Scales. El Monte, California: Arden Press, 1968.

748 Burns, R. H.; McCullen, Audrey; Cattell, Raymond B. "Teachers look at classroom behavior problems: a survey." Ment Hyg 55: 504-6, October, 1971.

749 Cattell, Raymond B., and Coan, Richard W. "Child personality structure as revealed in teachers' behavior ratings." J Clin Psychol 13(4): 315-27, October, 1957.

750 Chaney, James A. "The development of a scale for the minimal brain dysfunction syndrome in adolescents." Diss Abstr Int 34(4-B): 1741, October, 1973.

751 Conners, C. Keith. "A teacher rating scale for use in drug studies with children." Am J Psychiatry 126(6): 884-88, December, 1969.

752 Davids, Anthony. "An objective instrument of assessing hyperkinesis in children." J Learn Disabil 4(9): 499-501, November, 1971.

753 Dayton, C. M. Technical Manual: Pupil Classroom Behavior Scale. College Park, Maryland: University of Maryland, Research Center of the Interprofessional Research Commission on Pupil Personnel Services, 1967.

754 Dielman, T. E.; Cattell, Raymond B.; Rhoades, P. A. "Cross-validational evidence on the dimensions of problem behavior in the early grades." Multivariate Behav Res 7(1): 33-40, January, 1972.

755 Katz, Lilian G.; Peters, Donald L.; Stein, Nancy S. "Observing behavior in kindergarten and preschool classes: behavior survey instrument." Child Educ 44(6): 400-405, February, 1968.

756 Kupietz, Samuel; Bialer, Irv; Winsberg, Bertrand G. "A behavior rating scale for assessing improvement in behaviorally deviant children: a preliminary investigation." Am J Psychiatry 128(11): 1432-36, May, 1972.

757 Maurer, Katharine M. "Patterns of behavior of young children as revealed by a factor analysis of trait clusters." J Genet Psychol 59: 177-88, September, 1941.

758 Miller, Lovick C. "Louisville Behavior Check List for Males, six to twelve years of age." Psychol Rep 21(3): 885-96, December, 1967.

759 Mutimer, Dorothy D., and Rosemier, Robert A. "Behavior problems of children as viewed by teachers and the children themselves." J Consult Psychol 31(6): 583-87, December, 1967.

760 Noffsinger, Thomas. "Effects of reward and level of aspiration on an educational task with children identified by a problem behavior checklist." Diss Abstr Int 31(1-A): 253, July, 1970.

761 ————. "Effects of reward and level of aspiration on students with deviant behavior: Quays Behavior Problem Checklist." Except Child 37(5): 355-64, January, 1971.

762 Peterson, Donald R., and Cattell, Raymond B. "Personality factors in nursery school children as derived from parent ratings." J Clin Psychol 14(4): 346-55, October, 1958.

763 Peterson, Donald R., and Quay, Herbert C. Behavior Problem Checklist. Champaign, Illinois: Children's Research Center, University of Illinois Press, 1967.

764 Phillips, Beeman N. "Problem behavior in the elementary school." Child Dev 39(3): 895-903, September, 1968.

765 Quay, Herbert C.; Morse, William C.; Cutter, Richard L. "Personality patterns of pupils in special classes for the emotionally disturbed." Except Child 32(5): 297-301, January, 1966.

766 Quay, Herbert C., and Peterson, Donald R. Manual for the Behavior Problem Checklist. Champaign, Illinois: Children's Research Center, University of Illinois Press, 1967.

767 Quay, Herbert C., and Quay, Lorene C. "Behavior problems in early adolescence." Child Dev 36(1): 215-20, March, 1965.

768 Richards, T. W., and Simons, Marjorie P. "The Fels Child Behavior Scales." Genet Psychol Monogr 24(2): 259-309, November, 1941.

769 Richman, N., and Graham, P. J. "Behavioural screening questionnaire for use with three-year-old children: preliminary findings." J Child Psychol Psychiatry 12(1): 5-33, June, 1971.

770   Ross, Alan O.; Lacey, Harvey M.; Parton, David A.   "The development of a behavior checklist for boys."   Child Dev   36(4):   1013-27, December, 1965.

771   Rutter, Michael.   "A children's behavior questionnaire for completion by teachers: preliminary findings."   J Child Psychol Psychiatry   8(1):   1-11, May, 1966.

772   Saunders, Bruce T.   "Procedure for the screening, identification, and diagnosis of emotionally disturbed children in the rural elementary school."   Psychol Sch   9(2):   159-64, April, 1972.

773   Schrager, Jules M.; Lindy, Janet M.; Harrison, Saul I.; et. al.   "The hyperkinetic child: some consensually validated behavioral correlates."   Except Child   32(9):   635-37, May, 1966.

774   Speer, David C.   "The Behavior Problem Checklist (Peterson-Quay):   baseline data from parents of child guidance and nonclinic children."   J Consult Clin Psychol   36(2):   221-28, April, 1971.

775   Spivack, George, and Levine, Murray.   "The Devereux Child Behavior Rating Scales: a study of symptom behaviors in latency age atypical children."   Am J Ment Defic   68(6):   700-717, May, 1964.

776   Spivack, George, and Spotts, Jules.   Devereux Child Behavior Rating Scale Manual.   Devon, Pennsylvania: The Devereux Foundation, 1966.

777   Spivack, George, and Spotts, Jules.   "The Devereux Child Behavior Scale: symptom behaviors in latency age children."   Am J Ment Defic   69(6):   839-53, May, 1965.

778   Spivack, George, and Swift, Marshall S.   "The classroom behavior of children: a critical review of teacher administered rating scales."   J Spec Educ   7(1):   55-89, Spring, 1973.

779   Spivack, George, and Swift, Marshall S.   "The Devereux Elementary School Behavior Rating Scale: a study of the nature and organization of achievement related disturbed classroom behavior."   J Spec Educ   1(1):   71-91, Fall, 1966.

780   Spivack, George, and Swift, Marshall S.   Hahnemann High School Behavior Rating Scale (HHSB).   Philadelphia: Hahnemann Medical College and Hospital, Department of Mental Health Sciences, 1971.

781   Stewart, Mark A.   "Hyperactive children."   Sci Am   222:   94-98, April, 1970.

782   Stott, D. H.   "Classification of behavior disturbance among school-age students: principles, epidemiology and syndromes."   Psychol Sch   8(3):   232-39, July, 1971.

783   Strauss, Alfred A., and Kephart, Newell C.   "Behavior differences in mentally retarded children measured by a new behavior rating scale."   Am J Psychiatry   96:   1117-23, March, 1940.

784 Swift, Marshall S., and Spivack, George. "Academic success and classroom behavior in secondary schools." Except Child 39(5): 392-99, February, 1973.

785 Swift, Marshall S., and Spivack, George. "Achievement related classroom behavior of secondary school normal and disturbed students." Except Child 35(9): 677-84, May, 1969.

786 Swift, Marshall S., and Spivack, George. "Clarifying the relationship between academic success and overt classroom behavior: the Devereux Elementary School Behavior Rating Scale." Except Child 36(2): 99-104, October, 1969.

787 Victor, James B.; Halverson, Charles F., Jr.; Inoff, Gale; et. al. "Objective behavior measures of first and second grade boys' free play and teachers ratings on a behavior problem check-list." Psychol Sch 10(4): 439-43, October, 1973.

788 Wimberger, Herbert C., and Gregory, Robert J. "A behavior checklist for use in child psychiatry clinics." J Am Acad Child Psychiatry 7(4): 677-88, October, 1968.

789 Zedler, Empress. "A screening scale for children with high risk of neurological impairment." In: Association for Children with Learning Disabilities, 3rd, Tulsa, Oklahoma, 1966. Selected papers: International approach to learning disabilities of children and youth. Pittsburgh, 1967. 284p.

790 Ziv, Avner. "Children's behavior problems as viewed by teachers, psychologists, and children." Child Dev 41(3): 871-79, September, 1970.

SECTION IV

MANAGEMENT

A. Clinical Management: with Emphasis on the

Role of Psychopharmacology

791 Abdou, F. A. "Psychotropic drug therapy in children and adolescents." Va Med Mon 94(8): 464-67, August, 1967.

792 Annotated reference list on use of psychopharmacologic agents with children. Bethesda, Maryland: Psychopharmacology Service Center, April 14, 1958.

793 Arnold, L. Eugene. "The art of medicating hyperkinetic children: a number of practical suggestions." Clin Pediatr 12(1): 35-41, January, 1973.

794 ———. "Letter to editor." Pediatrics 48(3): 496-97, September, 1971.

795 Association for Research in Nervous and Mental Disease. The effect of pharmacologic agents on the nervous system, proceedings of the association, New York, 1957. Baltimore: Williams & Wilkins, 1959. 488p. (Its Research Publications, Vol. 37).

796 Bakwin, Harry, and Bakwin, Ruth M. Clinical management of behavior disorders in children. 3rd ed. Philadelphia: Saunders, 1966. 652p.

797 Baldwin, Ruth W., and Kenny, Thomas J. "Medical treatment of behavior disorders." In: Hellmuth, Jerome, ed. Learning disorders. Vol. 2. Seattle: Special Child Publications, 1966. 311-25.

798 Bateman, Barbara D., and Frankel, Herman. "Special education and the pediatrician." J Learn Disabil 5(4): 178-86, April, 1972.

799 Battista, Orlando. Mental drugs: chemistry's challenge to psychotherapy. Philadelphia: Childon, 1960. 155p.

800 Beavan, K. "Drugs to prevent dropouts." Times Educ Suppl 2877: 18, July 10, 1970.

801 Bedwell, H. Wade. "Medication for hyperactivity in the classroom." Sch Community 58(3): 39, November, 1971.

802 Bender, Lauretta. "Discussion of Eisenberg's paper." In: Fisher Seymour, ed. Child research in psychopharmacology. Springfield, Illinois: Thomas, 1959. 35-42.

803 Bender, Lauretta, and Faretra, Gloria. "Organic therapy in pediatric psychiatry." Dis Nerv Syst 22(4-Suppl.): 110-11, April, 1961.

804 Bender, Lauretta, and Nichtern, Sol. "Chemotherapy in child psychiatry." NY J Med 56(18): 2791-95, September 15, 1956.

805 Bendix, Selina. "Drug modification of behavior: a form of chemical violence against children?" J Clin Child Psychol 2(3): 17-19, Fall, 1973.

806 Berger, F. M. "Classification of psychoactive drugs according to their chemical structures and sites of action." In: Uhr, Leonard, and Miller, James G., eds. Drugs and behavior. New York: Wiley, 1960. 86-105.

807 Blanco, Ralph F. Prescriptions for children with learning and adjustment problems. Springfield, Illinois: Thomas, 1972. 298p.

808 Bouthilet, Lorraine, and Fisher, Seymour. "Reference list on the use of psychopharmacological agents with children." In: Fisher, Seymour, ed. Child research in psychopharmacology. Springfield, Illinois: Thomas, 1959. 170-206.

809 Bradley, J. E. "School problems and the physician." Curr Med Dig 25: 147-85, 1968.

810 Branan, K. "What can I do about hyperactive children and drugs." Scholastic Teach (Suppl.): 28-29, February 7, 1972.

811 Bruch, H. "Changing approaches to anorexia nervosa." Int Psychiatry Clin 7: 3-24, 1970.

812 Carek, Donald J., and Dobbs, Harold I. "An approach to behavior disorders--enuresis, encopresis, and hyperkinetic syndrome." Wis Med J 71(11): 250-54, November, 1972.

813 Chapman, Arthur H. Management of emotional problems of children and adolescents. Philadelphia: Lippincott, 1965. 315p.

814 Chess, Stella. "Hyperactive children: a rational approach to medication." Urban Rev 5(1): 33-35, January, 1972.

815 ———. "A rational approach to medication for hyperactive children." In: Pope, Lillie, ed. Issues in urban education and mental health. Brooklyn: Book-Lab, 1971. 12-17.

816 ———. "Temperamental individuality: a perspective for pediatricians." Feelings Their Med Significance 15(2): 1-6, March/April, 1973.

817 Claghorn, J.; Neblett, C.; Sutter, E. "The effect of drugs on hyperactivity in children with some observations of changes in mineral metabolism." J Nerv Ment Dis 153(2): 118-25, August, 1971.

818 "Classroom pushers: using drugs to control unruly children." Time 101: 65, February 26, 1973.

819 Coleman, Marry. "Serotonin concentrations in whole blood of hyperactive children." J Pediatr 78(6): 985-90, June, 1971.

820 Comly, Hunter H. "Drugs for emotionally disturbed children." Child House 3(2): 6-10, Spring, 1969.

821 ———. "Drugs for emotionally disturbed children: II." Child House 3(3): 10-13, Summer, 1969.

822 Conference on Child Research in Psychopharmacology, Washington, D. C., 1957. Child research in psychopharmacology. Edited by Seymour Fisher. Springfield, Illinois: Thomas, 1959. 216p.

823 Conners, C. Keith. "Drugs in management of children with learning disabilities." In: Tarnopol, Lester, ed. Learning disorders in children: diagnosis, medication, education. Boston: Little, Brown, 1971. 253-301.

824 ———. "Pharmacotherapy of behavior disorders in children." In: Quay, Herbert C., and Werry, John S., eds. Psychopathological disorders of childhood. New York: Wiley-Interscience, 1972. 316-47. (Series in psychology).

825 ———. "Psychopharmacologic treatment of children." In: DiMascio, Alberto, and Shader, Richard I., eds. Clinical handbook of psychopharmacology. New York: Science House, 1970. 281-87.

826 ———. "Recent drug studies with hyperkinetic children." J Learn Disabil 4(9): 476-83, November, 1971.

827 Conners, C. Keith, and Rothschild, Gerald H. "Drugs and learning in children." In: Hellmuth, Jerome, ed. Learning disorders. Vol. 3. Seattle: Special Child Publications, 1968. 191-223.

828 Cott, Allan. "Megavitamins: the orthomolecular approach to behavioral disorders and learning disabilities." Acad Ther 7(3): 245-58, Spring, 1972.

829 Cunningham, Constance P. "An exploratory study of the long term effects of drug use in hyperkinesis." Diss Abstr Int 34(9-A): 5752, March, 1974.

830 Davis, Karen V.; Sprague, Robert L.; Werry, John S. "Stereotyped behavior and activity level in severe retardates: the effects of drugs." Am J Ment Defic 73(5): 721-27, March, 1969.

831 "Debate on drugging for classroom control: school administrators opinion poll." Nations Sch 88: 39, July, 1971.

832 Delong, Arthur R. "What have we learned from psychoactive drug research on hyperactives?" Am J Dis Child 123(2): 177-80, February, 1972.

833 Denhoff, Eric. "The best management of learning disabilities calls for pediatric skill of a special sort." Clin Pediatr 12(7): 427-35, July, 1973.

834 Denhoff, Eric, ed. "Role of medication in the treatment of learning disabilities and related behavior disorders: special issue." J Learn Disabil 4(9): 466-534, November, 1971.

835 Dexheimer, Patrick; Memory, Catherine; Coleman, Nathan; et. al. "Psychopharmocological treatment as an intervention for hyperkinetic children: a team approach." In: American Psychological Association, 81st, Montreal, 1973. Proceedings. 8(pt. 2): 673-74, 1973.

836 DiPalms, J. R. "Drugs for the hyperactive child." RN 35: 61ff., May, 1972.

837 "Drugs and the hyperactive syndrome." Am Educ 7: 14, June, 1971.

838 "Drugs for learning." Time 96: 43-44, August 10, 1970.

839 Dyment, Paul G., and Robinson, Clare A. "Learning disabilities and the physician." Ohio State Med J 69(6): 445-47, June, 1973.

840 Edgington, Ruth. "Letter on drugs." Acad Ther 6(1): 47-50, Fall, 1970.

841 Eisenberg, Leon. "Basic issues in drug research with children: opportunities and limitations of a pediatric age group." In: Fisher, Seymour, ed. Child research in psychopharmacology. Springfield, Illinois: Thomas, 1959. 21-47.

842 ———. "Drug therapy of overactivity in children." Clin Proc Child Hosp 19(9): 253-55, September, 1963.

843 ———. "The management of the hyperkinetic child." Dev Med Child Neurol 8(5): 593-98, October, 1966.

844 ———. "Pharmacologic therapy of childhood behavior disorders." Feelings Their Med Significance 14(5): 1-4, September/October, 1972.

845 ———. "The role of drugs in treating psychiatric disorders in children." Children 11: 167-73, 1964.

846 ———. "Use of drugs in the treatment of disturbed children." Feelings Their Med Significance 7(6): 1-4, June, 1965.

847 Eisenberg, Leon, and Conners, C. Keith. "Psychopharmacology in childhood." In: Talbot, Nathan; Kagan, Jerome; Eisenberg, Leon, eds. Behavioral science in pediatric medicine. Philadelphia: Saunders, 1971. 397-423.

848 Elliot, Ian. "Chemistry and hyperkinesis." <u>Grade Teach</u> 88(9): 35, May/June, 1971.

849 Epstein, Estelle P.; Harrington, Nancy D.; Meagher, Judith A.; et. al. "Chemotherapy and the hyperkinetic child." <u>J Educ</u> 151(2): 47-60, December, 1968.

850 Erenberg, Gerald. "Mood-altering drugs and hyperkinetic children." <u>Pediatrics</u> 49(2): 308-9, February, 1972.

851 ————. "Treatment of the hyperactive child." <u>Pediatr Ann</u> 2(5): 56-79, May, 1973.

852 Eveloff, Herbert H. "Psychopharmacologic agents in child psychiatry." <u>Arch Gen Psychiatry</u> 14(5): 472-81, May, 1966.

853 Faigel, Harris C. "The adolescent with a learning problem: the need for insight." <u>Clin Pediatr</u> 12(10): 577-81, October, 1973.

854 Faretra, Gloria, and Gozun, Concepcion. "The use of drug combination in pediatric psychiatry." <u>Curr Ther Res</u> 6(5): 340-43, May, 1964.

855 Feighner, Anne C., and Feighner, John P. "Multimodality treatment of the hyperkinetic child." <u>Am J Psychiatry</u> 131(4): 459-63, April, 1974.

856 Fish, Barbara. "Drug therapy in child psychiatry: pharmacological aspects." <u>Compr Psychiatry</u> 1: 212-27, 1960.

857 ————. "Drug therapy in child psychiatry: psychological aspects." <u>Compr Psychiatry</u> 1: 55-61, 1960.

858 ————. "Drug use in psychiatric disorders of children." <u>Am J Psychiatry</u> 124(No. 8 Suppl.): 31-36, February, 1968.

859 ————. "The influence of maturation and abnormal development on the response of disturbed children to drugs." In: World Congress of Psychiatry, 3rd, Montreal, 1961. <u>Proceedings.</u> Vol. 2. Montreal: McGill University Press, 1961. 1341-44.

860 ————. "Methodology in child psychopharmacology." In: Efron, D. H., ed. <u>Psychopharmacology: a review of progress, 1957-67.</u> Washington, D. C.: Government Printing Office, 1968. 989-1001. (PHS Publication, No. 1836).

861 ————. "Treating hyperactive children." <u>JAMA</u> 218(9): 1427, November 29, 1971.

Fisher, Seymour, ed.
see Conference on Child Research in Psychopharmacology, Washington, D. C., 1957. <u>Child research in psychopharmacology.</u> (Item No. 822).

862 Fleming, Juanita W., ed. <u>Care and management of exceptional children.</u> New York: Appleton-Century-Crofts, 1973. 212p.

863 Freed, Herbert. The chemistry and therapy of behavior disorders in children. Springfield, Illinois: Thomas, 1962. 78p.

864 Freedman, Alfred M. "Drug therapy in behavior disorders." Pediatr Clin North Am 5(3): 573-94, August, 1958.

865 Freedman, Alfred M.; Effron, Abraham S.; Bender, Lauretta. "Pharmacotherapy in children with psychiatric illness." J Nerv Ment Dis 122: 479-86, 1955.

866 Freeman, Roger D. "Drug effects on learning in children: a selective review of the past thirty years." J Spec Educ 1(1): 17-44, Fall, 1966.

867 ———. "The drug treatment of learning disorders: continuing confusion." J Pediatr 81(1): 112-15, July, 1972.

868 ———. "Review of drug effects." In: International Conference of the Association for Children with Learning Disabilities, 5th, Boston, Massachusetts, 1968. Selected papers. San Rafael, California: Academic Therapy Publications, 1969. 505-7.

869 ———. "Review of medicine in special education: another look at drugs and behavior." J Spec Educ 4(3): 377-84, Summer, 1970.

870 ———. "Review of medicine in special education: medical-behavioral pseudorelationships." J Spec Educ 5(1): 93-100, Winter/Spring, 1971.

871 Friedman, Robert; Dale, Earle P.; Wagner, John H. "A long-term comparison of two treatment regimes for minimal brain dysfunction." Clin Pediatr 12(11): 666-71, November, 1973.

872 Gaddes, W. H. "A neuropsychological approach to learning disorders." J Learn Disabil 1(9): 523-34, September, 1968.

873 Greenberg, Lawrence M., and Lipman, Ronald S. "Pharmacotherapy of hyperactive children: current treatment practices." Clin Proc Child Hosp 27(4): 101-5, April, 1971.

874 George Von Hilsheimer, B. D. "Creeping reification: functional versus symptomatic treatment in the diagnosis 'minimal brain dysfunction.'" J Learn Disabil 6(3): 185-90, March, 1973.

875 Giardina, Teresa. "Help for the hyperactive and distractible child." Acad Ther 6(3): 313-16, Spring, 1971.

876 Grant, Quentin R. "Psychopharmacology in childhood emotional and mental disorders." J Pediatr 61(4): 626-37, October, 1962.

877 Green, Leila H. "Treatment suggestion: the hyperkinetic child." Int Bobath Alumni Assoc Newsl 3: 2-3, Summer, 1968.

878 Green, R. P. "Oral medications for minimal brain dysfunction in children." J Natl Med Assoc 65(2): 157-60, March, 1973.

879 Grossman, H. J. "Psychopharmacology in learning and behavioral disorders of children: a discussion of the bases for competency." In: Cruickshank, William, ed. The teacher of brain-injured children. Syracuse, New York: Syracuse University Press, 1966. 245-54.

880 Hammond, Jerrold E. "Drugs for the treatment of children with behavior disorders: toward a more specific use of them." Med Times 92: 421-26, May, 1964.

881 Harlin, Vivian K. "Help for the hyperkinetic child in school." J Sch Health 42(10): 587-92, December, 1972.

882 Hentoff, Nat. "Using drugs in classrooms." Current 126: 40-45, February, 1971.

883 "How successful are you with the hyperkinetic child?" Patient Care 4: 102ff., October 15, 1970.

884 Hutt, Corinne; Jackson, P. M.; Level, M. "Behavioral parameters and drug effects: a study of a hyperkinetic epileptic child." Epilepsia 7: 250-59, 1961.

885 "Hyperkineticism in children." Ill Med J 138: 618, December, 1970.

886 Ireland, Roderick. "Drugs and hyperactivity: process is due." Inequality Educ 8: 19-24, June, 1971.

887 Jones, D. "Psychopharmacological therapy with the mentally retarded." Ment Retard Abstr 3(1): 21-27, January, 1966.

888 Kearsley, Richard B. "The child, his doctor and his teacher." Child Educ 42(6): 341-44, February, 1966.

889 Kehne, Christine W. "Control of the hyperactive child via medication--at what cost to personality development: some psychological implications and clinical interventions." Am J Orthopsychiatry 44 (2): 237-38, March, 1974. (Abstract of paper).

890 Keiffer, E. "Miracle that misfired: mood altering drugs prescribed for overactive children." Good House 178: 82-83ff., January, 1974.

891 Knobel, Mauricio. "Newer dynamic considerations on psychopharmacology for the hyperkinetic child." In: World Congress of Psychiatry, 3rd, Montreal, 1961. Proceedings. Vol. 2. Montreal: McGill University Press, 1961. 1344-48.

892 ———. "Psychopharmacology of the hyperkinetic child: dynamic considerations." Arch Gen Psychiatry 6(3): 198-202, March, 1962.

893 Knobel, Mauricio; Mohamed, Salomon; Pasqualini, Gerardo. "Pharmacological treatment for behavior disorders in children." Int J Neuropsychiatry 2(6): 660-66, December, 1966.

894 Kornetsky, Conan. "Psychoactive drugs in the immature organism." Psychopharmacologia 17(2): 105-36, 1970.

895 Kraft, Irvin A. "Outpatient child psychopharmacotherapy." Curr Psychiatr Ther 9: 19-25, 1969.

896 Krakowski, Adam J. "The role of the physician in the management of the emotionally disturbed child." Psychosomatics 4(5-Management): 270-78, September/October, 1963.

897 Krausen, R. "Control drugs may damage in long-term." Times Educ Suppl 3049: 19, November 2, 1973.

898 Kugelmass, I. Newton. "Chemical therapy of mentally retarded children." Int Rec Med Gen Pract Clin 172(3): 119-36, March, 1959.

899 ————. "Psychochemotherapy of mental deficiency in children." Int Rec Med Gen Pract Clin 169(6): 323-38, June, 1956.

900 Ladd, E. T. "Pills for classroom peace? controversy over the use of drugs to improve school performance by controlling hyperactivity." Saturday Rev 53: 66-68, 81-82, November 21, 1970.

901 Laufer, Maurice W. "Medications, learning, and behavior." Phi Delta Kappan 52(3): 169-70, November, 1970.

902 Laufer, Maurice W.; Denhoff, Eric; Rubin, Eli Z. "Photo-Metrazol activation in children." Electroencephalogr Clin Neurophysiol 6(1): 1-8, February, 1954.

903 LaVeck, Gerald D., and Buckley, P. "The use of psychopharmacologic agents in retarded children with behavior disorders." J Chron Dis 13: 174-83, 1961.

904 Lesser, Leonard I. "Hyperkinesis in children: operational approach to management." Clin Pediatr 9(9): 548-52, September, 1970.

905 Lindsley, Donald B., and Henry, Charles E. "Effects of drugs on behavior and the electroencephalograms of children with behavior disorders." Psychosom Med 4(1): 140-49, January, 1942.

906 Lipman, Ronald S. "Pharmacotherapy of children." Psychopharmacol Bull 7(2): 14-27, April, 1971.

907 Lourie, Reginald S. "Psychoactive drugs in pediatrics." Pediatrics 34(5): 691-93, November, 1964.

908 Louttit, Richard T. "Chemical facilitation of intelligence among the mentally retarded." Am J Ment Defic 69(4): 495-501, January, 1965.

909 Lucas, Alexander R. "Psychopharmacologic treatment." In: Shaw, Charles R. The psychiatric disorders of childhood. New York: Appleton-Century-Crofts, 1966. 387-402.

910 McBride, Robert R. "Psychochemicals and the minimal brain dysfunction child." Acad Ther 8(3): 303-15, Spring, 1973.

911 "May continue therapy for minimal brain dysfunction for life." Pediatr News 8(6): 34ff., June, 1974.

912 Miller, Emanuel. "Psychopharmacology in childhood: a critique." In: Miller, E., ed. Foundations of child psychiatry. Oxford: Pergamon, 1968. 625-41.

913 Millichap, J. Gordon. "Drugs in management of minimal brain dysfunction." Ann NY Acad Sci 205: 321-34, February 28, 1973.

914 ———. "Management of hyperkinetic behavior in children with epilepsy." Mod Treat 6(6): 1233-46, November, 1969.

915 Millichap, J. Gordon, and Boldrey, Edwin E. "Studies in hyperkinetic behavior: II. Laboratory and clinical evaluations of drug treatments." Neurology 17(5): 467-71, May, 1967.

916 Millichap, J. Gordon, and Fowler, Glenn W. "Treatment of 'minimal brain dysfunction' syndromes." Pediatr Clin North Am 14(4): 767-77, November, 1967.

917 Murray, Joseph N. "Drugs to control classroom behavior?" Educ Leadership 31(1): 21-25, October, 1973.

918 ———. "Drugs to control classroom behavior?" Educ Dig 39: 13-15, January, 1974.

919 Novack, Harry S. "An educator's view of medication and classroom behavior." J Learn Disabil 4(9): 507-8, November, 1971.

920 Oettinger, Leon, Jr. "Learning disorders, hyperkinesis, and the use of drugs in children." Rehabil Lit 32: 162-67, 170, June, 1971.

921 ———. "The use of drugs in children with learning disorders." In: International Copenhagen Congress on the Scientific Study of Mental Retardation, 1964. Proceedings. Copenhagen: Det Berlingske Bogtrykkeri, 1964. 1: 256-59, 1964.

922 Olsen, Ralph. "Pediatric practice: whose mood are we altering?" Pediatrics 47(5): 961, May, 1971.

923 Ong, Beale H. "The pediatrician's role in learning disabilities." In: Myklebust, Helmer R., ed. Progress in learning disabilities. Vol. 1. New York: Grune & Stratton, 1968. 98-112.

924 Papazian, Clement. "Fact or fallacy: an open line between doctor and teacher." Claremont Read Conf Yearb 37: 167-72, 1973.

925 Paredes, A.; Gogerty, J. H.; West, L. J. "Psychopharmacology." Curr Psychiatr Ther 1: 54-85, 1961.

926 Paxton, Patricia W. "Effects of drug-induced behavior changes in hyperactive children on maternal attitude and personality." Diss Abstr Int 33(1-B): 447-48, July, 1972.

927 "Pep pills for pupils: use of stimulants to control hyperactive children in Omaha." Newsweek 76: 60-61, July 13, 1970.

928 "Pep pills for youngsters: treatment of hyperactive children in Omaha." US News World Rep 69: 49, July 13, 1970.

929 Powers, Hugh S. "Dietary measures to improve behavior and achievement." Acad Ther 9(3): 203-14, Winter, 1973-74.

930 "Proceedings of the panel on medication: medicating children with learning disabilities, parts I and II." In: Tarnopol, Lester, ed. Learning disorders in children: diagnosis, medication, education. Boston: Little, Brown, 1971. 119-205.

931 Rapoport, Judith L.; Lott, I. T.; Alexander, D. F.; et. al. "Urinary noradrenaline and playroom behavior in hyperactive boys." Lancet 2: 1141, November 28, 1970.

932 Rees, E. L. "Clinical observations on treatment of schizophrenic and hyperactive children with megavitamins." Orthomol Psychiatry 2 (3): 93ff., 1973.

933 Safer, Daniel J. "Drugs for problem school children." J Sch Health 41: 491-95, November, 1971.

934 Salk, Lee. "Emotional factors in pediatric practice." Pediatr Ann 2(5): 83-86, May, 1973.

935 Sarma, P. S. B., and Falk, Marshall A. "Drug treatment of hyperactivity in children." Ill Med J 144(2): 117-19, 156, August, 1973.

936 Schneyer, J. Wesley. "Drug therapy and learning in children." Read Teach 24(6): 561-63, March, 1971.

937 Smith, Forrest M., Jr. "Treatment of brain-damaged child continues to be a controversial issue." Tex Med 69(1): 109-10, January, 1968.

938 "Social ills and appetite pills." Ann Intern Med 75(4): 645-47, October, 1971.

939 Solomons, Gerald. "Drug therapy: initiation and follow-up." Ann NY Acad Sci 205: 335-44, February, 1973.

940 ————. "Monitoring drug therapy by telephone." Med Times 96: 205-10, 1968.

941 Sprague, Robert L. "Psychopharmacology and learning disabilities." J Oper Psychiatry 3: 56, 1972.

942 Stewart, Mark A., and Olds, Salley W. Raising a hyperactive child. New York: Harper & Row, 1973. 299p.

943 Teicher, J. D. "The new drugs and the child." Med Times 85: 1020-26, 1957.

944 Thompson, Travis I., and Schuster, Charles R. Behavioral pharma- cology. Englewood Cliffs, New Jersey: Prentice-Hall, 1968. 297p.

945 Tobiessen, Jon, and Karowe, Harris E. "Role for the school in the pharmacological treatment of hyperkinetic children." Psychol Sch 6(4): 340-46, October, 1969.

946 Topaz, Peter M. "Report on the Journal of Learning Disabilities preliminary study of drug abuse and minimal brain dysfunction." J Learn Disabil 4(9): 502-6, November, 1971.

947 Turner, E. J. "Mood-altering drugs." Pediatrics 48(3): 496-97, September, 1971.

948 Uhr, Leonard, and Miller, James G., eds. Drugs and behavior. New York: Wiley, 1961. 676p.

949 U. S. Congress. House. Committee on Government Operations. Spec- ial Studies Subcommittee. Federal involvement in the use of behavior modification drugs on grammar school children of the right to privacy inquiry, Hearings. 91st. Cong., 2nd. sess., 1970. Washington, D. C.: Government Printing Office, 1970. 175p.

950 U. S. Congress. Senate. Senator Mondale speaking on migrant farm- worker children and the drug "Ritalin." 93rd Cong., 2nd. sess., Sep- tember 9, 1970. Congressional Record. 116(pt. 23): 30974-77, 1970.

951 Vinnedge, H. "Drugs for children: the Omaha program and resulting involvement." New Repub 164: 13-15, March 13, 1971; Discussion 164: 28-29, April 10, 1971; April 17, 1971.

952 Weiss, G. "Review of the effects of drugs on children's behavior." In: International Conference of the Association for Children with Learning Disabilities, 6th, Fort Worth, Texas, 1969. Selected papers: Progress in parent information, professional growth, and public policy. Edited by John I. Arena. San Rafael, California: Academic Therapy Publications, 1969. 498-504.

953 ———. "Treatment of hyperactivity in children." Curr Psychiatr Ther 10: 26-29, 1970.

954 Welsch, Ellen B. "Potentially dangerous business of teaching with drugs." Am Sch Board J 161: 41-45, February, 1974.

955 Wender, Paul H. "Platelet serotonin level in children with 'mini- mal brain dysfunction.'" Lancet 2: 1012, November 8, 1969.

956 Wender, Paul H.; Epstein, Richard S.; Kopin, Irwin J.; et. al. "Urinary monoamine metabolities in children with minimal brain dys- function." Am J Psychiatry 127(10): 1411-15, April, 1971.

957 Werry, John S. "The use of psycho-active drugs in children." Ill Med J 131(6): 785-87ff., June, 1967.

958 Werry, John S.; Sprague, Robert L.; Weiss, G.; et. al. "Some clinical and laboratory studies of psychotropic drugs in children: an overview." In: Smith, W. Lynn, ed. Drugs and cerebral function. Springfield, Illinois: Thomas, 1970. 134-44.

959 Whitsell, Leon J. "Clinical pharmacology of psychotropic drugs." In: Tarnopol, Lester, ed. Learning disorders in children: diagnosis, medication, education. Boston: Little, Brown, 1971. 331-59.

960 Wiens, Arthur N.; Anderson, Kathryn A.; Matarazzo, Ruth. "Use of medication as an adjunct in the modification of behavior in the pediatric psychology setting." Prof Psychol 3(2): 157-63, Spring, 1972.

961 Willner, Milton M., and Gordon, Lee E. "Psychotropic drugs in children: pharmacotherapy as an adjunct to counseling or psycotherapy." Clin Pediatr 8(4): 193-200, April, 1969.

962 Witter, Charles. "Drugging and schooling." Trans-action 8: 30-34, July, 1971.

963 Worrell, J. B., and Bell, W. E. "Management of hyperactive behavior in children." Northwest Med 70: 43-46, 1971.

964 Wunderlich, Ray C. "Treatment of hyperactive children." Acad Ther 8(4): 375-90, Summer, 1973.

965 Zara, Martha M. "Effects of medication on learning in hyperactive four-year-old children." Diss Abstr Int 34(5-A): 2407, November, 1973.

966 Zrull, Joel P.; Westman, Jack C.; Arthur, Bettie; et. al. "An evaluation of methodology used in the study of psychoactive drugs for children." J Am Acad Child Psychiatry 5(2): 284-91, April, 1966.

1. Tranquilizers

a. General

967 Blough, Donald. "New test for tranquilizers." Science 127: 586-87, 1958.

968 Boatman, M. J., and Berlin, I. N. "Some implications of incidental experiences with psychopharmacologic drugs in a children's psychotherapeutic program." J Am Acad Child Psychiatry 1(3): 431-42, July, 1962.

969 Bradley, Charles. "Tranquilizing drugs in pediatrics." Pediatrics 21(2): 325-36, February, 1958.

970 Brummit, Houston. "The use of long-acting tranquilizers with hyperactive children." Psychosomatics 9(3): 157-59, 1968.

971 Clifford, S. H. "Tranquilizers." J Pediatr 53(6): 764-66, December, 1958.

972 Craft, M. "Mental disorder in the defective: the use of tranquilizers." Am J Ment Defic 64(1): 63-71, July, 1959.

973 Cytryn, Leon; Gilbert, Anita; Eisenberg, Leon. "The effectiveness
of tranquilizing drugs plus supportive psychotherapy in treating behavior disorders of children: a double-blind study of eighty outpa-
tients." Am J Orthopsychiatry 30(1): 113-29, January, 1960.

974 "Drug therapy for infant psychiatry." JAMA 165(11): 1474, November 16, 1957.

975 Freed, Herbert. "The current status of the tranquilizers and of
child analysis in child psychiatry." Dis Nerv Syst 22(8): 434-37,
August, 1961.

976 ————. "The tranquilizing drugs and the school child." Am Pract
Dig Treat 8: 377-80, 1957.

977 Freed, Herbert, and Frignito, M. "Tranquilizers in child psychiatry: current status on drugs, particularly phenothiazine." Pa Psychiatr Q 1: 39-48, 1961.

978 Geller, Stanley J. "Comparison of a tranquilizer and a psychic
energizer used in the treatment of children with behavioral disorders." JAMA 174(5): 481-84, October 1, 1960.

979 Rosenblum, Sidney. "Practices and problems in the use of tranquilizers with exceptional children." In: Trapp, E. Philip, and Himelstein, Philip, eds. Readings on the exceptional child. New York:
Appleton-Century-Crofts, 1962. 639-57.

980 Shaw, Charles R.; Lockett, H. J.; Lucas, Alexander R.; et. al.
"Tranquilizer drugs in the treatment of emotionally disturbed children:
I. Inpatients in a residential treatment center." J Am Acad Child
Psychiatry 2(4): 725-42, October, 1963.

b. Chlordiazepoxide

981 Kraft, Irvin A.; Ardali, Cohit; Duffy, James H.; et. al. "A clinical study of chlordiazepoxide used in psychiatric disorders of children." Int J Neuropsychiatry 1(5): 433-37, September/October, 1965.

982 Peterman, M. G., and Thomas, E. M. "The effects of methaminozep-
oxide (Librium) on seizures, EEG dysrhythmias and behavior disturbances in childhood convulsive disorders." Electroencephalogr Clin
Neurophysiol 14(2): 289, April, 1962.

983 Pilkington, T. L. "Comparative effects of Librium and Taractan on
behavior disorders of mentally retarded children." Dis Nerv Syst 22
(10): 573-75, October, 1961.

984 Vann, L. J. "Chlordiazepoxide, a tranquilizer with anticonvulsant
properties." Can Med Assoc J 86(3): 123-25, January 20, 1962.

c. Chlorpromazine

985 Bair, H. V., and Herold, W. "Efficacy of chlorpromazine in hyperactive mentally retarded children." AMA Arch Neurol Psychiatry 74
(4): 363-64, October, 1955.

986 Bakwin, Harry. "The uses of chlorpromazine in pediatrics." J Pediatr 48(2): 240-47, February, 1956.

987 Esen, Fatma M., and Durling, Dorothy. "Thorazine in the treatment
of mentally retarded children." Arch Pediatr 73: 168-73, 1956.

988 Flaherty, James A. "Effect of chlorpromazine medication on children with severe emotional disturbance." Del State Med J 27(8): 180-
84, August, 1955.

989 Freed, Herbert, and Peifer, Charles A. "Some considerations on the
use of chlorpromazine in a child psychiatric clinic." J Clin Exp Psychopath 17: 164-69, 1956.

990 Freed, Herbert, and Peifer, Charles A. "Treatment of hyperkinetic
emotionally disturbed children with prolonged administration of chlorpromazine." Am J Psychiatry 113(1): 22-26, July, 1956.

991 Freibergs, Vaira; Douglas, Virginia I.; Weiss, Gabrielle. "The
effect of chlorpromazine on concept learning in hyperactive children
under two conditions of reinforcement." Psychopharmacologia 13(4):
299-310, 1968.

992 Garfield, Sol L.; Helper, Malcolm M.; Wilcott, R. C.; et. al.
"Effects of chlorpromazine on behavior in emotionally disturbed children." J Nerv Ment Dis 135(2): 147-54, August, 1962.

993 Garrison, Mortimer, Jr. "Use of chlorpromazine and reserpine in
mentally defective children." Train Sch Bull 53(3): 55-63, May,
1956.

994 Gatski, Robert L. "Chlorpromazine in the treatment of emotionally
maladjusted children." JAMA 157(15): 1298-1300, April 9, 1955.

995 Geyer, Hal W. "Response to Thorazine (chlorpromazine) administration in hyperkinetic mongolism." Del State Med J 28(8): 189-90,
August, 1956.

996 ————. "Thorazine (chlorpromazine) and Serpasil therapy in a hyperactive patient of low mentality." Del State Med J 27(8): 187-89,
August, 1955.

997 Helper, Malcolm M.; Wilcott, R. C.; Garfield, Sol L. "Effects of
chlorpromazine on learning and related processes in emotionally disturbed children." J Consult Psychol 27(1): 1-9, February, 1963.

998 Hunt, Brian R.; Frank, Thomas; Krush, Thaddeus P. "Chlorpromazine
in the treatment of severe emotional disorders of children." Am J Dis
Child 91(3): 268-77, March, 1956.

999 Hunter, H., and Stephenson, G. M. "Chlorpromazine and trifluoperazine in the treatment of behavioural abnormalities in the severely subnormal child." Br J Psychiatry 109: 411-17, May, 1963.

1000 Ison, M. Gail. "The effects of Thorazine on Wechsler scores." Am J Ment Defic 62(3): 543-47, November, 1957.

1001 Korein, Julius, Fish, Barbara; Shapiro, Theodore; et. al. "EEG and behavioral effects of drug therapy in children: chlorpromazine and diphenhydramine." Arch Gen Psychiatry 24(6): 552-63, June, 1971.

1002 Lane, Gorham B.; Huber, Wm. G.; Smith, F. Loren. "The effect of chlorpromazine on the behavior of disturbed children." Am J Psychiatry 114(10): 937-38, April, 1958.

1003 Miksztal, M. Wesley. "Chlorpromazine (Thorazine) and reserpine in residential treatment of neuropsychiatric disorders in children." J Nerv Ment Dis 123(5): 477-79, May, 1956.

1004 Porteus, Stanley D. "Maze test reactions after chlorpromazine." J Consult Psychol 21(1): 15-21, February, 1957.

1005 Porteus, Stanley D., and Barclay, John E. "A further note on chlorpromazine: maze reactions." J Consult Psychol 21(4): 297-99, August, 1957.

1006 Rowley, Janet D.; Kaplitz, Sherman E.; Schwartz, Martin L. "The use of chlorpromazine in disturbed mentally retarded children." Ill Med J 116(2): 81-83, August, 1959.

1007 Tarjan, George; Lowery, Vincent E.; Wright, Stanley W. "Use of chlorpromazine in 278 mentally deficient patients." Am J Dis Child 94: 294-300, September, 1957.

1008 Weiss, Gabrielle; Minde, Klaus; Douglas, Virginia I.; et. al. "A comparison of the effects of chlorpromazine, dextroamphetamine and methlyphenidate on the behaviour and intellectual functioning of the hyperactive child." Can Med Assoc J 104(1): 20-25, January 9, 1971.

1009 Werry, John S.; Weiss, Gabrielle; Douglas, Virginia I.; et. al. "Studies on the hyperactive child: III. The effect of chlorpromazine upon behaviour and learning ability." J Am Acad Child Psychiatry 5 (2): 292-312, April, 1966.

d. Haloperidol

1010 Barker, Philip, and Fraser, Ian A. "A controlled trial of haloperidol in children." Br J Psychiatry 114: 855-57, July, 1968.

1011 Cunningham, M. A.; Pillai, V.; Rogers, W. J. B. "Haloperidol in the treatment of children with severe behaviour disorders." Br J Psychiatry 114(512): 845-54, July, 1968.

1012 Lucas, Alexander R. "Psychoactive drugs in the treatment of emotionally disturbed children: haloperidol and diazepam." Compr Psychiatry 10: 376-86, September, 1969.

e. Hydroxyzine

1013 Bowman, Peter W., and Blumberg, Edward. "Ataractic therapy of hyperactive, mentally retarded patients." J Maine Med Assoc 49(7): 272-73, July, 1958.

1014 Dougan, H. T. "Hydroxyzine syrup (Atarax) in the management of pediatric behavior problems." Med Times 90(5): 551-54, May, 1962.

1015 Piuck, Charlotte L. "Clinical impressions of hydroxyzine and other tranquilizers in a child guidance clinic." Dis Nerv Syst 24(8): 483-88, April, 1963.

1016 Segal, Leslie J., and Tansley, A. E. "A clinical trial with hydroxyzine (Atarax) on a group of maladjusted educationally subnormal children." J Ment Sci 103: 677-81, July, 1957.

f. Meprobamate

1017 Kraft, Irvin A.; Marcus, Irwin M.; Wilson, Wilma; et. al. "Methololigical problems in studying the effect of tranquilizers in children with special reference to meprobamate." South Med J 52(2): 179-85, February, 1959.

1018 Litchfield, Harry R. "Clinical evaluation of meprobamate in disturbed and pre-psychotic children." Ann NY Acad Sci 67(10): 828-31, May 8, 1957.

1019 Livingston, Samuel, and Pauli, Lydia L. "Meprobamate in the treatment of epilepsy of children." Am J Dis Child 94: 277-81, 1957.

1020 Zier, Adolfo. "Meprobamate (Miltown) as an aid to psychotherapy in an outpatient child guidance clinic." Am J Orthopsychiatry 29(2): 377-82, April, 1959.

g. Prochlorperazine

1021 Carter, C. H. "Prochlorperazine in emotionally disturbed, mentally defective children." South Med J 52(2): 174-78, February, 1959.

1022 Lapierre, Jean; Amin, Mohammed; Hattangadi, Sunder. "Prochlorperazine--a review of the literature since 1956." Can Psychiatr Assoc J 14(3): 267-74, June, 1969.

1023 Rosenblum, Sidney; Buoniconto, Pasquale; Graham, Bruce D. "Compazine vs. placebo: a controlled study with educable emotionally disturbed children." Am J Ment Defic 64(4): 713-17, January, 1960.

h. Promazine

1024 Benda, Hans. "Promazine in mental deficiency." Psychiatr Q 32 (3): 449-55, 1958.

1025 Esen, Fatma M., and Durling, Dorothy. "The treatment of fourteen mentally retarded boys with Sparine." Arch Pediatr 74(12): 471-74, December, 1957.

1026 Ilem, Priscilla G., and Osterheld, Roger G. "Adjunctive therapy of refractory epilepsy with promazine." Dis Nerv Syst 21(6): 326-29, June, 1960.

1027 Schulman, Jerome L., and Clarinda, Sister Mary. "The effect of promazine on the activity level of retarded children." Pediatrics 33 (2): 271-75, February, 1964.

i. Reserpine

1028 Carter, C. H. "The effects of reserpine and methyl-phenidylacetate (Ritalin) in mental defectives, spastics, and epileptics." Psychiatr Res Rep 4: 44-48, 1956.

1029 Graham, Bruce D.; Rosenblum, Sidney; Callahan, Roger J. "Placebo-controlled study of reserpine in maladjusted retarded children." Am J Dis Child 96(6): 690-95, December, 1958.

1030 Horenstein, Simon. "Resperine and chlorpromazine in hyperactive mental defectives." Am J Ment Defic 61(4): 525-29, January, 1957.

1031 Johnston, Alfred H., and Martin, Charles H. "The clinical use of reserpine and chlorpromazine in the care of the mentally deficient." Am J Ment Defic 62(2): 292-94, September, 1957.

1032 Lehman, Edward; Haber, Joseph; Lesser, Stanley R. "The use of reserpine in autistic children." J Nerv Ment Dis 125: 351-56, 1957.

1033 Rosenblum, Sidney; Callahan, Roger J.; Buoniconto, Pasquale; et. al. "The effects of tranquilizing medication (reserpine) on behavior and test performance of maladjusted, high-grade retarded children." Am J Ment Defic 62(4): 663-71, January, 1958.

1034 Timberlake, William H.; Belmont, Elizabeth H.; Ogonik, John. "The effect of reserpine in 200 mentally retarded children." Am J Ment Defic 62(1): 61-66, July, 1957.

1035 Zimmerman, Frederic T., and Burgemeister, Bessie B. "Effects of reserpine on the behavior problems of children." NY J Med 57: 3132-40, 1957.

1036 Zimmerman, Frederic T., and Burgemeister, Bessie B. "Preliminary report upon the effect of reserpine on epilepsy and behavior problems in children." Ann NY Acad Sci 61: 215-21, April 15, 1955.

j. Thioridazine

1037 Abbott, P.; Blake, A.; Vineze, L. "Treatment of the mentally retarded with thioridazine." Dis Nerv Syst 26(9): 583-85, September, 1965.

1038 Alderton, H. R., and Hoddinott, B. A. "Controlled study of the use of thioridazine in the treatment of hyperactive and aggressive children in a children's psychiatric hospital." Can Psychiatr Assoc J 9: 239-47, 1964.

1039 Alexandris, A. R., and Lundell, F. W. "Effect of thioridazine, amphetamine and placebo on the hyperkinetic syndrome and cognitive area in mentally deficient children." Can Med Assoc J 98(2): 92-96, January 13, 1968.

1040 Allen, Mary; Shannon, Gizella; Rose, Dorian. "Thioridazine hydrochloride in the behavior disturbance of retarded children." Am J Ment Defic 68(1): 63-68, July, 1963.

1041 Baldwin, Ruth W., and Kenny, Thomas J. "Thioridazine in the management of organic behavior disturbance in children." Curr Ther Res 8(8): 373-77, August, 1966.

1042 Connolly, James R. "Behavior disorders in mental retardates: treatment with thioridazine." Pa Med J 71(6): 67-69, June, 1968.

1043 Livingston, Samuel, and Pauli, Lydia L. "Management of hyperkinetic and handicapped children." JAMA 208(4): 694-95, April 28, 1969.

1044 Oettinger, Leon, Jr., and Simonds, Robert. "The use of thioridazine in the office management of children's behavior disorders." Med Times 90(6): 596-604, June, 1962.

1045 Schickedanz, D. I. Effects of thioridazine and methylphenidate on performance of a motor task and concurrent motor activity in retarded boys. Unpublished thesis. University of Illinois, 1967.

k. Trifluoperazine

1046 Beaudry, Philippe, and Gibson, David. "Effect of trifluoperazine on the behavior disorders of children with malignant emotional disturbance." Am J Ment Defic 64(5): 823-26, March, 1960.

1047 Desrochers, Jean-Leon, and Schiffmann, Wanda. "Short-term study on the use of trifluoperazine in behavior disorders in children." Union Med Can 90: 369-73, April, 1961.

1048 Fish, Barbara; Shapiro, Theodore; Campbell, Magda. "Long-term prognosis and the response of schizophrenic children to drug therapy: a controlled study of trifluoperazine." Am J Psychiatry 123(1): 32-39, July, 1966.

1049 LeVann, L. J. "Trifluoperazine dihydrochloride: an effective tranquilizing agent for behavioural abnormalities in defective children." Can Med Assoc J 80(2): 123-24, January 15, 1959.

1050 Smith, S. Wayne. "Trifluoperazine in children and adolescents with marked behavior problems." Am J Psychiatry 122(6): 702-3, December, 1965.

L. Other Tranquilizers

1051 Baldwin, Ruth W.; Kenny, Thomas J.; Badie, Davood. "A new drug for behavior problems in children: a preliminary report." Curr Ther Res 9(9): 457-61, September, 1967.

1052 Denhoff, Eric, and Shammas, Elias. "Diazepam as an aid in the
photo-Metrazol activation test." Dis Nerv Syst 29(11): 759-62, November, 1968.

1053 Effron, Abraham S., and Freedman, Alfred M. "Psychologic aspects
of pediatrics: the treatment of behavior disorders in children with
Benadryl." J Pediatr 42(2): 261-66, February, 1953.

1054 Gillie, Anne K. "The use of Pacatal in low-grade mental defectives." J Ment Sci 103: 402-5, April, 1957.

1055 Harman, Charles, and Winn, Don A. "Clinical experience with chlorprothixene in disturbed children—a comparative study." Int J Neuropsychiatry 2(1): 72-77, February, 1966.

1056 Kaplitz, Sherman E. "The use of perphenazine syrup in the severely
disturbed mentally retarded children." Ill Med J 130(6): 785-87,
December, 1966.

1057 Kenny, Thomas J.; Badie, Davood; Baldwin, Ruth W. "The effectiveness of a new drug, mesoridazine, and chlorpromazine with behavior
problems in children." J Nerv Ment Dis 147(3): 316-21, September,
1968.

1058 LaVeck, Gerald D.; DeLaCruz, Felix F.; Simundson, Eleanor. "Fluphenazine in the treatment of mentally retarded children with behavior
disorders." Dis Nerv Syst 21(2): 82-85, February, 1960.

1059 Low, N. L., and Myers, G. G. "Suvren in brain-injured children."
J Pediatr 52(3): 259-63, March, 1958.

1060 Molling, Peter A.; Lockner, Arthur W.; Sauls, Robert J.; et. al.
"Committed delinquent boys: the impact of perphenazine and of placebo." Arch Gen Psychiatry 7(1): 70-76, July, 1962.

1061 Oettinger, Leon. "Chlorprothixene in the management of problem
children." Dis Nerv Syst 23(10): 568-71, October, 1962.

1062 Waites, Lucius, and Keele, Doman K. "Fluphenazine in the management of disturbed mentally retarded children." Dis Nerv Syst 24(2):
113-14, February, 1963.

1063 Zrull, Joel P.; Westman, Jack C.; Arthur, Bettie; et. al. "A comparison of diazepam, d-amphetamine and placebo in the treatment of hyperkinetic syndrome in children." Am J Psychiatry 121(4): 388-89,
October, 1964.

2. Antidepressants

a. General

1064 Comly, Hunter H. "Cerebral stimulants for children with learning
disorders?" J Learn Disabil 4(9): 484-90, November, 1971.

1065 Conference on the Use of Stimulant Drugs in the Treatment of Behaviorally Disturbed Young School Children, Washington, D. C., 1971.
Report. Washington, D. C.: 1971. 8p. (Sponsored by the Office of
Child Development and the Office of the Assistant Secretary for Health
and Scientific Affairs, Department of Health, Education, and Welfare).

1066 Conners, C. Keith. Comparative effects of stimulant drugs in hyperkinetic children. Boston: Massachusetts General Hospital, Child
Development Laboratory, 1971. 35p. (ED 059 555).

1067 ————. "The effect of stimulant drugs on human figure drawings
in children with minimal brain dysfunction." Psychopharmacologia 19
(4): 329-33, 1971.

1068 ————. "Review of stimulant drugs in learning and behavior disorders." Psychopharmacol Bull 7(3): 39-40, July, 1971.

1069 ————. "Symposium: behavior modification by drugs: II. Psychological effects of stimulant drugs in children with minimal brain
dysfunction." Pediatrics 49(5): 702-8, May, 1972.

1070 Eisenberg, Leon. "The hyperkinetic child and stimulant drugs."
N Engl J Med 287(5): 249-50, August 3, 1972.

1071 ————. "Principles of drug therapy in child psychiatry with
special reference to stimulant drugs." Am J Orthopsychiatry 41(3):
371-79, April, 1971.

1072 ————. "Symposium: behavior modification by drugs: III. The
clinical use of stimulant drugs in children." Pediatrics 49(5):
709-15, May, 1972.

1073 Eisenberg, Leon; Lachman, Roy; Molling, Peter A.; et. al. "A psychopharmacologic experiment in a training school for delinquent boys:
methods, problems, findings." Am J Orthopsychiatry 33(3): 431-47,
April, 1963.

1074 Fish, Barbara. "The 'one child, one drug' myth of stimulants in
hyperkinesis." Arch Gen Psychiatry 25(3): 193-203, September, 1971.

1075 Fras, I. Letter: "Alternating caffeine and stimulants." Am J
Psychiatry 131: 228-29, February, 1974.

1076 Freedman, Daniel X. "Report of the Conference on the Use of Stimulant Drugs in the Treatment of Behaviorally Disturbed Young School
Children." J Learn Disabil 4(9): 523-30, November, 1971.

1077 ————. "Use of stimulant drugs in treating hyperactive children:
Drug Panel Report, Office of Child Development." Children 18: 111,
May, 1971.

1078 Hall, Peter H. "The effect of a stimulant drug (methamphetamine)
on cognitive impulsivity, planning, new learning, and social behavior
in hyperactive children." Diss Abstr Int 33(10-A): 5584, April,
1973.

1079 Hawkins, Mary E. "Don't dodge the drug question: stimulants."
Sci Teach 33(8): 33-34, November, 1966.

1080 "How coffee calms kids." Newsweek 82: 76, October 8, 1973.

1081 Kinsbourne, Marcel. "Stimulants for insomnia." N Engl J Med
288: 1129, May 24, 1974.

1082 Krippner, Stanley; Silverman, Robert; Cavallo, Michael; et. al.
"Study of hyperkinetic children receiving stimulant drugs." Acad Ther
8(3): 261-69, Spring, 1973.

1083 Loney, Jan, and Ordona, Truce T. "Cerebral stimulants and minimal
dysfunction: some questions, some answers, and some more questions."
Am J Orthopsychiatry 44(2): 243-44, March, 1974. (Abstract of
paper).

1084 McCabe, E. R., and McCabe, L. "Dissociation of learning to stimulant drug therapy." N Engl J Med 287: 825, October 19, 1972.

1085 McGaugh, James L., and Petrinovich, Lewis. "Comments concerning
the basis of learning enhancement with central nervous system stimulants." Psychol Reports 12(1): 211-14, February, 1963.

1086 Millichap, J. Gordon. "Drugs in the management of hyperkinetic
and perceptually handicapped children." JAMA 206(8): 1527-30, November 11, 1968.

1087 Satterfield, James H.; Cantwell, Dennis P.; Saul, Ronald E.; et.
al. "Response to stimulant drug treatment in hyperactive children--
prediction from EEG and neurological findings." J Autism Child Schizophr 3(1): 36-48, January/March, 1973.

1088 Schnackenberg, Robert C. "Caffeine as a substitute for Schedule
II stimulants in hyperkinetic children." Am J Psychiatry 130(7):
796-98, July, 1973.

1089 Shetty, Taranath. "Photic responses in hyperkinesis of childhood." Science 174: 1356-57, December 24, 1971.

1090 Solomons, Gerald. "Guidelines on the use and medical effects of
psychostimulant drugs in therapy." J Learn Disabil 4(9): 470-75,
November, 1971.

1091 "Stimulant drugs and learning disorders in children." JAMA 202
(3): 227, October 16, 1967.

1092 "Stimulants and the hyperkinetic youngster." Med World News 12
(10): 34K, March 12, 1971.

1093 Weiss, B., and Laties, V. G. "Enhancement of human performance
by caffeine and the amphetamines." Pharmacol Rev 14: 1-36, 1962.

b. Amphetamine

1094 American Academy of Pediatrics. Committee on Drugs. "Use of d-
amphetamine and related central nervous system stimulants in children."
Pediatrics 51(2): 302-5, February, 1973.

1095 "Amphetamine-type drugs for hyperactive children." Med Lett Drugs
Ther 14: 21-23, March, 1972.

1096 Arnold, L. E.; Kirilcuk, V.; Corson, S. A.; et. al. "Levoamphet-
amine and dextroamphetamine: differential effect on aggression and
hyperkinesis in children and dogs." Am J Psychiatry 130(2): 165-70,
February, 1973.

1097 Arnold, L. E.; Wender, Paul H.; McCloskey, K.; et. al. "Levoam-
phetamine and dextroamphetamine: comparative efficacy in the hyperkinetic syndrome: assessment by target symptoms." Arch Gen Psychiatry
27(6): 816-22, December, 1972.

1098 Baldessarini, Ross J. "Symposium: behavior modification by
drugs: I. Pharmacology of the amphetamines." Pediatrics 49(5):
694-701, May, 1972.

1099 Bazell, Robert J. "Panel sanctions amphetamines for hyperkinetic
children." Science 171: 1223, March 26, 1971.

1100 Bender, Lauretta, and Cottington, Frances. "The use of amphetamine sulfate (Benzedrine) in child psychiatry." Am J Psychiatry 99
(1): 116-21, July, 1942.

1101 Bradley, Charles. "Behavior of children receiving Benzedrine."
Am J Psychiatry 94: 577-85, November, 1937.

1102 ———. "Benzedrine and Dexedrine in the treatment of children's
behavior disorders." Pediatrics 5(1): 27-37, January, 1950.

1103 Bradley, Charles, and Bowen, Margaret. "Amphetamine therapy for
children's behavior disorders." Am J Orthopsychiatry 11(1): 92-103,
January, 1941.

1104 Bradley, Charles, and Bowen, Margaret. "School performance of
children receiving amphetamine (Benzedrine) sulfate." Am J Orthopsychiatry 10(4): 782-88, October, 1940.

1105 Buchsbaum, Monte, and Wender, Paul H. "Average evoked response in
normal and minimally brain dysfunctioned children treated with amphetamine: a preliminary report." Arch Gen Psychiatry 29(6): 764-70,
December, 1973.

1106 Buckley, Robert E. "A neurophysiologic proposal for the amphetamine response in hyperkinetic children." Psychosomatics 13(2): 93-
99, March, 1972.

1107 Burks, Harold F. "Effects of amphetamine therapy on hyperkinetic
children." Arch Gen Psychiatry 11(6): 604-9, December, 1964.

1108 Cole, Jonathan O. "The amphetamines in child psychiatry: a review." Semin Psychiatry 1(2): 174-78, 1969.

1109 ———. "Clinical uses of the amphetamines." In: Current Concepts on Amphetamine Abuse, Duke University, 1970. Proceedings. Edited by Everett H. Ellinwood and Sidney Cohen. Rockville, Maryland: National Institute of Mental Health; for sale by the Superintendent of Documents, U. S. Government Printing Office, 1972. 238p. (DHEW Publication, No. (HSM) 72-9085).

1110 Conners, C. Keith. "Stimulant drugs and cortical evoked responses in learning and behavior disorders in children." In: Cerebral Function Symposium, 2nd, Denver, 1970. Papers: drugs, development, and cerebral function. Compiled and edited by W. Lynn Smith. Springfield, Illinois: Thomas, 1972. 179-99.

1111 Conrad, W. G.; Dworkin, E. S.; Shai, A.; et. al. "Effects of amphetamine therapy and prescriptive tutoring on the behavior and achievement of lower class hyperactive children." J Learn Disabil 4(9): 509-17, November, 1971.

1112 Conrad, W. G., and Insel, Jonathan. "Anticipating the response to amphetamine therapy in the treatment of hyperkinetic children." Pediatrics 40(1): 96-98, July, 1967.

1113 Cutler, Mabelle; Little, J. W.; Strauss, Alfred A. "The effect of Benzedrine on mentally deficient children." Am J Ment Defic 45(1): 59-65, July, 1940.

1114 Cutts, K. K., and Jasper, Herbert H. "Effect of Benzedrine Sulfate and Phenobarbital on behavior problem children with abnormal electroencephalograms." Arch Neurol Psychiatry 41: 1138-45, 1939.

1115 Duvernoy, Wolf F. "Amphetamine effects." JAMA 215(12): 1987-88, March, 1971.

1116 Finnerty, D.; Greaney, J.; Soltys, J.; et. al. "The use of d-amphetamine with hyperkinetic children." Psychopharmacologia 21: 302-8, 1971.

1117 Fowlie, Barbara. "A parent's guide to amphetamine treatment of hyperkinesis." J Learn Disabil 6(6): 352-55, June/July, 1973.

1118 Freedman, Daniel X. "Amphetamine-type drugs for hyperactive children." Med Lett Drugs Ther 14: 21-23, March 31, 1972.

1119 Grinspoon, L., and Singer, S. B. "Amphetamines in the treatment of hyperkinetic children." Harv Educ Rev 43(4): 515-55, November, 1973.

1120 Kalant, Oriana J. The amphetamines: toxicity and addiction. 2nd ed. Springfield, Illinois: Thomas, 1973. 188p.

1121 Koret, Sydney. The effect of amphetamine sulfate upon the behavior and school performance of hyperactive children. Unpublished doctoral dissertation. Boston University, 1956.

1122 Lasagna, Louis, and Epstein, Lynn C. "The use of amphetamines in the treatment of hyperkinetic children." In: International Symposium on Amphetamines and Related Compounds. Edited by Erminio Costa and S. Garattini. New York: Raven, 1970. 849-64. (Proceedings of the Mario Negri Institute for Pharmacological Research).

1123 McConnell, Thomas R.; Cromwell, Rue L.; Bialer, Irv; et. al. "Studies in activity level: VII. Effects of amphetamine drug administration on the activity level of retarded children." Am J Ment Defic 68(5): 647-51, March, 1964.

1124 Mantegazza, P.; Muller, E. E.; Naimzada, M. K.; et. al. "Studies on the lack of correlation between hyperthermia, hyperactivity and anorexia induced by amphetamine." In: International Symposium on Amphetamines and Related Compounds. Edited by Erminio Costa and S. Garattini. New York: Raven, 1970. 559-75. (Proceedings of the Mario Negri Institute for Pharmacological Research).

1125 Martin, W. R.; Sloan, J. W.; Sapira, J. D.; et. al. "Physiologic subjective and behavioral effects of amphetamine, methamphetamine, ephedrine, phenmetrazine and methylphenidate in man." Clin Pharmacol Ther 12: 245-58, March/April, 1971.

1126 Molitch, Matthew, and Sullivan, John P. "Effects of Benzedrine Sulfate on children taking the New Stanford Achievement Test." Am J Orthopsychiatry 7(4): 519-22, October, 1937.

1127 Oettinger, Leon, Jr. Amphetamines, hyperkinesis and learning. CANHC Literature Distribution, P. O. Box 790, Lomita, California 90717. 1970. 1p.

1128 Snyder, Solomon H., and Meyerhoff, James L. "How amphetamine acts in minimal brain dysfunction." Ann NY Acad Sci 205: 310-20, February 28, 1973.

1129 Tec, Leon, and Levy, Harold B. "Amphetamines in hyperkinetic children." JAMA 216(11): 1864-65, June 14, 1971.

c. Deanol

1130 Clausen, J.; Fineman, M.; Henry, Charles E.; et. al. "The effect of Deaner (2-Dimethylaminoethanol) on mentally retarded subjects." Train Sch Bull 57(1): 3-12, May, 1960.

1131 Fields, Elmore M. "The effects of deanol in children with organic and functional behavior disorders." NY State J Med 61(6): 901-5, March 15, 1961.

1132 Jacobs, J. "A controlled trial of Deaner and a placebo in mentally defective children." Br J Clin Pract 19(2): 77-86, February, 1965.

1133 Kugel, Robert B., and Alexander, Theron. "The effect of a central nervous system stimulant (deanol) on behavior." Pediatrics 31(4): 651-55, April, 1963.

1134 Mebane, John C. "Use of deanol with disturbed juvenile offenders."
Dis Nerv Syst 21(11): 642-43, November, 1960.

1135 Oettinger, Leon, Jr. "The use of deanol in the treatment of disorders of behavior in children." J Pediatr 53(6): 671-75, December,
1958.

1136 Tapia, Fernando. "Medication of 'brain-damaged' children: a
double-blind study with deanol." Dis Nerv Syst 26(8): 490-95,
August, 1965.

1137 Tobias, Milton. "The disturbed child--a concept: usefulness of
deanol in management." Am Pract Dig Treat 10: 1759-66, October,
1959.

d. Dextroamphetamine

1138 Ambrosino, S. V., and Scuto, T. J. "Item analysis: parental attitude vs. dextroamphetamine." Behav Neuropsychiatry 3: 19-24,
June/July, 1971.

1139 Anton, Aron H., and Greer, Melvin. "Dextroamphetamine, catechola-
mines, and behavior: the effect of dextroamphetamine in retarded
children." Arch Neurol 21(3): 248-52, September, 1969.

1140 Barcai, Avner. "Predicting the response of children with learning
disabilities and behavior problems to dextroamphetamine sulfate: the
clinical interview and the finger twitch test." Pediatrics 47(1):
73-80, January, 1971.

1141 Conners, C. Keith. "The effects of Dexedrine on rapid discrimination and motor control of hyperkinetic children under mild stress." J
Nerv Ment Dis 142(5): 429-33, May, 1966.

1142 Conners, C. Keith; Eisenberg, Leon; Barcai, Avner. "Effect of
dextroamphetamine on children." Arch Gen Psychiatry 17(2): 478-85,
October, 1967.

1143 Conners, C. Keith; Rothschild, Gerald H.; Eisenberg, Leon. "Dextroamphetamine sulfate in children with learning disorders: effects
on perception, learning and achievement." Arch Gen Psychiatry 21(2):
182-90, August, 1969.

1144 Denhoff, Eric. "Effects of dextroamphetamine on hyperactive children: a controlled double-blind study." J Learn Disabil 4(9): 491-
98, November, 1971.

1145 Disenhouse, Harvey A. "An academic and social follow-up of children placed on Dexedrine or Ritalin for severe hyperactive or hyperkinetic disorders." Diss Abstr Int 33(4-A): 1549-50, October, 1972.

1146 Epstein, Lynn C.; Lasagna, Louis; Conners, C. Keith; et. al. "Correlation of dextroamphetamine excretion and response in hyperkinetic
children." J Nerv Ment Dis 146(2): 136-46, February, 1968.

1147 Ginn, Stephen A., and Hohman, Leslie B. "The use of dextroamphet-amine in severe behavior problems of children." South Med J 46(11): 1124-27, November, 1953.

1148 Greenberg, Lawrence M.; Deem, Michael A.; McMahon, Shirley A. "Effects of dextroamphetamine, chlorpromazine, and pydroxyzine on be-havior and performance in hyperactive children." Am J Psychiatry 129 (5): 532-39, November, 1972.

1149 Small, A.; Hibi, S.; Feinberg, I. "Effects of dextroamphetamine sulfate on EEG sleep patterns of hyperactive children." Arch Gen Psy-chiatry 25(4): 369-80, October, 1971.

1150 Steinberg, Grace G.; Troshinsky, Charles; Steinberg, Harry R. "Dextroamphetamine-responsive behavior disorder in school children." Am J Psychiatry 128(2): 174-79, August, 1971.

1151 Weiss, Gabrielle; Werry, John S.; Minde, Klaus; et. al. "Studies on the hyperactive child: V. The effects of dextroamphetamine and chlorpromazine on behavior and intellectual functioning." J Child Psy-chol Psychiatry 9(3/4): 145-56, December, 1968.

1152 Winsberg, Bertrand G.; Press, Mark; Bialer, Irv; et. al. "Dextro-amphetamine and methylphenidate in the treatment of hyperactive/aggres-sive children." Pediatrics 53(2): 236-41, February, 1974.

e. Imipramine

1153 Brown, David; Winsberg, Bertrand G.; Bialer, Irv; et. al. "Imip-ramine therapy and seizures: three children treated for hyperactive behavior disorders." Am J Psychiatry 130(2): 210-12, February, 1973.

1154 Huessy, Hans R., and Wright, Alice L. "The use of imipramine in children's behavior disorders." Acta Paedopsychiatr 37(7/8): 194-99, July/August, 1970.

1155 Rapoport, Judith L. "Childhood behavior and learning problems treated with imipramine." Int J Neuropsychiatry 1: 635-42, Novem-ber/December, 1965.

1156 Rapoport, Judith L.; Quinn, Patricia O.; Bradbard, Gail; et. al. "Imipramine and methylphenidate treatments of hyperactive boys." Arch Gen Psychiatry 30(6): 789-93, June, 1974.

1157 Waizer, Jonas; Hoffman, Stanley P.; Polizos, Polizoes; et. al. "Outpatient treatment of hyperactive school children with imipramine." Am J Psychiatry 131(5): 587-91, May, 1974.

1158 Winsberg, Bertrand G.; Bialer, Irv; Kupietz, Samuel; et. al. "Effects of imipramine and dextroamphetamine on behavior of neuropsy-chiatrically impaired children." Am J Psychiatry 128: 1425-31, May, 1972.

1159 Winsberg, Bertrand G.; Bialer, Irv; Kupietz, Samuel. "Imipramine fate and behavior in hyperactive children: pilot study." Psychopharmacol Bull 9: 45, 1973.

f. Methylphenidate

1160 Barnes, Kenneth R. Effects of methylphenidate and thioridazine on learning, reaction time and activity level in hyperactive emotionally disturbed children. Unpublished bachelor's thesis. University of Illinois, 1968.

1161 Beck, Leah; MacKay, Mary C.; Taylor, Reginald. "Methylphenidate: results of a children's psychiatric service." NY State J Med 70(23): 2897-2902, December 1, 1970.

1162 Blacklidge, Virginia Y., and Ekblad, Robert L. "The effectiveness of methylphenidate hydrochloride (Ritalin) on learning and behavior in public school educable mentally retarded children." Pediatrics 47(5): 923-26, May, 1971.

1163 Blue, Arthur W.; Lytton, George J.; Miller, Oren W. "The effect of methylphenidate on intellectually handicapped children." Am Psychol 15(7): 393, July, 1960. (Abstract of paper).

1164 Carter, C. H., and Maley, M. C. "Parental use of methylphenidate (Ritalin)." Dis Nerv Syst 18(4): 146-48, April, 1960.

1165 Charles, A. F. "Case of Ritalin: drugs for hyperactive children." New Repub 165: 17-19, October 23, 1971.

1166 Christensen, Donald E. "The combined effects of methylphenidate (Ritalin) and a classroom behavior modification program in reducing the hyperkinetic behaviors of institutionalized mental retardates." Diss Abstr Int 34(11-B): 5671, May, 1974.

1167 Cohen, Nancy J.; Douglas, Virginia I.; Morgenstern, Gert; et. al. "The effect of methylphenidate on attentive behavior and autonomic activity in hyperactive children." Psychopharmacologia 22(3): 282-94, 1971.

1168 Cohn, Howard D. "Methylphenidate and minimal brain dysfunction." N Engl J Med 285(20): 1150, November 11, 1971.

1169 Conley, Daniel P. "Effects of Ritalin on hyperkinetic children attending the Glendale elementary schools." Diss Abstr Int 34(3-A): 1072-73, September, 1973.

1170 Conners, C. Keith, and Eisenberg, Leon. "The effects of methylphenidate on symptomatology and learning in disturbed children." Am J Psychiatry 120(5): 458-64, November, 1963.

1171 Conners, C. Keith; Eisenberg, Leon; Sharpe, Lawrence. "Effects of methylphenidate (Ritalin) on paired-associate learning and Porteus Maze performance in emotionally disturbed children." J Consult Psychol 28(1): 14-22, February, 1964.

1172 Creager, Ray O., and VanRiper, Catharine. "The effect of methylphenidate on the verbal productivity of children with cerebral dysfunction." J Speech Hear Res 10(3): 623-28, September, 1967.

1173 Douglas, Virginia I.; Weiss, Gabrielle; Minde, Klaus. "Learning
disabilities in hyperactive children and the effect of methylphenidate." Can Psychol 10: 201, 1969. (Abstract).

1174 Ellis, M. J.; Witt, Peter A.; Reynolds, Ronald; et. al. "Methylphenidate and the activity of hyperactives in the informal setting."
Child Dev 45(1): 217-20, March, 1974.

1175 Fischer, K. C., and Wilson, W. P. "Methylphenidate and the hyperkinetic state." Dis Nerv Syst 32(10): 695-98, October, 1971.

1176 Froelich, Robert E., and Heckel, Robert V. "The psychological effects of methylphenidate." J Clin Exp Psychopath Q Rev Psychiatry
Neurol 23(2): 91-98, June, 1962.

1177 Greenwold, Warren E., and Jones, Philip R. "The effect of methylphenidate on behavior of three school children: a pilot investigation." Except Child 38(3): 261-63, November, 1971.

1178 Haddock, Samuel T. "Usefulness of methylphenidate." N Engl J Med
286(7): 375, February 17, 1972.

1179 Hoffman, Stanley P.; Engelhardt, David M.; Margolis, Reuben A.;
et. al. "Response to methylphenidate in low socioeconomic hyperactive
children." Arch Gen Psychiatry 30(3): 354-59, March, 1974.

1180 Knights, Robert M., and Hinton, George G. "The effects of methylphenidate (Ritalin) on the motor skills and behavior of children with
learning problems." J Nerv Ment Dis 148: 643-53, 1969.

1181 Levy, James M.; Jones, B. E.; Croley, Hugh T. "Effects of methylphenidate (Ritalin) on drug-induced drowsiness in mentally retarded
patients." Am J Ment Defic 62(2): 284-87, September, 1957.

1182 Lucas, Alexander R., and Weiss, Morris. "Methylphenidate hallucinosis." JAMA 217(8): 1079-81, August 23, 1971.

1183 Mackay, Mary C.; Beck, Leah; Taylor, Reginald. "Methylphenidate
for adolescents with minimal brain dysfunction." NY State J Med 73:
550-54, February 15, 1973.

1184 Martin, D. M. "Hyperkinetic behavior disorders in children:
clinical results with methylphenidate hydrochloride." West Med 8:
23-27, January, 1967.

1185 Nichamin, Samuel J., and Barahal, G. D. "Faulty neurologic integration with perceptual disorders in children: a two dimentional program of methylphenidate and psychologic management." Mich Med 67
(17): 1071-75, September, 1968.

1186 Robin, S. S., and Bosco, J. J. "Ritalin for school children: the
teachers' perspective." J Sch Health 43(10): 624-28, December, 1973.

1187 Satterfield, James H.; Cantwell, Dennis P.; Lesser, Leonard I.; et. al. "Physiological studies of the hyperkinetic child: I." Am J Psychiatry 128(11): 1418-24, May, 1972.

1188 Schnackenberg, Robert C., and Bender, E. P. "The effect of methylphenidate hydrochloride on children with minimal brain dysfunction syndrome and subsequent hyperkinetic syndrome." Psychiatr Forum 2(2): 32-36, 1971.

1189 Schwartz, Martin L.; Pizzo, S. V.; McKee, P. A. "Minimal brain dysfunction and methylphenidate." N Engl J Med 285: 293, July 29, 1971.

1190 Sleator, Esther K., and Neumann, Alice W. Von. "Methylphenidate in the treatment of hyperkinetic children--recommendations on diagnosis, dosage, and monitoring." Clin Pediatr 13(1): 19-24, January, 1974.

1191 Solomons, Gerald. "The role of methylphenidate and dextroamphetamine in hyperactivity in children." J Iowa Med Soc 6(11): 658-61, November, 1971.

1192 Sprague, Robert L.; Barnes, Kenneth R.; Werry, John S. "Methylphenidate and thioridazine: learning, reaction time, activity and classroom behavior in disturbed children." Am J Orthopsychiatry 40 (4): 615-28, July, 1970.

1193 Spring, Carl; Greenberg, Lawrence M.; Scott, Jimmy; et. al. "Reaction time and effect of Ritalin on children with learning problems." Percept Mot Skills 36(1): 75-82, February, 1973.

1194 Sykes, Donald H.; Douglas, Virginia I.; Morgenstern, Gert. "The effect of methylphenidate (Ritalin) on sustained attention in hyperactive children." Psychopharmacologia 25(3): 262-74, 1972.

1195 Sykes, Donald H.; Douglas, Virginia I.; Weiss, Gabrielle; et. al. "Attention in hyperactive children and the effect of methylphenidate (Ritalin)." J Child Psychol Psychiatry 12(2): 129-39, August, 1971.

1196 Tec, Leon. "Additional observation on methylphenidate in hyperactive children." Am J Psychiatry 127(10): 1424, April, 1971.

1197 "Teenagers with minimal brain dysfunction respond to methylphenidate as infants do." Pediatr News 8(3): 76, March, 1974.

1198 "Those mean little kids: methylphenidate therapy for hyperkinetic syndrome." Time 92: 92-94, October 18, 1968.

1199 Willey, Robert F. "Abuse of methylphenidate (Ritalin)." N Engl J Med 285: 464, August 19, 1971.

1200 Witt, Peter A. "Dosage effects of methylphenidate on the activity level of hyperactive children." Diss Abstr Int 32(10-A): 5631-32, April, 1972.

1201 Zimmerman, Frederic T., and Burgemeister, Bessie B. "Action of methylphenidylacetate (Ritalin) and reserpine in behavior disorders in children and adults." Am J Psychiatry 115(4): 323-28, October, 1958.

1202 Zrull, Joel P. "Discussion of an article by C. Keith Conners and Leon Eisenberg: the effects of methylphenidate on symptomatology and learning in disturbed children." Am J Psychiatry 120(5): 463, November, 1963.

g. Other Antidepressants

1203 Conners, C. Keith; Taylor, Eric; Meo, Grace; et. al. "Magnesium pemoline and dextroamphetamine: a controlled study in children with minimal brain dysfunction." Psychopharmacologia 26: 321-36, 1972.

1204 Davies, T. S. "A monoamine oxidase inhibitor (Niamid) in the treatment of the mentally subnormal." J Ment Sci 107: 115-18, January, 1961.

1205 Hoffer, A. "Treatment of hyperkinetic children with nicotinamide and pyridoxine." Can Med Assoc J 107: 111-12, July 22, 1972.

1206 Kraft, Irvin A.; Ardali, Cohit; Duffy, James H.; et. al. "Use of amitriptyline in childhood behavioral disturbances." Int J Neuropsychiatry 2(6): 611-14, December, 1966.

1207 Krakowski, Adam J. "Amitriptyline in treatment of hyperkinetic children: a double-blind study." Psychosomatics 6(5): 355-60, September/October, 1965.

1208 Kurland, Albert A.; Dorf, Herman J.; Michaux, Mary; et. al. "Cypenamine treatment of mentally retarded children." Curr Ther Res 9(6): 293-305, June, 1967.

1209 Kurtis, Leslie B. "Clinical study of the response to nortriptyline on autistic children." Int J Neuropsychiatry 2(4): 298-301, August, 1966.

1210 Oettinger, Leon. "Meratran: preliminary report of a new drug for the treatment of behavior disorders in children." Dis Nerv Syst 16 (9): 299-302, September, 1955.

1211 Soblen, Robert A., and Saunders, John C. "Monoamine oxidase inhibitor therapy in adolescent psychiatry." Dis Nerv Syst 22(2): 96-100, February, 1961.

1212 Spencer, D. A. "Ronyl (pemoline) in overactive mentally subnormal children." Br J Psychiatry 117: 239-40, August, 1970.

1213 Triantafillou, M. "Pemoline in overactive mentally handicapped children." Br J Psychiatry 121: 577, November, 1972.

1214 Watter, N. "Modification of hyperkinetic behavior by nortriptyline." Va Med Mon 100(2): 123-26, February, 1972.

3. Other Drugs

1215 Albert, K.; Hoch, P.; Waelsch, H. "Glutamic acid and mental deficiency." J Nerv Ment Dis 114(6): 471-91, December, 1951.

1216 Albert K.; Hoch, P.; Waelsch, H. "Preliminary report on the effect
of glutamic acid administration in mentally retarded subjects." J Nerv
Ment Dis 104(3): 263-74, September, 1946.

1217 Annell, A. L. "Lithium in the treatment of children and adolescents." Acta Psychiatr Scand (Suppl) 207: 19-30, 1969.

1218 Bruce, A. G. "Lucidril for autism." NY Med J 73: 173, March,
1971.

1919 Campbell, Magda; Fish, Barbara; Korein, Julius; et. al. "Lithium
and chlorpromazine: a controlled crossover study of hyperactive
severely disturbed young children." J Autism Child Schizophr 2(3):
234-63, July/September, 1972.

1220 Conners, C. Keith; Kramer, R.; Rothschild, Gerard H.; et. al.
"Treatment of young delinquent boys with dilphenylhydantoin and methylphenidate: a controlled comparison." Arch Gen Psychiatry 24(2):
156-60, February, 1971.

1221 Dyson, William L., and Barcai, Avner. "Treatment of children of
lithium-responding parents." Curr Ther Res 12(5): 286-90, May, 1970.

1222 Freedman, Alfred M.; Kremer, M. W.; Robertiello, R. C.; et. al.
"The treatment of behavior disorders in children with Tolserol." J
Pediatr 47(3): 369-72, September, 1955.

1223 Greenhill, Lawrence; Buchsbaum, Monte; Rieder, R. O.; et. al.
"Lithium-carbonate in treatment of hyperactive children." Arch Gen
Psychiatry 28(5): 636-40, May, 1973.

1224 Gross, Mortimer D., and Wilson, William C. "Behavior disorders of
children with cerebral dysrhythmias: successful treatment of subcon-
vulsive dysrhythmia with anticonvulsants." Arch Gen Psychiatry 11
(6): 610-19, December, 1964.

1225 Gupta, P. D., and Virmani, V. "Clinical trial of jatamansone
(Valeranone) in hyperkinetic behaviour disorders." Neurol India 16:
168-73, October/December, 1968.

1226 Hava, F. A. "Lithium, the hyperactive child, and manic depressive
illness." J Arkansas Med Soc 69: 299-300, March, 1973.

1227 Kneebone, G. M. "The use of sulthiame 'Ospolot' in the epileptic
child with the hyperkinetic syndrome." Med J Aust 2: 1096-97, December 14, 1968.

1228 Lefkowitz, M. M. "The effects of diphenylhydantoin on disruptive
behavior: study of male delinquents." Arch Gen Psychiatry 20(6):
643-51, June, 1969.

1229 Looker, Andrew, and Conners, C. Keith. "Diphenylhydantoin in children with severe temper tantrums." Arch Gen Psychiatry 23(1): 80-89, July, 1970.

1230 Lyons, G. D., and Cranfield, C. C. "Ketamine hydrochloride as a pre-anesthetic agent in children." Laryngoscope 81(6): 813-17, June, 1971.

1231 Pasamanick, Benjamin. "Anticonvulsant drug therapy of behavior problem children with abnormal electroencephalograms." AMA Arch Neurol Psychiatry 65: 752-66, 1951.

1232 Smith, W. Lynn, and Weyl, T. C. "The effects of ethosuximide (Zarontin) on intellectual functions of children with learning deficits and cortical brain dysfunction." Curr Ther Res 10(6): 265-69, June, 1968.

1233 Tec, Leon. "Efficacy of diphenylhydantoin in childhood psychiatric disorders." Am J Psychiatry 124(8): 1138-39, February, 1968.

1234 Walker, Charlotte F., and Kirkpatrick, Barbara B. "Dilantin treatment for behavior problems and normal EEG." Am J Psychiatry 103: 484-92, January, 1947.

1235 Whitehead, Paul L., and Clark, Lincoln D. "Effect of lithium carbonate, placebo, and thioridazine on hyperactive children." Am J Psychiatry 127(6): 824-25, December, 1970.

1236 Zimmerman, Frederic T., and Burgemeister, Bessie B. "A controlled experiment of glutamic acid therapy: first report summarizing thirteen years of study." AMA Arch Neurol Psychiatry 81(5): 639-48, May, 1959.

1237 Zimmerman, Frederic T., and Burgemeister, Bessie B. "Permanency of glutamic acid treatment." AMA Arch Neurol Psychiatry 65: 291-98, 1951.

4. Adverse Effects

1238 Baldwin, Ronald L., and Peters, John E. "Hematologic complications from tranquilizers in children." South Med J 61(10): 1072-75, October, 1968.

1239 Barcai, Avner. "Emergence of neurotic conflict in some children after successful administration of dextroamphetamine." J Child Psychol Psychiatry 10(4): 269-76, December, 1969.

1240 DiMascio, A.; Soltys, J.; Shader, R. "Psychotropic drug side effects in children." In: Shader, Richard I., and DiMascio, Alberto. Psychotropic drug side effects: clinical and theoretical perspectives. Baltimore: Williams & Wilkins, 1970. 235-60.

1241 Golden, Gerald S. "Gilles de la Tourette's syndrome following methylphenidate administration." Dev Med Child Neurol 16(1): 76-78, February, 1974.

1242 Greenberg, Laurence M.; McMahon, Shirley A.; Deem, Michael A. "Side effects of dextroamphetamine therapy of hyperactive children." West J Med 120(2): 105-9, February, 1974.

1243 "The growth of children given stimulant drugs." Nutr Rev 31(3): 91-92, March, 1973.

1244 Hooshmand, H. "Toxic effects of anticonvulsants: general principles." Pediatrics 53(4): 555-56, April, 1974.

1245 Lennard, Henry L.; Epstein, Leon J.; Bernstein, Arnold; et. al. "Hazards implicit in prescribing psychoactive drugs: mystification in drug use and models of drug action are reviewed." Science 169: 438-41, July 31, 1970.

1246 Mattson, Richard H., and Calverley, John R. "Dextroamphetamine-sulfate-induced dyskinesias." JAMA 204(5): 400-402, April 29, 1968.

1247 Ney, Philip G. "Psychosis in a child associated with amphetamine administration." Can Med Assoc J 97(17): 1026-29, October 21, 1967.

1248 Randrup, A., and Mundvak, I. "Stereotyped activities produced by amphetamines in several animal species and man." Psychopharmacologia 11: 300-310, 1967.

1249 Rothschild, C. J., and Nicol, H. "Allergic reaction to methylphenidate." Can Med Assoc J 106: 1064, May 20, 1972.

1250 Safer, Daniel J., and Allen, Richard. "Factors influencing suppressant effects of two stimulant drugs on the growth of hyperactive children." Pediatrics 51(4): 660-67, April, 1973.

1251 Safer, Daniel J.; Allen, Richard; Barr, Evelyn. "Depression of growth in hyperactive children on stimulant drugs." N Eng J Med 287: 217-20, August 3, 1972.

1252 Teitelbaum, Daniel T. "Poisoning with psychoactive drugs." Pediatr Clin North Am 17(3): 557-67, August, 1970.

5. Surgical Therapy

1253 Balasubramaniam, V.; Kanaka, T. S.; Ramamurthi, B. "Surgical treatment of hyperkinetic and behavior disorders." Int Surg 54: 18-23, July, 1970.

1254 Balasubramaniam, V., and Ramamurthi, B. "Stereotaxic amygdalotomy in behavior disorders." Confin Neurol 32: 367-73, 1970.

1255 Breggin, Phyllis. "Underlying a method: is psychosurgery an acceptable treatment for 'hyperactivity' in children?" Ment Hyg 58 (1): 19-21, Winter, 1974.

1256 Bucy, P. C. "The surgical treatment of abnormal involuntary movements." J Neurosurg Nurs 2: 31-39, July, 1970.

1257 Narabayashi, H., and Uno, M. "Long range results of stereotactic amygdalotomy for behavior disorders." Confin Neurol 27: 168-71, 1966.

1258 "Stereotactic neurosurgery for aggressive behavior." Med J Aust 1: 779-80, April 21, 1973.

1259 Wood, Matthew W., and Rowland, Joseph P. "Bilateral anterior thalamotomy for the hyperactive child." South Med J 61(1): 36-39, January, 1968.

6. Placebo Studies

1260 Beecher, Henry K. "The powerful placebo." JAMA 159(17): 1602-6, December 24, 1965.

1261 Kurland, Albert A. "Placebo effect." In: Uhr, Leonard, and Miller, James G., eds. Drugs and behavior. New York: Wiley, 1960. 156-65.

1262 Liberman, R. "An analysis of the placebo phenomenon." J Chronic Dis 15: 761, 783, July, 1962.

1263 McDermott, John F. "A specific placebo effect encountered in the use of Dexedrine in a hyperactive child." Am J Psychiatry 12(9): 923-24, March, 1965.

1264 Mooney, W. E. "The placebo: a bibliography (1955-1960)." Psychiatr Commun 4: 21-26, 1961.

7. Psychotherapy

1265 Allen, Frederick H. Psychotherapy with children. New York: Norton, 1942. 311p.

1266 Anderson, Robert P. "Let's treat discouragement too: MBD children." Acad Ther 7(2): 131-37, Winter, 1971-72.

1267 Aronson, Leonard J. "The psychologist and minimal brain dysfunction: ten steps to maximum incompetence." Ment Hyg 55(4): 523-25, October, 1971.

1268 Bender, Lauretta. "Art and therapy in the mental disturbances of children." J Nerv Ment Dis 86(3): 249-63, September, 1937.

1269 ———. "Psychological treatment of the brain-damaged child." Q J Child Behav 3: 323-33, 1951.

1270 Berlin, Irving. "A psychiatric view of learning disorders." In: Ross Conference on Pediatric Research, 61st, Columbus, Ohio, 1971. Report. Edited by John H. Menkes, and Richard J. Schain. Columbus, Ohio: Ross Laboratories, 1971. 40-47.

1271 Bond, Earl D., and Smith, Lauren H. "Post-encephalitic behavior disorders: a ten year review of the Franklin School." Am J Psychiatry 92: 17-33, July, 1935.

1272 Carter, John L., and Miller, Phillis K. "Creative art for minimally brain-injured children." Acad Ther 6(3): 245-52, Spring, 1971.

1273 Cermark, Sharon A.; Abelson, C.; Stein, F. "Hyperactive children and an activity group-therapy model." Am J Occup Ther 27(6): 311-15, September, 1973.

1274 Conners, C. Keith; Eisenberg, Leon; Sharpe, Lawrence. "A controlled study of the differential application of outpatient psychiatric treatment for children." Jap J Child Psychiatry 6: 125-32, 1965.

1275 Dietz, E. "Case analysis: consultation and counseling: case of Willie Pace, a Negro student." Elem Sch Guid Couns 8(2): 140-45, December, 1973.

1276 Doris, John, and Solnit, Albert J. "Treatment of children with brain damage and associated school problems." J Am Acad Child Psychiatry 2(4): 618-35, October, 1963.

1277 Eisenberg, Leon. "Brief psychotherapy versus drugs: fitting the treatment to the illness." In: Segal, Julius, ed. The mental health of the child: program reports of the NIMH. Rockville, Maryland: Program Analysis and Evaluation Branch, Office of Program Planning and Evaluation, 1971. 401-11. (PHS Publication, No. 2168).

1278 Eisenberg, Leon; Gilbert, Anita; Cytryn, Leon; et. al. "The effectiveness of psychotherapy alone and in conjunction with perphenazine or placebo in the treatment of neurotic and hyperkinetic children." Am J Psychiatry 117(2): 1088-93, June, 1961.

1279 Eysenck, H. J. "The effects of psychotherapy." In: Eysenck, Hans J., ed. Handbook of abnormal psychology: an experimental approach. London: Pitman, 1960. 675-725.

1280 Freed, Herbert; Abrams, J.; Peifer, Charles A. "Reading disability: a new therapeutic approach and its implications." J Clin Exp Psychopath Q Rev Psychiatry Neurol 20: 251-59, 1959.

1281 Frostig, Marianne, and Horne, David. "An approach to the treatment of children with learning disorders." In: Hellmuth, Jerome, ed. Learning disorders. Vol. 1. Seattle: Special Child Publications, 1965. 293-305.

1282 Fuentes, Pedro A. "Minimal brain dysfunction syndrome: a reexamination of its affective and social aspects." Diss Abstr Int 34 (6-B): 2928-29, December, 1973.

1283 Furman, Seymour, and Feighner, Anne C. "Video feedback in treating hyperactive children: a preliminary report." Am J Psychiatry 130(7): 792-96, July, 1973.

1284 Gallagher, James J. "Psychology and special education--the future: where the action is." Psychol Sch 6(3): 219-26, July, 1969.

1285 Garrard, Sterling D., and Richmond, Julius B. "Psychological aspects of the management of children with defects or damage of the central nervous system." Pediatr Clin North Am 4: 1033-48, November, 1957.

1286 Ginott, Haim G. Group psychotherapy with children: the theory and practice of play-therapy. New York: McGraw-Hill, 1961. 208p.

1287 Goodman, Jerome D. "Short-term treatment in child psychiatry." Am Fam Physician 3(1): 80-85, January, 1971.

1288 Halpern, Howard M. A parent's guide to child psychotherapy. New York: Barnes, 1963. 178p.

1289 Hamilton, Gordon. Psychotherapy in child guidance. New York: Columbia University Press, 1947. 340p.

1290 Holt, Fred D., and Kicklighter, Richard H., comps. Psychological services in the schools: readings in preparation, organization, and practice. Dubuque, Iowa: Brown, 1971. 312p.

1291 Hood-Williams, J. "The results of psychotherapy with children: a revaluation." J Consult Psychol 24(1): 84-88, February, 1960.

1292 Kahn, Jane; Buchmueller, A. D.; Gildea, Margaret. "Group therapy for parents of behavior problem children in public schools: failure of the program in a Negro school." Am J Psychiatry 108(5): 351-57, November, 1951.

1293 Knobel, Mauricio. "The environmental 'antidrug' effect." Psychiatry 23(4): 403-7, November, 1960.

1294 ———. "A syndromic approach to 'acting out' children." Dis Nerv Syst 20(2): 80-87, February, 1959.

1295 Kok, J. F. W. Structopathic children: I. Description of disturbance type and strategies. Portland, Oregon: International Scholarly Book Services, 1972. 125p.

1296 ———. Structopathic children: II. Results of experimental research of structuring group therapy. Portland, Oregon: International Scholarly Book Services, 1972. 122p.

1297 Levitt, Eugene E. "Psychotherapy with children: a further evaluation." Behav Res Ther 1(1): 45-51, May, 1963.

1298 ———. "The results of psychotherapy with children." J Consult Psychol 21(3): 189-96, June, 1957.

1299 Minde, Klaus, and Werry, John S. "Intensive psychiatric teacher counseling in a low socio-economic area: a controlled evaluation." Am J Orthopsychiatry 39(4): 595-608, July, 1969.

1300 Moore, Nancy. "Diagnosis? hyperkinesis, prescription? music!" Music J 27: 29, 46-47, November, 1969.

1301 Newman, Ruth G. "The assessment of progress in the treatment of hyperaggressive children with learning disturbances within a school setting." Am J Orthopsychiatry 29(3): 633-43, July, 1959.

1302 Reger, Roger, and Dawson, Antoinette. "The hyperactive educable mentally retarded child: occupational therapy program." Am J Occup Ther 16(4): 182-84, July/August, 1962.

1303 Scott, Thomas J. "Use of music to reduce hyperactivity in children." Am J Orthopsychiatry 40(4): 677-80, July, 1970.

1304 Shaw, Charles R. When your child needs help: a psychiatrist looks at the emotional problems of children. New York: Morrow, 1972. 309p.

1305 Smith, B. S., and Phillips, E. H. "Treating a hyperactive child." Phys Ther 50(4): 506-10, April, 1970.

1306 Solnit, Albert J., and Stark, M. H. "Pediatric management of school learning problems of underachievement." N Engl J Med 261: 988-93, November 12, 1959.

1307 Splitter, S. R., and Kaufman, M. "A new treatment for underachieving adolescents: psychotherapy combined with nortriptyline medication." Psychosomatics 7: 171-74, 1966.

1308 Weight, L.; Woodcock, J.; Scott, R. "Treatment of sleep disturbance in a young child by conditioning." South Med J 63: 173-76, February, 1970.

1309 Wender, Paul. "The minimal brain dysfunction syndrome in children: I. The syndrome and its relevance to society; II. A psychological and biochemical model for the syndrome." J Nerv Ment Dis 155(1): 55-71, July, 1972.

1310 Werry, John S. "The psychiatrist and society." Discoverer 5(3): 1-12, 1968.

B. Educational Management: Hyperkinesis and

Learning Disorders: Educational Implications

1311 Abrams, Jules C. "Learning disabilities: a complex phenomenon." Read Teach 23: 299-303ff., January, 1970.

1312 Anderson, Robert P. The child with learning disabilities and guidance. Boston: Houghton-Mifflin, 1970. 83p.

1313 Bannatyne, Alexander. Language, reading, and learning disabilities: psychology, neuropsychology, diagnosis and remediation. Springfield, Illinois: Thomas, 1971. 787p.

1314 Barr, Karen L., and McDowell, Richard L. "Comparison of learning disabled and emotionally disturbed children on three deviant classroom behaviors." Except Child 39(1): 60-62, September, 1972.

1315   Bateman, Barbara D.   "Educational implications of minimal brain dysfunction." Ann NY Acad Sci   205: 245-50, February 28, 1973.

1316   ———. "Learning disabilities--yesterday, today and tomorrow." Except Child 31(4): 167-77, December, 1964.

1317   Birch, Herbert G., and Bortner, Morton. "Brain damage: an educational category?" In: Bortner, Morton, ed. The evaluation and education of children with brain damage. Springfield, Illinois: Thomas, 1968. 3-11.

1318   Black, F. William. "Neurological dysfunction and reading disorders." J Learn Disabil 6(5): 313-16, May, 1973.

1319 Blackham, Garth J. The deviant child in the classroom. Belmont, California: Wadsworth, 1967. 191p.

1320   Bortner, Morton, ed. The evaluation and education of children with brain damage. Springfield, Illinois: Thomas, 1968. 269p.

1321   Bradfield, Robert H.; Brown, Josephine; Kaplan, Phyllis; et. al. "Special child in the regular classroom." Except Child 39(5): 384-90, February, 1973.

1322   Bricklin, Barry, and Bricklin, Patricia M. Bright child, poor grades: the psychology of underachievement. New York: Delacorte, 1967. 173p.

1323   Brody, Charles; Plutchik, Robert; Reilly, Edwina; et. al. "Personality and problem behavior of third grade children in the regular classroom." Psychol Sch 10(2): 196-99, April, 1973.

1324   Carrier, Neil A.; Malpass, Leslie F.; Orton, Kenneth D. Responses of bright, normal, and retarded children to learning tasks. Carbondale, Illinois: Southern Illinois University, 1961. 128p. (Office of Education Cooperative Research Project, No. 578).

1325   Carter, Pauline, and Lockey, Ann. "Teaching the hyperactive child." Provo Papers Summer: 124-31, 1967.

1326   Clements, Sam D., and Peters, John E. "Psychoeducational programming for children with minimal brain dysfunctions." Ann NY Acad Sci 205: 46-51, February 28, 1973.

1327   Cohen, S. Allan. "Minimal brain dysfunction and practical matters such as teaching kids to read." Ann NY Acad Sci 205: 251-61, February 28, 1973.

1328   Conners, C. Keith. "Information processing in children with learning disabilities and brain damage: some experimental approaches." In: Association for Children with Learning Disabilities, 3rd, Tulsa, 1966. Selected papers: International approach to learning disabilities of children and youth. Pittsburgh, 1967. 284p.

1329   Cruickshank, William M. "Some issues facing the field of learning disability." J Learn Disabil 5(7): 380-88, August/September, 1972.

1330 Cruickshank, William M.; Bentzen, F. A.; Ratzeburg, F. H.; et. al. A teaching method for brain-injured and hyperactive children: a demonstration pilot study. Syracuse, New York: Syracuse University Press, 1961. 576p.

1331 Cruickshank, William M.; Junkala, John B.; Paul, James L. The preparation of teachers of brain-injured and hyperactive children. Syracuse, New York: Syracuse University Press, 1968. 203p. (Syracuse University. Special Education and Rehabilitation Monograph Series, No. 8).

1332 Cutts, Norma E., and Moseley, Nicholas. Teaching the disorderly pupil in elementary and secondary school. New York: Longmans, Green, 1957. 170p.

1333 De Hirsch, Katrina. "Learning disabilities: an overview." Bull NY Acad Med 50(4): 459-79, April, 1974.

1334 Denckla, Martha B. "Research needs in learning disabilities: a neurologists point of view." J Learn Disabil 6(7): 441-50, August/September, 1973.

1335 Denhoff, Eric, and Kovack, Harry S. "Syndromes of cerebral dysfunction: medical aspects that contribute to special education methods." In: Haring, Norris G., and Schiefelbusch, Richard L., eds. Methods in special education. New York: McGraw-Hill, 1967. 351-83.

1336 Dunn, Lloyd M. "Minimal brain dysfunction: a dilemma for educators." In: Haywood, H. Carl, ed. Brain damage in school age children. Washington, D. C.: Council for Exceptional Children, 1968. 161-81.

1337 Durbin, Mary Lou, and Kaye, Clement L. "Classroom research: materials and the severely retarded." Mich Educ J 40: 501, 526, March 1, 1963.

1338 Ebersole, Marylou; Kephart, Newell C.; Ebersole, James B. Steps to achievement for the slow learner. Columbus, Ohio: Merrill, 1968. 196p.

1339 Edwards, R. Philip; Alley, Gordon R.; Snider, William. "Academic achievement and minimal brain dysfunction in mentally retarded children." Except Child 37(7): 539-40, March, 1971.

1340 Edwards, R. Philip; Alley, Gordon R.; Snider, William. "Academic achievement and minimal brain dysfunction." J Learn Disabil 4(3): 134-38, March, 1971.

1341 Ellingson, Careth. The shadow children: a book about children's learning disorders. Chicago: Topaz Books, 1967. 254p.

1342 Faas, Larry A., comp. Learning disabilities: a book of readings. Springfield, Illinois: Thomas, 1972. 257p.

1343 Fargo, George A. "Classroom behaviors of emotionally disturbed and brain-injured children." Diss Abstr 24(6): 2357, December, 1963.

1344 Fouracre, Maurice H. "Learning characteristics of brain-injured children." Except Child 24(5): 210-12, 223, January, 1968.

1345 Francis-Williams, Jessie. "Special educational problems of children with minimal cerebral dysfunction." Spastics Q 14(2): 12-17, 1965.

1346 Friedman, Fay T. MBD--an éducational puzzlement. Buffalo: D'Youville College, 1965. 17p. (ED 032 130).

1347 Frierson, Edward C., and Barbe, Walter B., eds. Educating children with learning disabilities: selected readings. New York: Appleton-Century-Crofts, 1967. 502p.

1348 Gallagher, James J. "New educational treatment models for children with minimal brain dysfunction." Ann NY Acad Sci 205: 383-89, February 28, 1973.

1349 ———. The tutoring of brain-injured mentally retarded children: an experimental study. Springfield, Illinois: Thomas, 1960. 194p.

1350 Gates, Maxine F. "A comparison of the learning characteristics of hyperactive and hypoactive children with related central nervous system dysfunctions." Diss Abstr 30(1-A): 166-67, July, 1969.

1351 Gofman, Helen F., and Allmond, Bayard W., Jr. "Learning and language disorders in children: II. The school-age child." Curr Probl Pediatr 1(11): 3-60, September, 1971.

1352 Gordon, Ronnie; White, Donna; Diller, Leonard. "Performance of neurologically impaired pre-school children with educational materials." Except Child 38(5): 428-37, January, 1972.

1353 Gordon, Sol. "Sense and nonsense about brain injury and learning disabilities." Acad Ther 5(4): 249-54, Summer, 1970.

1354 Graubard, Paul S. "The relationship between academic achievement and behavior dimensions." Except Child 37(10): 755-57, Summer, 1971.

1355 Grimm, Jeffrey A. "A problem solving model for teaching remedial arithmetic to handicapped young children." J Abnorm Child Psychol 1 (1): 26-39, January/March, 1973.

1356 Hager, James L. "Educator's role with hyperkinetic children." Phi Delta Kappan 54(5): 338-39, January, 1973.

1357 Hallahan, Daniel P. "Learning disabilities in historical and psychoeducational perspective." Diss Abstr Int 33(5-A): 2169, November, 1972.

1358 Hallahan, Daniel P., and Cruickshank, William M. Psychoeducational foundations of learning disabilities. Englewood Cliffs, New Jersey: Prentice-Hall, 1973. 317p.

1359 Hammill, Donald D., and Bartel, Nettie R. Educational perspectives in learning disabilities. New York: Wiley, 1971. 420p.

1360 Hammond, Jerrold E. "Learning and behavior problems of children."
Va Med Mon 89(6): 379-85, June, 1962.

1361 Haring, Norris G., and Phillips, E. Lakin. Educating emotionally
disturbed children. New York: McGraw-Hill, 1962. 322p.

1362 Haring, Norris G., and Schiefelbusch, Richard L., eds. Methods in
special education. New York: McGraw-Hill, 1967. 430p.

1363 Hellmuth, Jerome, ed. Learning disorders. Seattle: Special Child
Publications, 1965-68. 3v.

1364 Hewett, Frank M. "Educational engineering with emotionally disturbed children." Except Child 33(7): 459-67, March, 1967.

1365 ———. The emotionally disturbed child in the classroom: a
developmental strategy for educating children with maladaptive behavior. Boston: Allyn & Bacon, 1968. 373p.

1366 ———. "A hierarchy of educational tasks for children with learning disorders." Except Child 31(4): 207-14, December, 1964.

1367 Hewett, Frank M.; Taylor, F. D.; Artuso, A. A. "The Santa Monica
Project: evaluation of an engineered classroom design with emotionally disturbed children." Except Child 35(7): 523-29, March, 1969.

1368 Jacquot, W. S.; Allen, Louise; Landreth, Garry L.; et. al.
"Learning disabilities: a team approach." Elem Sch J 70: 248-52,
February, 1970.

1369 Johnson, Doris J., and Myklebust, Helmer R. Learning disabilities:
educational principles and practices. New York: Grune & Stratton,
1967. 336p.

1370 Jolles, Isaac. "A public school demonstration class for children
with brain damage." Am J Ment Defic 60: 582-88, January, 1956.

1371 Kaliski, Lotte. "The brain-injured child--learning by living in a
structured setting." Am J Ment Defic 63(4): 688-95, January, 1959.

1372 ———. "Educational therapy for brain injured retarded children."
Am J Ment Defic 60: 71-76, July, 1955.

1373 Kappelman, Murray M.; Luck, Elizabeth; Ganter, Robert L. "Profile
of the disadvantaged child with learning disorders." Am J Dis Child
121(5): 371-79, May, 1971.

1374 Katz, Davis, and Wolfe, Harvey R. Teaching brain injured children:
a handbook for teachers and supervisors. Brooklyn: New York City
Board of Education, 1967. (ED 019 788).

1375 Keogh, Barbara K. 'Hyperactivity and learning disorders: review
and speculation." Except Child 38(2): 101-9, October, 1971.

1376 ———. "Hyperactivity and learning problems: implications for
teachers." Acad Ther 7(1): 47-50, Fall, 1971.

1377 Kephart, Newell C. The brain injured child in the classroom. Chicago: National Society for Crippled Children and Adults, 1963. 14p.

1378 ———. "Educational problems of the brain-injured child." Educ Rep 3: 8-10, 1962.

1379 ———. Learning disability: an educational adventure. West Lafayette, Indiana: Kappa Delta Pi Press, 1968. 133p.

1380 ———. The slow learner in the classroom. Columbus, Ohio: Merrill, 1960. 292p.

1381 Kinsbourne, Marcel. "School problems." Pediatrics 52(5): 697-710, November, 1973.

1382 Kirk, Samuel A. "What is special about special education?: the child who is mentally handicapped." Except Child 19(4): 138-42, January, 1953.

1383 Knoblock, Peter. "Open education for emotionally disturbed children." Except Child 39(5): 358-65, February, 1973.

1384 Knoblock, Peter, and Johnson, John L., eds. "The teaching-learning process in educating emotionally disturbed children." In: Conference on the Education of Emotionally Disturbed Children, 3rd, Syracuse University, 1967. Proceedings. Syracuse, New York: Syracuse University, Division of Special Education and Rehabilitation, 1967. 141p. (ED 023 235).

1385 Krauch, V. "Hyperactive engineering." Am Educ 7(5): 12-16, June, 1971.

1386 Learning disabilities due to minimal brain dysfunction: hope through research. Washington, D. C.: U. S. Dept. of Health, Education and Welfare, National Institute of Neurological Diseases and Stroke, 1971. 22p. (PHS Publication, No. 1646).

1387 Learning disabilities: introduction to educational and medical management. Edited by Lester Tarnopol. Springfield, Illinois: Thomas, 1969. 389p.

1388 Learning disorders in children: diagnosis, medication, education. Edited by Lester Tarnopol. Boston: Little, Brown, 1971. 366p.

1389 Lesley College Annual Graduate Symposium, 3rd, Cambridge, Massachusetts, 1967. Educational implications of psychopathology for brain-injured children. Edited by Boris Gertz. Cambridge, Massachusetts: Lesley College, Graduate School of Education, 1967. 43p. (ED 021 366).

1390 Levy, Harold B. Square pegs, round holes: the learning-disabled child in the classroom and at home. Boston: Little, Brown, 1973. 250p.

1391 Long, Nicholas J.; Morse, William C.; Newman, Ruth G.; eds. Conflict in the classroom: the education of children with problems. 2nd ed. Belmont, California: Wadsworth, 1971. 587p.

1392 Lordi, W. M. "Minimal brain syndrome and learning disabilities in childhood." Va Med Mon 99(9): 972-75, September, 1972.

1393 McCarthy, James J., and McCarthy, Joan F. Learning disabilities. Boston: Allyn & Bacon, 1969. 138p.

1394 McCarthy, Jeanne M. "Education: the base of the triangle." Ann NY Acad Sci 205: 362-67, February 28, 1973.

1395 McGrady, Harold J. "Learning disabilities: implications for medicine and education." J Sch Health 41(5): 227-34, May, 1971.

1396 Magnifico, L. X. Education for the exceptional child. New York: Longmans, Green, 1958. 371p.

1397 Mallison, Ruth. Education as therapy: suggestions for work with neurologically impaired children. Seattle: Special Child Publications, 1968. 166p.

1398 Margolese, Arthur. "The relation of hypercusis to hyperkinesis among regular classroom pupils as compared to educationally handicapped pupils." Diss Abstr Int 32(4-A): 1945, October, 1971.

1399 Marrone, R. T., and Anderson, Nancy. "Innovative public school programming for emotionally disturbed children." Am J Orthopsychiatry 40(4): 694-701, July, 1970.

1400 Mehegan, Charles, and Dreifuss, Fritz E. "Hyperlexia: exceptional reading ability in brain-damaged children." Neurology 22(11): 1105-11, November, 1972.

1401 Mekler, Lucy. "My son the reader." Acad Ther 7(4): 473-76, Summer, 1972.

1402 Mesinger, John F. "Emotionally disturbed and brain-damaged children--should we mix them?" Except Child 32(4): 237-38, December, 1965.

1403 Michael-Smith, Harold, and Morgenstern, Murry. "Learning disorders: an overview." In: Hellmuth, Jerome, ed. Learning disorders. Vol. 1. Seattle: Special Child Publications, 1965. 169-96.

1404 Miller, Floyd. "Getting Billy into the game." Am Educ 9(1): 22-27, January/February, 1973.

1405 Muller, M. E. "Teaching reading to the brain injured child." Clgh House J 9: 29-41, 1968.

1406 Murphy, John F. "Learning by listening: a public school approach to learning disabilities." Acad Ther 8(2): 167-89, Winter, 1972-73.

1407 Myers, Patricia, and Hammill, Donald D. Methods for learning disorders. New York: Wiley, 1969. 313p.

1408 Myklebust, Helmer R. "Learning disabilities: definition and overview." In: Myklebust, Helmer R., ed. Progress in learning disabilities. Vol. 1. New York: Grune & Stratton, 1968. 1-15.

1409 ———. "Learning disorders: psychoneurological disturbances in
children." Rehabil Lit 25(12): 354-60, 1965.

   Myklebust, Helmer R., ed.
      see Progress in learning disabilities. (Item No. 1416).

1410 Myklebust, Helmer R., and Boshes, Benjamin. "Psychoneurological
learning disorders in children." Arch Pediatr 77: 247-56, June,
1960.

1411 Nichamin, Samuel J. "Reading disorders in children." JAMA 207
(13): 2438-39, March 31, 1969.

1412 Ohio. Division of Special Education. Ohio programs for neurologically handicapped children. Edward C. Grover and Joseph H. Todd, joint
authors. Columbus, Ohio: 1967. 74p.

1413 Petersen, Wretha. "Classroom management for the neurologically
impaired." In: Hellmuth, Jerome, ed. Learning disorders. Vol. 1.
Seattle: Special Child Publications, 1965. 389-406.

1414 Potter, Robert E., and Orlich, Donald C. "Learning disabilities
· of pupils with average intelligence." Education 91(1): 92-95, Sep-
tember/October, 1970.

1415 Prechtl, H. F. R. "Reading difficulties as a neurological problem
in childhood." In: Money, John, ed. Reading disability. Baltimore:
Johns Hopkins, 1962. 187-93.

1416 Progress in learning disabilities. Edited by Helmer R. Myklebust.
New York: Grune & Stratton, 1968-

1417 Quay, Herbert C. "The facts of educational exceptionality: a
conceptual framework for assessment, grouping, and instruction."
Except Child 35(1): 25-32, September, 1968.

1418 ———. "Some basic consideration in the education of emotionally
disturbed children." Except Child 30(1): 27-31, September, 1963.

1419 Rabinovitch, Ralph D. "Reading and learning disabilities." In:
Arieti, S., ed. American handbook of psychiatry. New York: Basic
Books, 1959. 857-69.

1420 Rappaport, Sheldon R. Public education for children with brain
dysfunction. Syracuse, New York: Syracuse University Press, 1969.
219p.

1421 Reed, Homer B. C. "Brain damage, intelligence, and education."
Nat Bus Educ Q 38(2): 19-27, March, 1970.

1422 Rosenbloom, Lewis. "Learning disabilities and hyperkinesis." Dev
Med Child Neurol 14(3): 394-95, June, 1972.

1423 Rossi, Albert O. "The educationally handicapped child." NY State J Med 67(21): 2823-27, November 1, 1967.

1424 Rubin, Eli Z., and Simson, Clyde B. "A special class program for the emotionally disturbed child in school: a proposal." Am J Orthopsychiatry 30(1): 144-53, January, 1960.

1425 Ryckman, David B. Learning disabilities: theoretical approaches. New York: MSS Educational Publishing Company, 1971. 186p.

1426 Sapir, Selma G., and Nitzburg, A. C., eds. Children with learning problems: readings in a developmental-interaction approach. New York: Brunner/Mazel, 1973. 709p.

1427 Saunders, Bruce T. "Effect of the emotionally disturbed child in the public school classroom." Psychol Sch 8(1): 23-26, January, 1971.

1428 Scholand, J. "The school nurse teacher's role in the life of the hyperactive child with learning disabilities." J NY Sch Nurse Teach Assoc 3: 35-40, Winter, 1972.

1429 Sheer, Daniel E. "Is there a common factor in learning for brain-injured children?" Except Child 21(1): 10-12, October, 1954.

1430 Siegel, Ernest. Helping the brain-injured child. New York: New York Association for Brain-Injured Children, 1961. 158p.

1431 Silver, Archie A.; Hagin, Rosa A.; Hersh, Marilyn F. "Reading disability: teaching through stimulation of deficit perceptual areas." Am J Psychiatry 37(4): 744-52, July, 1967.

1432 Silver, Larry B. "The neurologic learning disability syndrome." Am Fam Physician 4(1): 95-102, July, 1971.

1433 Smith, Bert K. Your nonlearning child: his world of upside-down. Boston: Beacon, 1968. 175p.

1434 Smith, B. S., and Ishee, B. "Specific learning disabilities." Todays Educ 61: 18-22, January, 1972.

1435 Stephens, Thomas M. Directive teaching of children with learning and behavioral handicaps. Columbus, Ohio: Merrill, 1970. 195p. (ED 043 982).

1436 Strauss, Alfred A. "The education of the brain-injured child." In: Magary, James F., and Eichorn, John R., eds. The exceptional child: a book of readings. New York: Holt, Rinehart & Winston, 1960. 135-43.

1437 Strauss, Alfred A., and Lehtinen, Laura E. Psychopathology and education of the brain-injured child: I. Fundamentals and treatment. II. Progress in theory and clinic. New York: Grune & Stratton, 1947-1955. 2v.

1438 Swift, Marshall S.; Spivack, George; Danset, A.; et. al. "Classroom behavior and academic success of French and American elementary school children." Int Rev Appl Psychol 20: 1-11, 1972.

Tarnopol, Lester, ed.
see Learning disabilities: introduction to educational and medical management. (Item No. 1387).

Tarnopol, Lester, ed.
see Learning disorders in children: diagnosis, medication, education. (Item No. 1388).

1439 Thelander, H. E.; Phelps, J. K.; Kirk, E. W. "Learning disabilities associated with lesser brain damage." J Pediatr 53(4): 405-9, October, 1958.

1440 Thomas, Evan W. Brain-injured children, with special reference to Doman-Delacato methods of treatment. Springfield, Illinois: Thomas, 1969. 178p.

1441 Thompson, Lloyd J. "Learning disabilities: an overview." Am J Psychiatry 130(4): 393-99, April, 1973.

1442 U. S. Congress. House. Committee on Education and Labor. Subcommittee on Education. Children with learning disabilities act of 1969, Hearings. 91st. Cong., 1st sess., on H. R. 8660 and H. R. 9065.. July 8, 9, and 10, 1969. Washington, D. C.: U. S. Government Printing Office, 1969. 236p.

1443 Valett, Robert E. The remediation of learning disabilities: a handbook of psychoeducational resource programs. Palo Alto, California: Fearon, 1967. 1v. (unpaged).

1444 Vuckovich, D. Michael. "Pediatric neurology and learning disabilities." In: Myklebust, Helmer R., ed. Progress in learning disabilities. Vol. 1. New York: Grune & Stratton, 1968. 16-38.

1445 Wallace, Gerald, and Kauffman, James M. Teaching children with learning problems. Columbus, Ohio: Merrill, 1973. 282p.

1446 Wasserman, Edward; Asch, Harvey; Snyder, Elkan E. "A neglected aspect of learning disabilities: energy level output." J Learn Disabil 5(3): 130-35, March, 1972.

1447 Weber, Elmer W. Mentally retarded children and their education. Springfield, Illinois: Thomas, 1963. 338p.

1448 Weir, Homer E., and Anderson, Robert L. "Organic and organizational aspects of school adjustment problems." JAMA 166(14): 1708-10, April 5, 1958.

1449 Werry, John S., and Quay, Herbert C. "Observing the classroom behavior of elementary school children." Except Child 35(6): 461-68, February, 1959.

1450 Wigglesworth, R. "Some special and educational aspects of minimal cerebral dysfunction." J Spec Educ 54: 2-5, 1965.

1451 Wood, Frank H. "The educator's role in team planning of therapeutic educational placements for children with adjustment and learning problems." Except Child 34(5): 337-40, January, 1968.

1452 Wortman, R. A. "Learning disabilities or learning problems?" Nat Elem Princ 50: 48-52, April, 1971.

1453 Zedler, Empress Y. "Educational programming for pupils with neurologically based language disorders." J Learn Disabil 3(12): 618-28, December, 1970.

1. Behavior Therapy

1454 Allen, K. Eileen. "Behavior modification: what teachers of young exceptional children can do." Teach Except Child 4(3): 119-27, Spring, 1972.

1455 Allen, K. Eileen, and Harris, Florence R. "Elimination of a child's excessive scratching by training the mother in reinforcement procedures." Behav Res Ther 4(2): 79-84, May, 1966.

1456 Allen, K. Eileen; Hart, B. M.; Buell, J. S.; et. al. "Effects of social reinforcement on isolate behavior of a nursery school child." Child Dev 35(2): 511-18, June, 1964.

1457 Allen, K. Eileen; Henke, Lydia B.; Harris, Florence R.; et. al. "Control of hyperactivity by social reinforcement of attending behavior." J Educ Psychol 58(4): 231-37, August, 1967.

1458 Allen, K. Eileen; Turner, Keith D.; Everett, Paulette M. "A behavior modification classroom for head start children with problem behaviors." Except Child 37(2): 119-27, October, 1970.

1459 Anderson, D. Application of behavior modification techniques to the control of a hyperactive child. Unpublished master's thesis. University of Oregon, 1964.

Anderson, Lauriel E., ed.
see Helping the adolescent with the hidden handicap. (Item No. 1511).

1460 Baer, Donald M. "A technique of social reinforcement for the study of child behavior: behavior avoiding reinforcement of withdrawal." Child Dev 33(4): 847-48, December, 1962.

1461 Baer, Donald M.; Wolf, Montrose M.; Risley, Todd R. "Some current dimensions of applied behavior analysis." J Appl Behav Anal 1(1): 91-97, Spring, 1968.

1462 Barrish, Harriet H.; Saunders, Muriel; Wolf, Montrose M. "Good behavior game: effects of individual contingencies for group consequences on disruptive behavior in a classroom." J Appl Behav Anal 2(2): 119-24, Summer, 1969.

1463 Becker, Wesley; Madsen, Charles H., Jr.; Arnold, C. R.; et. al.
"The contingent use of teacher attention and praise in reducing classroom behavior problems." J Spec Educ 1(3): 287-307, Spring, 1967.

1464 Berkowitz, Pearl H., and Rothman, Esther P. The disturbed child:
recognition and psychoeducational therapy in the classroom. New York:
New York University Press, 1960. 204p.

1465 Bernal, M. "Behavioral feedback and the modification of brat behaviors." J Nerv Ment Dis 148: 375-85, 1969.

1466 Birnbrauer, J. S.; Bijou, Sidney W.; Wolf, Montrose M. "Program-
med instruction in the classroom." In: Ullmann, Leonard P., and Krasner, Leonard, eds. Case studies in behavioral modification. New York:
Holt, Rinehart & Winston, 1965. 358-63.

1467 Blackham, Garth J., and Silberman, Adolph. Modification of child
behavior. Belmont, California: Wadsworth, 1971. 186p.

1468 Blanco, Ralph F. "Fifty recommendations to aid exceptional children." Psychol Sch 7(1): 29-37, January, 1970.

1469 ———. "A focus on remediation in school psychology." J Sch
Psychol 9(3): 261-79, 1971.

1470 Blinder, Barton J.; Freeman, Daniel M.; Stunkard, Albert J. "Behavior therapy of anorexia nervosa: effectiveness of activity as a
reinforcer of weight gain." Am J Psychiatry 126(8): 1093-98, February, 1970.

1471 Bradfield, Robert H., ed. Behavior modification of learning disabilities. San Rafael, California: Academic Therapy Publications,
1971. 172p.

1472 Briskin, Alas S., and Gardner, William I. "Social reinforcement
in reducing inappropriate behavior." Young Child 24(2): 84-89, December, 1968.

1473 Broadhead, Geoffrey D. "The role of educational physical activity
programs in the modification of selected parameters of the behavior of
educable mentally retarded children and minimally brain injured children of elementary school age." Diss Abstr 29(12-A): 4305-6, June,
1969.

1474 Brown, Daniel G. Behavior modification in child and school mental
health: an annotated bibliography on applications with parents and
teachers. Rockville, Maryland: National Institute of Mental Health;
for sale by the Superintendent of Documents. U. S. Government Printing Office, Washington, D. C., 1971. 41p. (DHEW Publication, No. 71-
9043).

1475 ———. Reinforcing productive classroom behavior: a teacher's
guide to behavior modification. New York: Behavioral Publications,
1972. 43p.

1476 Brown, Donald Watkins. "Operant conditioning of attending and verbal imitation of deaf children with deviant behaviors." Diss Abstr 28(12-A): 4904-5, June, 1968.

1477 Brown, James C., and Teague, David G. "Behavior modification in the school: a team approach." Sch Couns 18(2): 111-16, November, 1970.

1478 Brown, Lou, and Foshee, James G. "Comparative techniques for increasing attending behavior of retarded students." Educ Train Ment Retard 6(1): 4-11, February, 1971.

1479 Brown, Paul, and Elliott, Rogers. "Control of aggression in a nursery school class." J Exp Child Psychol 2(2): 103-7, June, 1965.

1480 Burns, Barbara J. "The effect of self-directed verbal commands on arithmetic performance and activity level of urban hyperactive children." Diss Abstr Int 33(4-B): 1782-83, October, 1972.

1481 Chapel, J. L. "Behavior modification techniques with children and adolescents." Can Psychiatr Assoc J 15: 315-18, June, 1970.

1482 Christensen, D. E. Reduction of hyperactive behaviors by conditioning procedures alone and combined with methylphenidate (Ritalin). Unpublished M. A. thesis. Urbana, Illinois: University of Illinois, 1972.

1483 Clarizio, Harvey F., and Yelon, Stephen M. "Learning theory approaches to classroom management: rationale and intervention techniques." J Spec Educ 1(3): 267-74, Spring, 1967.

1484 Collins, Ronald C. Treatment of disruptive classroom behavior problems by employment of a partial-milieu consistency program: final report. Eugene, Oregon: Oregon University, 1967. 145p. (ED 013 468).

1485 Cromwell, Rue L. The development of behavior dimensions for emotionally disturbed children--a study of relevant indicators for classroom techniques, therapies, methods, and prognosis: interim report. Nashville, Tennessee: Vanderbilt University, 1967. 171p. (ED 019 783).

1486 Culbertson, Frances M. "An effective, low-cost approach to the treatment of disruptive school children." Psychol Sch 11(2): 183-87, April, 1974.

1487 Curry, D. R. "Case studies in behavior modification." Psychol Sch 7(4): 330-35, October, 1970.

1488 "Doman-Delacato treatment of neurologically handicapped children." Dev Med Child Neurol 10(2): 243-46, April, 1968.

1489 Doubros, Steve G., and Daniels, Gary J. "An experimental approach to the reduction of overactive behavior." Behav Res Ther 4(4): 251-58, November, 1966.

1490 Drass, Sarah D., and Jones, Reginald L. "Learning disabled children as behavior modifiers." J Learn Disabil 4(8): 418-25, October, 1971.

1491 Ebner, Michael J. "An investigation of the role of the social environment in the generalization and persistence of the effect of a behavior modification program." Diss Abstr 28(9-B): 3874-75, March, 1968.

1492 Edelson, Richard I., and Sprague, Robert L. "Conditioning of activity level in a classroom with institutionalized retarded boys." Am J Ment Defic 78(4): 384-88, January, 1974.

1493 Edgington, Ruth, and Clements, Sam D. Indexed bibliography on the educational management of children with learning disabilities (minimal brain dysfunction). Chicago: Argus Communications, 1967. 109p.

1494 Edson, Thomas. "Physical education: a substitute for hyperactivity and violence." J Health Phys Educ Recreat 40(7): 79-81, September, 1969.

1495 Ellis, Errington. The physical management of developmental disorders. London: Spastics Society Medical Education and Information Unit/Heinemann Medical Books, 1967. 50p. (Clinics in developmental medicine, No. 26).

1496 Engelhardt, Leah; Sulzer, Beth; Altekruse, Michael. "Counselor as a consultant in eliminating out-of-seat behavior." Elem Sch Guide Couns 5(3): 196-204, March, 1971.

1497 Fargo, George A.; Behrns, Charlene; Nolen, Patricia A. Behavior modification in the classroom. Belmont, California: Wadsworth, 1970. 344p.

1498 Flynn, Regina, and Hopson, Buena. Inhibitory training: an alternative approach to development of controls in hyperactive children. 1972. 18p. (ED 067 596).

1499 Forness, S. R. "Behavioristic approach to classroom management and motivation." Psychol Sch 7(4): 356-63, October, 1970.

1500 Galambos, Jeanette. Discipline and self-control: a program manual and study guide. Project Head Start, Office of Child Development, U.S. Department of Health, Education, and Welfare. Washington, D. C.: U.S. Government Printing Office, 1969. 28p.

1501 Gardner, James M., and Watson, Luke S., Jr. "Behavior modification of the mentally retarded: an annotated bibliography." Ment Retard Abstr 6(2): 181-93, April/June, 1969.

1502 Glavin, John P.; Quay, Herbert C.; Annesley, Frederick; et. al. "Experimental resource room for behavior problem children." Except Child 38(2): 131-37, October, 1971.

1503 Glavin, John P.; Quay, Herbert C.; Werry, John S. "Behavioral and academic gains of conduct problem children in different classroom settings." Except Child 37(6): 441-46, February, 1971.

1504 Glennon, C. A., and Nason, D. E. "Managing the behavior of the hyperkinetic child: what research says." Read Teach 27: 815-24, May, 1974.

1505 Graziano, Anthony M., ed. Behavior therapy with children. Chicago: Aldine-Atherton, 1971. 458p.

1506 Gropper, G. L.; Kress, G. C.; Hughes, R.; et. al. "Training teachers to recognize and manage social and emotional problems in the classroom." J Teach Educ 19(4): 477-85, Winter, 1968.

1507 Hall, R. Vance; Lund, Diane; Jackson, Deloris. "Effects of teacher attention on study behavior." J Appl Behav Anal 1(1): 1-12, Spring, 1968.

1508 Hanley, Edward M. "Review of research involving applied behavior analysis in the classroom." Rev Educ Res 40(5): 597-625, December, 1970.

1509 Harris, E. "Dealing with disruptive pupils: with a study-discussion program." PTA Mag 63: 19-21, 36-37, March, 1969.

1510 Harris, Florence R.; Wolf, Montrose M.; Baer, Donald M. "Effects of adult social reinforcement on child behavior." Young Child 20: 8-17, 1964.

1511 Helping the adolescent with the hidden handicap. Edited by Lauriel E. Anderson with the assistance of the Adolescent Committee, CANHC. Los Angeles: California Association for Neurologically Handicapped Children, 1970. 151p.

1512 Herman, W. L. "Techniques for dealing with children's behavior." Elem Sch J 69: 198-203, January, 1969.

1513 Homme, L. E.; De Baca, P. C.; Devine, J. V.; et. al. "Use of the Premack principle in controlling the behavior of nursery school children." J Exp Anal Behav 6(4): 544, October, 1963.

1514 Husted, John R.; Hall, Patricia; Agin, Bill. "The effectiveness of time-out in reducing maladaptive behavior of autistic and retarded children." J Psychol 79(2): 189-96, November, 1971.

1515 Johnston, Margaret K.; Kelley, C. Susan; Harris, Florence R.; et. al. "An application of reinforcement principles to development of motor skills of a young child." Child Dev 37(2): 379-87, June, 1966.

1516 Kallan, Cynthia A. "Rhythm and sequencing in an intersensory approach to learning disability." J Learn Disabil 5(2): 68-74, February, 1972.

1517 Kennedy, Daniel A., and Thompson, Ina. "Use of reinforcement techniques with a first grade boy." Personnel Guid J 46(4): 366-70, December, 1967.

1518 Kinsley, Donald E. "The effects of operant conditioning techniques upon select behaviors of neurologically handicapped children." Diss Abstr Int 30(9-A): 3792, March, 1970.

1519 Kiphard, E. J. "Behavioral integration of problem children through remedial physical education." J Health Phys Educ Recreat 41(4): 45-47, April, 1970.

1520 Knowles, Patsy L.; Prutsman, Thomas D.; Raduege, Virginia. "Behavior modification of simple hyperkinetic behavior and letter discrimination in a hyperactive child." J Sch Psychol 6(2): 157-60, Winter, 1968.

1521 Kounin, Jacob S.; Friesen, Wallace V.; Norton, A. Evangeline. "Managing emotionally disturbed children in regular classrooms." J Educ Psychol 57(1): 1-13, February, 1966.

1522 Krasner, Leonard, and Ullmann, Leonard P., eds. Research in behavior modification: new developments and implications. New York: Holt, Rinehart & Winston, 1965. 403p.

1523 Krop, Harry. "Modification of hyperactive behavior of a brain-damaged, emotionally disturbed child." Train Sch Bull 68(1): 49-54, May, 1971.

1524 Lovitt, Thomas C. "Behavior modification: the current scene." Except Child 37(2): 85-91, October, 1970.

1525 ———. "Self-management projects with children with behavioral disabilities." J Learn Disabil 6(3): 138-50, March, 1973.

1526 Madsen, Charles H.; Becker, Wesley; Thomas, Don R.; et. al. "An analysis of the reinforcing function of 'sit-down' commands." In: Parker, R. K., ed. Readings in educational psychology. Boston: Allyn & Bacon, 1968. 265-78.

1527 Madsen, Charles H.; Becker, Wesley; Thomas, Don R. "Rules, praise, and ignoring: elements of elementary classroom control." J Appl Behav Anal 1(2): 139-50, Summer, 1968.

1528 Marr, John P.; Miller, Elizabeth R.; Straub, Richard R. "Operant conditioning of attention with a psychotic girl." Behav Res Ther 4 (2): 85-87, May, 1966.

1529 Martin, Garry L. "Can you manage the overactive child?" Consultant 11: 63ff., August, 1971.

1530 Martin, Garry L., and Powers, Richard B. "Attention span: an operant conditioning analysis." Except Child 33(8): 565-70, April, 1967.

1531 Meichenbaum, Donald, and Goodman, Joseph. "Reflection-impulsivity and verbal control of motor behavior." Child Dev 40(3): 785-98, September, 1969.

1532 Miklich, Donald R. "Operant conditioning procedures with systematic desensitization in a hyperkinetic asthmatic boy." J Behav Ther Exp Psychol 4(2): 177-82, June, 1973.

1533 Miller, Robert W., and Miller, Joyce L. Dealing with behavioral problems in the elementary school. West Nyack, New Jersey: Parker, 1969. 207p.

1534 Mitchell, Dewayne W., and Crowell, Phyllis J. "Modifying inappropriate behavior in an elementary art class." Elem Sch Guid Couns 8 (1): 34-42, October, 1973.

1535 Nessler, Mary E. "Behavior modification: implications for the school counselor." J Educ 153(4): 12-17, April, 1971.

1536 Newman, Ruth G. "The acting-out boy." Except Child 22(5): 186-90, 204-6, February, 1956.

1537 Nixon, Stewart B. "Increasing the frequency of attending responses in hyperactive distractible youngsters by use of operant and modeling procedures." Diss Abstr 26(11): 6517, May, 1966.

1538 Nolen, Patricia A.; Kunzelmann, Harold P.; Haring, Norris G. "Behavioral modification in a junior high learning disabilities classroom." Except Child 34(3): 163-68, November, 1967.

1539 Novy, Pamela; Burnett, Joseph; Powers, Maryann; et. al. "Modifying attending-to-work behavior of a learning disabled child." J Learn Disabil 6(4): 217-21, April, 1973.

1540 O'Leary, K. Daniel, and Becker, Wesley. "Behavior modification of an adjustment class: a token reinforcement program." Except Child 33(9): 637-42, May, 1967.

1541 O'Leary, K. Daniel; Becker, Wesley; Evans, M. B.; et. al. "A token reinforcement program in a public school: a replication and systematic analysis." J Appl Behav Anal 2(1): 3-14, Spring, 1969.

1542 Osborne, J. Grayson. "Free-time as a reinforcer in the management of classroom behavior." J Appl Behav Anal 2(2): 113-18, Summer, 1969.

1543 Packard, Robert G. "The control of 'classroom attention': a group contingency for complex behavior." J Appl Behav Anal 3(1): 13-28, Spring, 1970.

1544 Palmieri, Jean C. "Learning problem children in the open concept classroom." Acad Ther 9(1): 91-97, Fall, 1973.

1545 Parry, Penny A. "The effect of reward on the performance of hyperactive children." Diss Abstr Int 34(12-B, pt. 1): 6220, June, 1974.

1546 Patterson, G. R. "An application of conditioning techniques to the control of a hyperactive child." In: Ullmann, Leonard P., and Krasner, Leonard, eds. Case studies in behavior modification. New York: Holt, Rinehart & Winston, 1965. 370-75.

1547 Patterson, G. R., and Brodsky, G. "A behaviour modification programme for a child with multiple problem behaviours." J Child Psychol Psychiatry 7(3/4): 277-95, December, 1966.

1548 Patterson, G. R.; Jones, R.; Whittier, J.; et. al. "A behavior modification technique for the hyperactive child." Behav Res Ther 2 (3): 217-26, January, 1965.

1549 Patterson, G. R.; Jones, R.; Whittier, J.; et. al. "A behavior modification technique for the hyperactive child." In: Graziano, Anthony M., ed. Behavior therapy with children. Chicago: Aldine-Atherton, 1971. 340-351.

1550 Perline, Irvin H., and Levinsky, David. "Controlling maladaptive classroom behavior in the severely retarded." Am J Ment Defic 73(1): 74-78, July, 1968.

1551 Phillips, Beeman N. Dimensions of problem behavior in the elementary school. Washington, D. C.: American Educational Research Association, 1968. 15p. (ED 020 558).

1552 Phillips, E. Lakin. "The use of the teacher as an adjunct therapist in child guidance." Psychiatry 20(4): 407-10, November, 1957.

1553 Pigeon, Grace, and Enger, Ann. "Increasing assignment completion and accuracy in a hyperactive first-grade student." Sch Appl Learn Theory 4(3): 24-30, June, 1972.

1554 Pihl, Robert F. "Conditioning procedures with hyperactive children." Neurology 17(4): 421-23, April, 1967.

1555 Pollack, C. "A conditioning approach to frustration reaction in minimally brain-injured children." J Learn Disabil 1: 681-88, 1968.

1556 Provencal, Gerald, and MacCormak, J. Paul. "Using a token economy to modify incorrigible behavior on a school bus: a case report." Sch Appl Learn Theory 4(1): 27-32, October, 1971.

1557 Quay, Herbert C. "Dimensions of problem behavior in children and their interaction in the approaches in behavior modification." Kansas Stud Educ 16: 6-13, 1966.

1558 Quay, Herbert C.; Werry, John S.; McQueen, Marjorie; et. al. "Remediation of the conduct problem child in the special class setting." Except Child 32(8): 509-15, April, 1966.

1559 Rollins, Howard A.; McCandless, Boyd R.; Thompson, Marion; et. al. "Project success environment: an extended application of contingency management in inner-city schools." J Educ Psychol 66(2): 167-78, April, 1974.

1560 Ross, Alan O. "The application of behavior principles by therapeutic education." J Spec Educ 1(3): 275-86, Spring, 1967.

1561 Rost, Kim J., and Charles, Don C. "Academic achievement of brain
injured and hyperactive children in isolation." Except Child 34(2):
125-26, October, 1967.

1562 Rumm, Mary K., and Kronick, Doreen. "An open letter to a teacher
of neurologically impaired children." Acad Ther 5(1): 75-78, Fall,
1969.

1563 Sarason, Irwin G.; Glaser, Edward M.; Fargo, George A. Reinforcing
productive classroom behavior: a teacher's guide to behavior modification. New York: Behavioral Publications, 1972. 43p.

1564 Schmidt, G. W., and Ulrich, R. E. "Effects of group contingent
events upon classroom noise." J Appl Behav Anal 2(3): 171-79, Fall,
1969.

1565 Shores, Richard E., and Haubrich, Paul A. "Effect of cubicles in
educating emotionally disturbed children." Except Child 36(1): 21-
24, September, 1969.

1566 Sidman, M. "Operant techniques." In: Bachrach, A. J., ed.
Experimental foundations of clinical psychology. New York: Basic
Books, 1962. 170-210.

1567 Smith, Judith M., and Smith, Donald E. P. "Behavior modification
of classroom behavior of a disadvantaged kindergarten boy by social
reinforcement and isolation." J Exp Child Psychol 7: 203-19, 1969.

1568 Snow, David L., and Brooks, Robert B. "Behavior modification
techniques in the school setting." J Sch Health 44(4): 198-205,
April, 1974.

1569 Solomon, Robert W., and Wahler, Robert G. "Peer reinforcement
control of classroom problem behavior." J Appl Behav Anal 6(1): 49-
56, Spring, 1973.

1570 Sprague, Robert L. "Minimal brain dysfunction from a behavioral
viewpoint." Ann NY Acad Sci 205: 349-61, February 28, 1973.

1571 Stetter, D. "Into the classroom with behavior modification."
Sch Couns 19: 110-14, November, 1971.

1572 Tate, B. G., and Baroff, George S. "Aversive control of self-in-
jurious behavior in a psychotic boy." Behav Res Ther 4(4): 281-87,
November, 1966.

1573 Tharp, Roland G., and Wetzel, Ralph J. Behavior modification in
the natural environment. New York: Academic Press, 1969. 236p.

1574 Thomas, Don R.; Becker, Wesley; Armstrong, Marianne. "Production
and elimination of disruptive classroom behavior by systematically
varying teacher's behavior." J Appl Behav Anal 1(1): 35-45, Spring,
1968.

1575 Tramontana, J. "Review of research on behavior modification in the home and school." Educ Tech 11: 61-64, February, 1971.

1576 Turnure, James E. "Control of orienting behavior in children under five years of age." Dev Psychol 4(1): 16-24, January, 1971.

1577 Twardosz, Sandra, and Sajwaj, Thomas. "Multiple effects of a procedure to increase sitting in a hyperactive, retarded boy." J Appl Behav Anal 5(1): 73-78, Spring, 1972.

1578 Ullmann, Leonard P., and Krasner, Leonard, eds. Case studies in behavior modification. Chicago: Holt, Rinehart & Winston, 1965. 401p.

1579 Walker, Hill M., and Buckley, Nancy K. "The use of positive reinforcement in conditioning attending behavior." J Appl Behav Anal 1 (3): 245-50, Fall, 1968.

1580 Ward, J. "Modification of deviant classroom behavior." Br J Educ Psychol 41(3): 304-13, November, 1971.

1581 Ward, M. H. Experimental modification of "hyperactive" behavior. Unpublished B. S. thesis. University of Illinois, 1966.

1582 Watson, Luke S., Jr. Child behavior modification: a manual for teachers, nurses, and parents. New York: Pergamon, 1973. 147p.

1583 Wehlan, Richard F., and Haring, Norris G. "Modification and maintenance of behavior through systematic application of consequences." Except Child 32(5): 281-89, January, 1966.

1584 Werry, John S., and Wollersheim, Janet P. "Behavior therapy with children: a broad overview." J Am Acad Child Psychiatry 6(2): 346-70, April, 1960.

1585 Whitman, Myron A., and Whitman, Joan. "Behavior modification in the classroom." Psychol Sch 8(2): 176-86, April, 1971.

1586 Whitman, Thomas L. "Reducing hyperactive behavior in a severely retarded child." Ment Retard 9(3): 17-19, June, 1971.

1587 Wolf, Montrose M.; Giles, David K.; Hall, R. Vance. "Experiments with token reinforcement in a remedial classroom." Behav Res Ther 6 (1): 51-64, February, 1968.

1588 Wolf, Montrose M.; Hanley, Edward L.; King, Louise A.; et. al. "The timer-game: a variable interval contingency for the management of out-of-seat behavior." Except Child 37(2): 113-17, October, 1970.

1589 Woody, Robert H. Behavioral problem children in the schools: recognition, diagnosis and behavioral modification. New York: Appleton-Century-Crofts, 1969. 264p.

1590 Worland, Julien. "Effects of reward and punishment on behavior control in hyperactive and normal boys." Diss Abstr Int 34(12-B, pt. 1): 6227, June, 1974.

1591 Wright, Lance, and McKenzie, Clancy. "Talking group therapy for learning-disabled children." Read Teach 23(4): 339-46, January, 1970.

1592 Zimmerman, Elaine F., and Zimmerman, J. "The alteration of behavior in a special classroom situation." J Exp Anal Behav 5(1): 59-60, January, 1962.

C. Parental Management

1593 Abrams, Jules C. "Parental dynamics: their role in learning disabilities." Read Teach 23(8): 751-55, 760, May, 1970.

1594 Advani, Kan. Involving parents in the behavior modification program of their children in home and school: a research project. Kingston, Ontario, Canada: Frontenac County Board of Education, 1973. 38p. (ED 084 755).

1595 Bannatyne, Alexander, and Bannatyne, Maryl. How your children can learn to live a rewarding life: behavior modification for parents and teachers. Springfield, Illinois: Thomas, 1973. 119p.

1596 Barsch, R. H. "Counseling the parents of the brain-damaged child." J Rehabil 27: 1-3, 1961.

1597 ———. "Explanations offered by parents and siblings for brain-damaged children." Except Child 27: 286-91, January, 1961.

1598 Berko, Frances G.; Berko, Martin J.; Thompson, Stephanie C. Management of brain-damaged children: a parents' and teachers' guide. Springfield, Illinois: Thomas, 1970. 73p.

1599 Bernal, M. "Training parents in child management." In: Bradfield, Robert H., ed. Behavior modification of learning disabilities. San Rafael, California: Academic Therapy Publications, 1971. 41-67.

1600 Brown, George W. "Suggestions for parents." J Learn Disabil 2 (2): 97-106, February, 1969.

1601 Brutten, Milton; Richardson, Sylvia O.; Mangel, Charles. Something's wrong with my child: a parents' book about children with learning disabilities. New York: Harcourt Brace Jovanovich, 1973. 246p.

1602 Daniels, Lloyd K. "Parental treatment of hyperactivity in a child with ulcerative colitis." J Behav Ther Exp Psychiatry 4(2): 183-85, June, 1973.

1603 Chess, Stella, and Thomas, Alexander. Your child is a person: a psychological approach to parenthood without guilt. New York: Viking, 1965. 213p.

1604 Doman, Glenn J. What to do about your brain-injured child, or your brain-damaged, mentally retarded, mentally deficient, cerebral-palsied, emotionally disturbed, spastic, flaccid, rigid, epileptic, autistic, athetoid, hyperactive child. Garden City, New York: Doubleday, 1974. 291p.

1605 Engeln, Richard; Knutson, John; Laughy, Linwood; et. al. "Behaviour modification techniques applied to a family unit--a case study." J Child Psychol Psychiatry 9(3/4): 245-52, December, 1968.

1606 Gardner, Richard A. "Psychogenic problems of brain-injured children and their parents." J Am Acad Child Psychiatry 7(3): 471-91, July, 1968.

1607 Gildea, Margaret, and Buchmueller, A. D. "A group therapy project with parents of behavior problems in children in public schools." Am J Psychiatry 106: 46-52, 1949.

1608 Hart, Jane, and Jones, Beverly. Where's Hannah?: a handbook for parents and teachers of children with learning disorders. New York: Hart, 1968. 272p.

1609 Hawkins, Robert P.; Peterson, Robert F.; Schweid, Edda; et. al. "Behavior therapy in the home." J Exp Child Psychol 4(1): 99-107, September, 1966.

1610 Jenkins, Richard L. "Hyperkinesis: making the parents understand their child." Med Insight 3: 48-49ff., June, 1971.

1611 Lindsley, O. E. "An experiment with parents handling behavior at home." Johnstone Bull 9: 27-36, 1966.

1612 Love, Harold D. The emotionally disturbed child: a parent's guide for parents who have problem children. Springfield, Illinois: Thomas, 1970. 105p.

1613 Luszki, Walter A. "Strictly for parents: controlling the brain-damaged hyperactive child." J Learn Disabil 1(11): 672-80, December, 1968.

1614 Melton, David. When children need help: an up-to-date handbook of guidance for parents of children who have been diagnosed as brain-injured, mentally retarded, cerebral palsied, learning disabled or as slow learners. New York: Crowell, 1972. 257p.

1615 Minde, Klaus. A parents' guide to hyperactivity in children. Quebec Association for Children with Learning Disabilities, 6338 Victoria Avenue, Montreal 252, Quebec, Canada, 1971. 24p.

1616 Mira, Mary. "Results of a behavior modification training program for parents and teachers." Behav Res Ther 8(3): 309-11, August, 1970.

1617 Nelson, Arnold E. "An analysis of communication effectiveness between parents and the hyperactive child." Diss Abstr Int 34(6-B): 2905, December, 1973.

1618 Nicholson, Georgia. Handbook of family activities for parents of learning disabled children. Tennessee: Bristol City Board of Education, n.d. 13p. (ED 085 956).

1619 Pinkerton, Philip. "Parental acceptance of the handicapped child (illustrated with recorded case extracts)." Dev Med Child Neurol 12 (2): 207-12, April, 1970.

1620 Reistroffer, Mary, and McVey, Helen. Parental survival and the hyperactive child. Available from: Publications, Business Office, 432 North Lake Street, Madison, Wisconsin. 54706.

1621 Salzinger, Kurt; Feldman, Richard S.; Portnoy, Stephanie. "Training parents of brain-injured children in the use of operant conditioning procedures." Behav Ther 1(1): 4-32, March, 1970.

1622 Sibley, S.; Abbot, M.; Cooper, B. Child management: a program for parents and teachers. Ann Arbor, Michigan: Ann Arbor Publishers, 1964.

1623 Siegel, Ernest. The exceptional child grows up: guidelines for understanding and helping the brain-injured adolescent and young adult. New York: Dutton, 1974. 227p.

1624 Sluyter, David J., and Hawkins, Robert P. "Delayed reinforcement of classroom behavior by parents." J Learn Disabil 5(1): 16-24, January, 1972.

1625 Wahler, Robert G.; Winkel, Gary H.; Peterson, Robert F.; et. al. "Mothers as behavior therapists for their own children." Behav Res Ther 3(2): 113-24, September, 1965.

1626 Wender, Paul H. The hyperactive child: a handbook for parents. New York: Crown, 1973. 120p.

1627 Zeilberger, Jane; Sampen, Sue E.; Sloane, Howard N. "Modification of a child's problem behaviors in the home with the mother as a therapist." J Appl Behav Anal 1(1): 47-53, Spring, 1968.

SECTION V

RELATED RESEARCH

A. Psychological Studies

1. Activity Level

1628 Bell, Richard Q. "Adaptation of small wristwatches for mechanical recording of activities in infants and children." J Exp Child Psychol 6(2): 302-5, June, 1968.

1629 Buxbaum, Edith. "Activity and aggression in children." Am J Orthopsychiatry 17(1): 161-66, January, 1947.

1630 Cratty, Bryant J. Motor activity and the education of retardates. Philadelphia: Lea and Febiger, 1969. 233p.

1631 Cromwell, Rue L. "Theory and research in activity level." Train School Bull 59(4): 134-41, February, 1963.

1632 Cromwell, Rue L.; Baumeister, A.; Hawkins, W. F. "Research in activity level." In: Ellis, Norman R., ed. Handbook of mental deficiency: psychological theory and research. New York: McGraw-Hill, 1963. 632-63.

1633 Cromwell, Rue L., and Foshee, James G. "Studies in activity level: IV. Effects of visual stimulation during task performance in mental defectives." Am J Ment Defic 65(2): 248-51, September, 1960.

1634 Cromwell, Rue L.; Palk, Bob E.; Foshee, James G. "Studies in activity level: V. The relationships among eyelid conditioning, intelligence, activity level, and age." Am J Ment Defic 65(6): 744-48, May, 1961.

1635 Dettweiler, Lawrence E. "Activity level, inhibition of response, and disruptive behavior in the classroom." Diss Abstr Int 32(5-B): 3027, November, 1971.

1636 Dimitroff, M. L. "Motor skills of hyperactive children." Am J Orthopsychiatry 42(5): 746, October, 1972.

1637 Duffy, Elizabeth. Activation and behavior. New York: Wiley, 1962. 384p.

1638 Ellis, Norman R., and Pryer, Ronald S. "Quantification of gross bodily activity in children with severe neuropathology." Am J Ment Defic 63(6): 1034-37, May, 1959.

1639 Fish, Barbara. "A study of motor development in infancy and its relationship to psychological functioning." Am J Psychiatry 117(12): 1113-18, June, 1961.

1640 Foshee, James G. "Studies in activity level: I. Simple and complex task performance in defectives." Am J Ment Defic 62(4): 882-86, March, 1958.

1641 Gardner, William I.; Cromwell, Rue L.; Foshee, James G. "Studies in activity level: II. The effects of distal visual stimulation in organics, familials, hyperactives and hypoactives." Am J Ment Defic 63(6): 1028-33, May, 1959.

1642 Garfield, John C. "Motor impersistence in normal and brain-damaged children." Neurology 14(7): 623-30, July, 1964.

1643 Grunewald-Zuberbier, E.; Grunewald, G.; Rasche, A. "Telemetric measurement of motor activity in maladjusted children under different experimental conditions." Psychiatr Neurol Neurochir 75: 371-81, September/October, 1972.

1644 Herron, R. E., and Ramsden, R. W. "Continuous monitoring of overt human body movement by radio telemetry: a brief review." Percept Mot Skills 24(3, pt. 2): 1303-8, June, 1967.

1645 Hutt, Corinne; Hutt, Sidney J.; Ounsted, Christopher. "A method for the study of children's behaviour." Dev Med Child Neurol 5(3): 233-45, June, 1963.

1646 Irwin, Orvis C. "The amount and nature of activities of newborn infants under constant external stimulating conditions during the first ten days of life." Genet Psychol Monogr 8(1): 1-92, July, 1930.

1647 Johnson, Charles F. "Hyperactivity and the machine: the actometer." Child Dev 42(6): 2105-10, December, 1971.

1648 ———. "Limits on the measurement of activity level in children using ultrasound and photoelectric cells." Am J Ment Defic 77(3): 301-10, November, 1972.

1649 Kaspar, Joseph C.; Millichap, J. Gordon; Backus, Reno; et. al. "A study of the relationship between neurological evidence of brain damage in children and activity and distractibility." J Consult Clin Psychol 36(3): 329-37, June, 1971.

1650 Kravitz, Harvey, and Boehm, John J. "Rhythmic habit patterns in infancy: their sequence, age of onset, and frequency." Child Dev 42(2): 399-413, June, 1971.

1651 Luisada, Paul V. "REM deprivation and hyperactivity in children." Chicago Med Sch Q 28: 97-108, 1969.

1652 Maccoby, Eleanor; Dowley, Edith M.; Hagen, John W. "Activity level and intellectual functioning in normal preschool children." Child Dev 36(3): 761-70, September, 1965.

1653 McFarland, J. N.; Peacock, L. J.; Watson, J. A. "Mental retardation and activity level in rats and children." Am J Ment Defic 71(3): 376-80, November, 1966.

1654 Massari, David; Hayweiser, Lois; Meyer, William J. "Activity level and intellectual functioning in deprived preschool children." Dev Psychol 1(3): 286-90, May, 1969.

1655 Massey, Philip S.; Lieberman, Allen; Batarseh, Gabriel. "Measure of activity level in mentally retarded children and adolescents." Am J Ment Defic 76(2): 259-60, September, 1971.

1656 Pope, Lillie. "Motor activity in brain-injured children." Am J Orthopsychiatry 40(5): 784-94, October, 1970.

1657 ———. "Motor activity in brain-injured children." In: Frazier, James R., ed. Readings on the behavior disorders of childhood. New York: MSS Information Corporation, 1972. 45-56.

1658 ———. "A study of motor activity in brain-injured children." Diss Abstr Int 30(6-A): 2384, December, 1969.

1659 Pope, Lillie, and Pope, M. "Measurement of motor activity." Percept Mot Skills 29(1): 315-19, August, 1969.

1660 Schaffer, H. R. "Activity level as a constitutional determinant of infantile reaction to deprivation." Child Dev 37(3): 595-602, September, 1966.

1661 Schulman, Jerome L., and Reisman, John J. "An objective measure of hyperactivity." Am J Ment Defic 64(3): 455-56, November, 1959.

1662 Shaffer, David; McNamara, Nancy E.; Pincus, J. H. "Controlled observations on patterns of activity, attention, and impulsivity in brain-damaged and psychiatrically disturbed boys." Psychol Med 4: 2-18, February, 1974.

1663 Spradlin, Joseph E.; Cromwell, Rue L.; Foshee, James G. "Studies in activity level: III. Effects of auditory stimulation in organisms, familials, hyperactives and hypoactives." Am J Ment Defic 64(4): 754-55, January, 1960.

1664 Sprague, Robert L., and Toppe, Lorraine K. "Relationship between activity level and delay of reinforcement in the retarded." J Exp Child Psychol 3(4): 390-97, July, 1966.

1665 Talkington, Larry W., and Hutton, W. Oren. "Hyperactive and non-hyperactive institutionalized retarded residents." Am J Ment Defic 78(1): 47-50, July, 1973.

1666 Tizard, Barbara. "Controlled study of all-night sleep in overactive imbecile children." Am J Ment Defic 73(2): 209-13, September, 1968.

1667 Wade, Michael G. "Biorhythms and activity level of institutionalized mentally retarded persons diagnosed hyperactive." Am J Ment Defic 78(3): 262-67, November, 1973.

1668 Weston, Donald L. "Motor activity and depression in juvenile delinquents." Diss Abstr 19: 2391-92, 1959.

1669 Willerman, Lee. "Activity level and hyperactivity in twins." Child Dev 44(2): 288-93, June, 1973.

1670 Wolff, Peter H. "Observations on newborn infants." Psychosom Med 21(2): 110-18, March/April, 1959.

2. Attention/Distractibility

1671 Adams, Jerry; Hayden, Benjamin S.; Canter, Arthur. "The relationship between the Canter background interference procedure and the hyperkinetic behavior syndrome." J Learn Disabil 7(2): 110-15, February, 1974.

1672 Alabiso, Frank P. "The inhibitory functions of attention in reducing hyperactive behavior." Diss Abstr Int 32(12-B, pt. 1): 7299-7300, June, 1972.

1673 ————. "Inhibitory functions of attention in reducing hyperactive behavior." Am J Ment Defic 77(3): 259-82, November, 1972.

1674 Anderson, Robert P.; Halcomb, Charles G.; Doyle, Robert B. "The measurement of attention deficits." Except Child 39(7): 534-39, April, 1973.

1675 Anderson, Robert P.; Halcomb, Charles G.; Gordon, William; et. al. "Measurement of attention distractibility in learning disabled children." Acad Ther 9(5): 261-66, Spring, 1974.

1676 "Attention span brief but useful in hyperactivity." Pediatr News 8(3): 81, March, 1974.

1677 Bakan, Paul E. Attention. Princeton, New Jersey: Van Nostrand, 1966. 225p.

1678 Bee, Helen L. "Parent-child interaction and distractibility in nine-year-old children." Merrill-Palmer Q 13(3): 175-90, July, 1967.

1679 Bestor, Mary F. "A study of attention in young children." Child Dev 5(4): 368-80, December, 1934.

1680 Birch, Robert W. "Attention span, distractibility and inhibitory potential in good and poor readers." Diss Abstr 28(11-B): 4742, May, 1968.

1681 Bremer, David A. "Attention during reading in hyperactive boys: reactions to distracting stimuli and to rewards." Diss Abstr Int 34 (12-B, pt. 1): 6206, June, 1974.

1682 Brown, Muriel W. "Continuous reaction as a measurement of attention." Child Dev 1(4): 255-91, December, 1930.

1683 Campanelli, Peter A. "Sustained attention in children with brain damage." In: American Psychological Association, 76th, San Francisco, 1968. Proceedings. 3: 661-62, 1968.

1684 Carrington, Frederick M. "The effects of music therapy on the attention span of hyperactive mental retardates." Diss Abstr Int 34 (7-A): 3864, January, 1974.

1685 Cohen, Nancy J. "Psychophysiological concomitants of attention in hyperactive children." Diss Abstr Int 32(1-B): 553, July, 1971.

1686 Cruse, Daniel B. "The effects of distraction upon the performance of brain-injured and familial retarded children." In: Trapp, E. Philip and Himelstein, Philip, eds. Readings on the exceptional child. New York: Appleton-Century-Crofts, 1962. 492-500.

1687 Douglas, Virginia I. "Stop, look and listen: the problem of sustained attention and impulse control in hyperactive and normal children." Can J Behav Sci 4(4): 259-82, October, 1972.

1688 Doyle, Robert B. "The effects of distraction and attention deficits among children with learning disabilities on a vigilance task." Diss Abstr Int 34(9-B): 4658, March, 1974.

1689 Dykman, Roscoe A.; Ackerman, Peggy T.; Clements, Sam D.; et. al. "Specific learning disabilities: an attentional deficit syndrome." In: Myklebust, Helmer R. Progress in learning disabilities. New York: Grune & Stratton, 1971. 56-93.

1690 Dykman, Roscoe A.; Walls, Robert C.; Suzuki, Tetsuko; et. al. "Children with learning disabilities: conditioning, differentiation, and the effect of distraction." Am J Orthopsychiatry 40(5): 766-82, October, 1970.

1691 Fisher, Lawrence. "Attention deficit in brain-damaged children." Am J Ment Defic 74(4): 502-8, January, 1970.

1692 ———. "A comparison of matched groups of brain-damaged children on externally validated attention measures." Diss Abstr 29(10-B): 3911, April, 1969.

1693 Freudman, Judith D. "Reflection--impulsivity and pupil attentive behavior in the classroom." Diss Abstr Int 34(10-B): 5166, April, 1974.

1694 Gilmore, John V. "The factor of attention in underachievement." J Educ 150(3): 41-66, February, 1968.

1695 Golden, Beverly. "A comparison of the distractibility of intellectually normal and mentally retarded subjects." Diss Abstr 16(9):
1718, 1956.

1696 Gutteridge, M. V. The duration of attention in young children.
London: Oxford University Press, 1936. (Melbourne University Educational Research Series, No. 41).

1697 Herring, Amanda, and Koch, Helen L. "A study of some factors influencing the interest span of preschool children." J Genet Psychol
38: 249-75, December, 1930.

1698 Leontiev, A. "The development of voluntary attention in children."
J Genet Psychol 40(1): 52-83, March, 1932.

1699 Maes, John L. "The role of attention in psychotherapy." J Educ
150(3): 82-91, February, 1968.

1700 Magdol, Miriam S. "Problems in attention: clearing up the terminology." Acad Ther 8(2): 141-52, Winter, 1972-73.

1701 Moyer, Kenneth E., and Von Haller Gilmer, B. "Attention spans of
children for experimentally designed toys." J Genet Psychol 87(1):
187-201, September, 1955.

1702 Moyer, Kenneth E., and Von Haller Gilmer, B. "The concept of attention spans in children." Elem Sch J 54(6): 464-66, February,
1954.

1703 Nelson, Terry F. "The effects of training in attention deployment
on observing behavior in reflective and impulsive children." Diss
Abstr 29(7-B): 2659, January, 1969.

1704 Nixon, S. Ways by which overly active students can be taught to
concentrate on study activity. Stanford, California: Stanford University School of Education, 1966. 104p. (ED 010 550).

1705 Reger, Roger. "Stimulating the distractible child." Elem Sch J
64(1): 42-48, October, 1963.

1706 Robertshaw, Carroll S. "An investigation of attention to task behavior, arithmetic performance and behavior problems in first grade
children." Diss Abstr Int 32(10-A): 5642, April, 1972.

1707 Santostefano, Sebastiano, and Stayton, Samuel. "Training the preschool retarded child in focusing attention: a program for parents."
Am J Orthopsychiatry 37(4): 732-43, July, 1967.

1708 Schulman, Jerome L.; Throne, Frances M.; Casper, Joseph C. "Studies on distractibility." Train Sch Bull 59(4): 142-49, February,
1963.

1709 Shacter, Helen S. "Intelligence as a causal factor determining
differences in sustained attention in preschool children." J Appl
Psychol 17: 478-88, 1933.

1710 Simpson, D. Dwayne, and Nelson, Arnold E. "Attention training through breathing control to modify hyperactivity." J Learn Disabil 7(5): 274-83, May, 1973.

1711 Simpson, D. Dwayne, and Nelson, Arnold E. Breathing control and attention training: a preliminary study of a psychophysiological approach to self control of hyperactive behavior in children: final report. Forth Worth, Texas: Texas Christian University, Institute of Behavioral Research, 1972. 60p.

1712 Simpson, D. Dwayne, and Nelson, Arnold E. "Breathing control and attention training: a preliminary study of a psychophysiological approach to self control of hyperactive behavior in children." Res Educ 7: 31-32, 1972.

1713 Sykes, Donald H. Sustained attention in hyperactive children. Unpublished doctoral dissertation. McGill University, 1969.

1714 Sykes, Donald H.; Douglas, Virginia I.; Morgenstern, Gert. "Sustained attention in the hyperactive child and the effect of methylphenidate." Can Psychol 10: 216, 1969. (Abstract).

1715 Sykes, Donald H.; Douglas, Virginia I.; Morgenstern, Gert. "Sustained attention in hyperactive children." J Child Psychol Psychiatry 14(3): 213-20, September, 1973.

1716 Turnure, James E. "Children's reactions to distractors in a learning situation." Dev Psychol 2(1): 115-22, January, 1970.

1717 ———. "Children's reactions to distraction: a developmental approach." Diss Abstr 27(1-B): 321, July, 1966.

1718 ———. "Distractibility in the mentally retarded: negative evidence for an orienting inadequacy." Except Child 37(3): 181-86, November, 1970.

1719 Whitman, Myron A., and Sprague, Robert L. "Learning and distractibility in normals and retardates." Train Sch Bull 65(3): 89-101, November, 1968.

1720 Zuk, Gerald H. "Over-attention to moving stimuli as a factor in the distractibility of retarded and brain-injured children." Train Sch Bull 59(4): 150-60, February, 1963.

1721 Zurif, E. The hyperkinetic syndrome including its effect on prolonged visual attention. Unpublished M. Sc. thesis. McGill University, 1963.

3. Perceptual Processes: Cognition,

Reflection-impulsivity, Concept Formation

1722 Ayers, A. J. "Tactile functions: their relation to hyperactive and perceptual motor behavior." Am J Occup Ther 18: 6-11, January/ February, 1964.

1723 Ault, Ruth L.; Crawford, David E.; Jeffrey, W. E. "Visual scan-
ning strategies of reflective, impulsive, fast-accurate, and slow-in-
accurate children on the matching familiar figures test." Child Dev
43(4): 1412-17, December, 1972.

1724 Becker, Laurence D. "Modifiability of conceptual tempo in educationally 'high risk' children." Diss Abstr Int 34(11-A): 7072, May,
1974.

1725 Bell, Richard Q.; Weller, George M.; Waldrop, Mary F. "Newborn
and preschooler: organization of behavior and relations between
periods." Monogr Soc Res Child Dev 36(1/2): 1-145, April/July, 1971.

1726 Bender, Morris B. Disorders in perception. Springfield, Illinois:
Thomas, 1952. 109p.

1727 Berlyne, D. E. Conflict, arousal, and curiosity. New York:
McGraw-Hill, 1960. 350p.

1728 Bijou, Sidney W. "Experimental studies of child behavior, normal,
and deviant." In: Krasner, Leonard, and Ullmann, Leonard P., eds.
Research in behavior modification. New York: Holt, Rinehart & Winston, 1965. 56-81.

1729 Birch, Herbert G., and Demb, Howard. "The formation and extinc-
tion of conditional reflexes in 'brain-damaged' and mongoloid children."
J Nerv Ment Dis 129(2): 162-70, August, 1959.

1730 Bjorklund, David F., and Butter, Eliot J. "Can cognitive impulsivity be predicted from classroom behavior?" J Genet Psychol 123
(2nd half): 185-94, December, 1973.

1731 Boydstun, James A.; Ackerman, Peggy T.; Stevens, Douglas A.; et. al.
"Physiologic and motor conditioning and generalization in children with
minimal brain dysfunction." Cond Reflex 3(2): 81-104, April/June,
1968.

1732 Campbell, Susan B. "Cognitive styles in normal and hyperactive
children." Diss Abstr Int 30(11-B): 5233, May, 1970.

1733 ———. "Cognitive styles in reflective, impulsive, and hyperactive boys and their mothers." Percept Mot Skills 36(1): 747-52,
June, 1973.

1734 Campbell, Susan B.; Douglas, Virginia I.; Morgenstern, Gert.
"Cognitive styles in hyperactive children and the effect of methylphenidate." J Child Psychol Psychiatry 12(1): 55-67, June, 1971.

1735 Cohen, Nancy J., and Douglas, Virginia I. "Characteristics of the
orienting response in hyperactive and normal children." Psychophysiology 9: 238-45, 1972.

1736 Cohen, Nancy J.; Douglas, Virginia I.; Morgenstern, Gert. "Psychophysiological concomitants of hyperactivity in children." Can Psychol
10: 199, 1969. (Abstract).

1737 Conners, C. Keith, and Greenfield, David. "Habituation of motor startle in anxious and restless children." J Child Psychol Psychiatry 7(2): 125-32, October, 1966.

1738 Coopersmith, Stanley. The antecedents of self-esteem. San Francisco: Freeman, 1967. 283p.

1739 Court, J. H. "Psychological monitoring of interventions into educational problems with psychoactive drugs." J Learn Disabil 4(7): 359-63, August/September, 1971.

1740 Cratty, Bryant J. Movement, preception and thought. Peek Publications, 4067 Transport Street, Palo Alto, California, 94303. 1969. 77p. (EC 030 709).

1741 ―――. Perceptual-motor behavior and educational processes. Springfield, Illinois: Thomas, 1969. 265p.

1742 Crowe, Patricia B. "Aspects of body image in children with the symptoms of hyperkinesis." Diss Abstr Int 33(4-B): 1785, October, 1972.

1743 Cushing, H. M. "A perseverative tendency in preschool children: a study in personality differences." Arch Psychol 108, 1929.

1744 Drake, D. M. "Perceptual correlates of impulsive and reflective behavior." Dev Psychol 2: 202-14, 1970.

1745 Elliott, Robert T. "Concept formation ability of 'brain-injured' children of normal intelligence." Diss Abstr 27(11-A): 3718-19, May, 1967.

1746 Farnham-Diggory, Sylvia. Self, future, and time: a developmental study of the concepts of psychotic, brain-damaged, and normal children. Chicago: University of Chicago Press, for the Society for Research in Child Development, 1966. 63p.

1747 Finneran, Mary P. "Visual perception in children with a hyperactive behavior syndrome." Diss Abstr 25(6): 3687-88, December, 1964.

1748 Freibergs, Vaira. Concept learning in hyperactive and normal children. Unpublished Ph. D. thesis. McGill University, 1965.

1749 Freibergs, Vaira, and Douglas, Virginia I. "Concept learning in hyperactive and normal children." J Abnorm Psychol 74(3): 388-95, June, 1969.

1750 Frostig, Marianne; Maslow, Phyllis; Lefever, D. Welty; et. al. "Visual perceptual development and school adjustment and progress." Am J Orthopsychiatry 33(2): 367-68, March, 1963.

1751 Gallagher, James J. "A comparison of brain-injured and non-brain-injured mentally retarded children on several psychological variables." Monogr Soc Res Child Dev 22(2, Whole No. 65): 1-79, 1957.

1752 Gratton, L. "Object concept and object relations in childhood psychosis: a pilot study." Can Psychiatr Assoc J 16: 347-54, August, 1971.

1753 Hallahan, Daniel P. "Cognitive styles: preschool implications for the disadvantaged." J Learn Disabil 3(1): 4-9, January, 1970.

1754 Hewett, Frank M. "Conceptual models for viewing minimal brain dysfunction: developmental psychology and behavioral modification." Ann NY Acad Sci 205: 38-45, February 28, 1973.

1755 Jacobs, Nora T. "A comparison of hyperactive and normal boys in terms of reaction time, motor time, and decision-making time, under conditions of increasing task complexity." Diss Abstr Int 33(3-A): 1045, September, 1972.

1756 Jones, Mary C., and Bayley, Nancy. "Physical maturing among boys as related to behavior." J Educ Psychol 41(3): 129-48, March, 1950.

1757 Juliano, Daniel B. "Conceptual tempo, activity and concept learning in hyperactive and normal children." Diss Abstr Int 34(8-A): 4875, February, 1974.

1758 Kagan, Jerome. "Impulsive and reflective children." In: Krumboltz, J. D., ed. Learning and the educational process. Chicago: Rand McNally, 1965. 133-61.

1759 ———. "Reflection-impulsivity and reading ability in primary grade children." Child Dev 36(3): 609-28, September, 1965.

1760 ———. "Reflection-impulsivity: the generality and dynamics of conceptual tempo." J Abnorm Psychol 7(1): 17-24, February, 1966.

1761 Kagan, Jerome; Pearson, Leslie; Welch, Lois. "Conceptual impulsivity and inductive reasoning." Child Dev 37(3): 583-94, September, 1966.

1762 Kagan, Jerome; Pearson, Leslie; Welch, Lois. "The modificability of an impulsive tempo." J Educ Psychol 57(6): 359-65, December, 1966.

1763 Kagan, Jerome; Rosman, B. L.; Kay, Deborah; et. al. "Information processing in the child: significance of analytic and reflective attitudes." Psychol Monogr 78(1, Whole No. 578): 1-37, 1964.

1764 Karlitz, Samuel, and Fisichelli, V. R. "The cry thesholds of normal infants and those with brain damage." J Pediatr 61(5): 679-85, November, 1962.

1765 Manheimer, Dean I., and Mellinger, Glen D. "Personality characteristics of the child accident repeater." Child Dev 38(2): 491-513, June, 1967.

1766 Mordock, John B. "Effects of stress on perceptual-motor functioning of adolescents with learning difficulties." Percept Mot Skills 29(pt. 2): 883-86, December, 1969.

1767 Nelson, Janine A. "A comparative study of the perceptual and conceptual development of hyperactive and normal boys." Diss Abstr Int 30(7-B): 3392-93, January, 1970.

1768 Palkes, Helen S.; Stewart, Mark A.; Freedman, Judith. "Improvement in maze performance of hyperactive boys as a function of verbal-training procedures." J Spec Educ 5(4): 337-42, Winter, 1971.

1769 Palkes, Helen S.; Stewart, Mark A.; Kahana, Boaz. "Porteus maze performance of hyperactive boys after training in self-directed verbal commands." Child Dev 39(3): 817-26, September, 1968.

1770 Rappaport, Sheldon R. "Behavioral disorder and ego development in a brain-injured child." Psychoanal Study Child 16: 423-50, 1961.

1771 Reed, James C., and Reed, Homer B. C., Jr. "Concept formation ability and nonverbal abstract thinking among older children with chronic cerebral dysfunction." J Spec Educ 1(2): 157-61, Winter, 1967.

1772 Santostefano, Sebastiano. "Cognitive controls and exceptional states in children." J Clin Psychol 20(2): 213-18, April, 1964.

1773 Santostefano, Sebastiano, and Paley, Evelyn. "Development of cognitive control in children." Child Dev 35(3): 939-49, September, 1964.

1774 Santostefano, Sebastiano; Rutledge, Louis; Randall, David. "Cognitive styles and reading disability." Psychol Sch 2(1): 57-62, January, 1965.

1775 Sarason, Seymour B.; Davidson, K. S.; Lighthall, F. F.; et. al. Anxiety in elementary school children: a report of research. New York: Wiley, 1960. 351p.

1776 Silver, Archie A. "Postural and righting responses in children." J Pediatr 41(4): 493-98, October, 1952.

1777 Skorina, Jane K. "A study of the effects of Ritalin intervention upon the perceptual competencies of children diagnosed as giving evidence of psychoneurological learning disabilities." Diss Abstr Int 34(11-A): 7055-56, May, 1974.

1778 Spring, Carl. Perceptual-speed deficit in reading disability children. Washington, D. C.: National Center for Educational Research and Development, 1972. 25p.

1779 Sroufe, L. Alan; Sonies, Barbara C.; West, Winifred D.; et. al. "Anticipatory heart rate deceleration and reaction time in children with and without referral for learning disability." Child Dev 44(2): 267-73, June, 1973.

1780 Stevens, Douglas A.; Boydstun, James A.; Ackerman, Peggy T.; et. al. "Reaction time, impulsivity, and autonomic lability in children with minimal brain dysfunction." In: American Psychological Association, 76th, San Francisco, 1968. Proceedings. 3: 367-68, 1968.

1781 Stevens, Douglas A.; Stover, Curtis E.; Backus, Joe T. "The hyperkinetic child: effect of incentives on the speed of rapid tapping."
J Consult Clin Psychol 34(1): 56-59, February, 1970.

1782 Strauss, Alfred A., and Werner, Heinz. "Disorders of conceptual
thinking in the brain-injured child." J Nerv Ment Dis 96: 153-72,
August, 1942.

1783 Switzer, Janet. "Developmental differences in place and name sequence learning in normal, hyperactive, and hypoactive eight- and
twelve-year-old boys." Diss Abstr 22(7): 2482, January, 1962.

1784 Terrace, H. S. "Stimulus control." In: Honig, W. K. Operant
behavior: areas of research and application. New York: Appleton-
Century-Crofts, 1966. 271-344.

1785 Ward, William C. "Reflection-impulsivity in kindergarten children." Child Dev 39(3): 867-74, September, 1968.

1786 Weithorn, Corinne J. "The relationship between hyperactivity and
impulsive responsiveness in elementary school children." Diss Abstr
Int 30(8-B): 3899, February, 1970.

1787 Werner, Heinz. "Thought disturbance with reference to figure-background impairment in brain-injured children." Confin Neurol 9: 255-
63, 1949.

1788 Werner, Heinz, and Weir, Alastair. "The figure-ground syndrome in
the brain-injured child." Int Rec Med Gen Pract Clin 169(6): 362-67,
June, 1956.

1789 Zucker, Joseph S., and Stricker, George. "Impulsivity-reflectivity
in preschool headstart and middle class children." J Learn Disabil
10(1): 578-83, October, 1968.

B. Sociological Studies

1790 Alkire, Armand A. "Social power and communication within families
of disturbed and nondisturbed preadolescents." J Pers Soc Psychol 13
(4): 335-49, December, 1969.

1791 Baldwin, Alfred L. "Socialization and the parent child relationship." Child Dev 19(3): 127-36, September, 1948.

1792 Becker, Wesley. "The relationship of factors in parental ratings
of self and each other to behavior of kindergarten children as rated
by mothers, fathers, and teachers." J Consult Psychol 24(6): 507-27,
December, 1960.

1793 Bott, H. "Observation of play activities in a nursery school."
Genet Psychol Monogr 4: 44-88, 1928.

1794 Bryan, Tanis S. "An observational analysis of classroom behaviors
of children with learning disabilities." J Learn Disabil 7(1): 26-
34, January, 1974.

1795 Campbell, Susan B. "Mother-child interaction in reflective, impulsive, and hyperactive children." Dev Psychol 8(3): 341-49, March, 1973.

1796 Cantwell, Dennis P. "Parents of hyperactive children: cause or effect?" Med Insight 5: 24-28, December, 1973.

1797 Carver, John N., and Carver, Nellie E. The family of the retarded child. Syracuse, New York: Syracuse University, Division of Special Education and Rehabilitation and the Center on Human Policy, 1972. 156p.

1798 Cockrell, Dura-Louise. "A study of the play of children of preschool age by an unobserved observer." Psychol Monogr 17(6): 377-469, December, 1935.

1799 Conger, John J., and Miller, Wilbur C. Personality, social class and delinquency. New York: Wiley, 1966. 249p.

1800 Despert, Juliette L. The emotionally disturbed child: an inquiry into family patterns. New York: Doubleday, 1970. 339p.

1801 Dielman, T. E., and Cattell, Raymond B. "The prediction of behavior problems in six- to eight-year-old children from mothers' reports of child-rearing practices." J Clin Psychol 28(1): 13-17, January, 1972.

1802 Gelfand, Carol C. "The effects of an altered interpersonal environment on minimally brain-damaged children." Diss Abstr Int 34(3-B): 1274-75, September, 1973.

1803 Gibson, H. B., and West, D. J. "Social and intellectual handicaps as precursors of early delinquency." Br J Criminol 10: 21-32, 1970.

1804 Ginsburg, Ethel L. "The relation of parental attitudes to variations in hyperactivity." Smith Coll Stud Social Work 4: 27-54, 1933.

1805 Gordon, Sol, and Golob, R. S., eds. Recreation and socialization for the brain-injured child. East Orange, New Jersey: New Jersey Association for Brain-Injured Children, 1967. 110p.

1806 Hertzig, Margaret E., and Birch, Herbert G. "Neurological organization in psychiatrically disturbed adolescents: a comparative consideration of sex differences." Arch Gen Psychiatry 19(5): 528-37, November, 1968.

1807 Kalverboer, A. F. "Observation of exploratory behavior of preschool children alone and in the presence of the mother." Psychiatr Neurol Neurochir 74: 43, 1971.

1808 Kanner, Leo, and Eisenberg, Leon. "Childhood problems in relation to the family." Pediatrics 20(1): 155-64, July, 1957.

1809 Karlsson, Kathryn A. "Hyperactivity and environmental compliance." Diss Abstr Int 34(2-A): 861, August, 1973.

1810 Lee, Douglas, and Hutt, Corinne. "A play-room designed for filming children: a note." J Child Psychol Psychiatry 5(3/4): 263-65, December, 1964.

1811 Levy, John. "A quantitative study of behavior problems in relation to family constellation." Am J Psychiatry 10(4): 637-54, January, 1931.

1812 Love, Harold D. Exceptional children in a modern society. 2nd ed. Dubuque, Iowa: Kendall-Hunt, 1967. 184p. (ED 036 004). also: Dubuque, Iowa: Brown, 1967. 171p.

1813 Morrison, James R., and Stewart, Mark A. "Psychiatric status of legal families of adopted hyperactive children." Arch Gen Psychiatry 28(6): 888-91, June, 1973.

1814 Peterson, Donald R.; Becker, Wesley; Hellmer, L. A.; et. al. "Parental attitudes and child adjustment." Child Dev 30(1): 119-30, March, 1959.

1815 Peterson, Donald R.; Becker, Wesley; Shoemaker, Donald J.; et. al. "Child behavior problems and parental attitudes." Child Dev 32(1): 151-52, March, 1961.

1816 Schwartz, Louisa. "The use and misuse of parental guilt in cases of children with minimal brain dysfunction." Ann NY Acad Sci 205: 368-72, February 28, 1973.

1817 Quay, Herbert C., and Peterson, Donald R. "Personality factors in the study of juvenile delinquency." Except Child 26(9): 472-76, May, 1960.

1818 Sarvis, Mary A. "Evil self image: a common denomination in learning problems." Ment Hyg 49(2): 308-10, April, 1965.

1819 Silver, Larry B. "Frequency of adoption in children with the neurological learning disability syndrome." J Learn Disabil 3(6): 306-10, June, 1970.

1820 Slater, Eleanor. "Types, levels and irregularities of response to a nursery school situation of forty children observed with special reference to the home environment." Monogr Soc Res Child Dev 4(2): 1-90, 1939.

1821 Solomon, Daniel; Houlihan, Kevin A.; Busse, Thomas V.; et. al. "Parent behavior and child academic achievement, achievement striving, and related personality characteristics." Genet Psychol Monogr 83 (2nd half): 173-273, May, 1971.

1822 Sutherland, I. "Study of a hyperkinetic syndrome and resultant social disability in childhood." In: World Congress of Psychiatry, 3rd, Montreal, 1961. Proceedings. 724-25.

1823 Tizard, Barbara. "Observations of over-active imbecile children in controlled and uncontrolled environments: I. Classroom studies." Am J Ment Defic 72(4): 540-47, January, 1968.

1824 ————. "Observations of over-active imbecile children in control-led and uncontrolled environments: II. Experimental studies." Am J Ment Defic 72(4): 548-53, January, 1968.

1825 Tuckman, Jacob, and Regan, Richard A. "Size of family and behav-ioral problems in children." J Genet Psychol 111(2nd half): 151-60, December, 1967.

1826 VanAlstyne, Dorothy. Play behavior and choice of play materials of preschool children. Chicago: University of Chicago Press, 1932. 104p.

1827 Weisskopf, B. "Learning disorders in children: behavioral and emotional aspects of child and family." South Med J 62(7): 811-15, July, 1969.

1828 Willerman, Lee. "Social aspects of minimal brain dysfunction." Ann NY Acad Sci 205: 164-72, February 28, 1973.

C. Follow-up and Longitudinal Studies

1829 Baumann, M. C.; Ludwig, F. A.; Alexander, R. H.; et. al. A five-year study of brain-damaged children. Springfield, Illinois: Mental Health Center, 1962. 44p.

1830 Birch, Herbert G.; Thomas, Alexander; Chess, Stella. "Behavioral development in brain-damaged children." Arch Gen Psychiatry 11(6): 596-603, December, 1964.

1831 Brown, Asa James. "A longitudinal study of the hyperkinetic syn-drome in children: kindergarten through grade three." Diss Abstr Int 30(5-A): 1857, November, 1969.

1832 Chess, Stella; Thomas, Alexander; Birch, Herbert G. "Characteris-tics of the individual child's behavioral responses to the environment." Am J Orthopsychiatry 29(4): 791-802, October, 1959.

1833 Cohen, Nancy J.; Weiss, Gabrielle; Minde, Klaus. "Cognitive styles in adolescents previously diagnosed as hyperactive." J Child Psychol Psychiatry 13(3): 203-9, September, 1972.

1834 Denhoff, Eric. "The natural life history of children with minimal brain dysfunction." Ann NY Acad Sci 205: 188-205, February 28, 1973.

1835 Dykman, Roscoe A.; Peters, John E.; Ackerman, Peggy T. "Experi-mental approaches to the study of minimal brain dysfunction: a follow-up study." Ann NY Acad Sci 205: 93-108, February 28, 1973.

1836 Feldhusen, John F.; Benning, James J.; Thurston, John R. "Predic-tion of delinquency, adjustment, and academic achievement over a five-year period with the Kvaraceus delinquency proneness scale." J Educ Res 65(8): 375-81, April, 1972.

1837 Glavin, John P. "Persistence of behavior disorders in children." Except Child 38(5): 367-76, January, 1972.

1838 ———. "'Spontaneous' improvement in emotionally disturbed children." Diss Abstr 28(9-A): 3503, March, 1967.

1839 Guze, S. B.; Wolfgram, E. D.; McKinney, J. K.; et. al. "Psychiatric illness in the families of convicted criminals: a study of 519 first degree relatives." Dis Nerv Syst 28(10): 651-59, October, 1967.

1840 Hammar, S. L. "School underachievement in the adolescent: a review of seventy-three cases." Pediatrics 40(3): 373-81, September, 1967.

1841 Harper, P. A.; Fischer, L. K.; Rider, R. V. "Neurological and intellectual status of prematures at three to five years of age." J Pediatr 55(6): 679-90, December, 1959.

1842 Huessy, Hans R.; Metoyer, Marie; Townsend, Marjorie. "Eight-ten year follow-up of children treated in rural Vermont for behavioral disorder." Am J Orthopsychiatry 43(2): 236-38, March, 1973.

1843 Ireton, Harold; Thwing, Edward; Gravem, Howard. "Infant mental development and neurological status, family socioeconomic status, and intelligence at age four." Child Dev 41(4): 937-45, December, 1970.

1844 Kagan, Jerome, and Moss, Howard A. Birth to maturity: a study in psychological development. New York: Wiley, 1962. 381p.

1845 Kalverboer, A. F.; Touwen, B. C. L.; Prechtl, H. F. R. "Follow-up of infants at risk of minor brain dysfunction." Ann NY Acad Sci 205: 173-87, February 28, 1973.

1846 Keldgord, Robert E. "Brain damage and delinquency: a question and a challenge." Acad Ther 4(2): 93-99, Winter, 1968-69.

1847 Koppitz, Elizabeth M. Children with learning disabilities: a five-year follow-up study. New York: Grune & Stratton, 1971. 218p.

1848 ———. "Special class pupils with learning disabilities: a five-year follow-up study." Acad Ther 8(2): 133-39, Winter, 1972-73.

1849 Laufer, Maurice W. "Long-term management and some follow-up findings on the use of drugs with minimal cerebral syndromes." J Learn Disabil 4(9): 518-22, November, 1971.

1850 Macfarlane, Jean W.; Allen, Lucile; Honzik, Marjorie P. A developmental study of the behavior problems of normal children between twenty-one months and fourteen years. Berkeley and Los Angeles: University of California Press, 1954. 221p. (California University Publications in Child Development, V. 2).

1851 Mellsop, Graham W. "Psychiatric patients seen as children and adults: childhood predictors of adult illness." J Child Psychol Psychiatry 13(2): 91-101, June, 1972.

1852 Mendelson, Wallace B.; Johnson, Noel; Stewart, Mark A. "Hyperactive children as teenagers: a follow-up study." J Nerv Ment Dis 153 (4): 273-79, October, 1971.

1853 Menkes, M. M.; Rowe, J. S.; Menkes, J. H. "A twenty-five year follow-up study on the hyperkinetic child with minimal brain dysfunction." Pediatrics 39(3): 393-99, March, 1967.

1854 Minde, Klaus; Lewin, D.; Weiss, Gabrielle; et. al. "The hyperactive child in elementary school: a five-year, controlled follow-up." Except Child 38(3): 215-21, November, 1971.

1855 Minde, Klaus; Weiss, Gabrielle; Mendelson, Nancy. "A five-year follow-up study of ninety-one hyperactive school children." J Am Acad Child Psychiatry 11(3): 595-610, July, 1972.

1856 Morris, Don P., and Dozier, Elizabeth. "Subtler organic factors in behavior disorders of childhood: follow-up studies." South Med J 58 (10): 1213-16, October, 1965.

1857 Morris, H. H., Jr.; Escoll, P. J.; Wexler, R. "Aggressive behavior disorders of childhood: a follow-up study." Am J Psychiatry 112(12): 991-97, June, 1956.

1858 Nichol, Hamish. "Children with learning disabilities referred to psychiatrists: a follow-up study." J Learn Disabil 7(2): 118-22, February, 1974.

1859 O'Neal, Patricia, and Robins, Lee N. "The relation of childhood behavior problems to adult psychiatric status: a thirty-year follow-up study of 150 subjects." Am J Psychiatry 114(11): 961-69, May, 1958.

1860 Quitkin, F., and Klein, D. F. "Two behavioral syndromes in young adults related to possible minimal brain dysfunction." J Psychiatr Res 7: 131-42, December, 1969.

1861 Rifkin, Arthur; Levitan, Steven J.; Galewski, Joel; et. al. "Emotionally unstable character disorder--a follow-up study: II. Prediction of outcome." Biol Psychiatry 4(1): 81-88, February, 1972.

1862 Ritvo, S.; McCollum, A. T.; Omwarke, E.; et. al. "Some relations of constitution, environment, and personality as observed in a longitudinal study of child development." In: Solnit, Albert J., and Provence, Sally, eds. Modern perspectives in child development. New York: International Universities Press, 1963. 107-44.

1863 Robins, Lee N. Deviant children grown up: a sociological and psychiatric study of sociopathetic personality. Baltimore: Williams & Wilkins, 1966. 351p.

1864 Robins, Lee N., and O'Neal, Patricia. "Mortality, mobility and crime: problem children thirty years later." Am Sociol Rev 23(2): 162-71, April, 1958.

1865 Rubin, Rosalyn, and Balow, Bruce. "Learning and behavior disorders: longitudinal study." Except Child 38(4): 293-99, December, 1971.

1866 Shipe, Dorothy; Vandenberg, Steven; Williams, R. D. B. "Neonatal Apgar ratings as related to intelligence and behavior in preschool children." Child Dev 39(3): 861-66, September, 1968.

1867 Stewart, Mark A.; Mendelson, Wallace B.; Johnson, Noel E. "Hyperactive children as adolescents: how they describe themselves." Child Psychiatry Hum Dev 4(1): 3-11, Fall, 1973.

1868 Stewart, Mark A.; Pitts, Ferris N.; Craig, Alan G.; et. al. "The hyperactive child syndrome." Am J Orthopsychiatry 36(5): 861-67, October, 1966.

1869 Stott, D. H., and Wilson, D. M. "The prediction of early-adult criminality from school-age behaviour." Int J Soc Psychiatry 14(1): 5-8, Winter, 1967-68.

1870 Tarnopol, Lester. "Delinquency and learning disabilities." In: Tarnopol, Lester, ed. Learning disabilities: introduction to educational and medical management. Springfield, Illinois: Thomas, 1969. 305-30.

1871 ———. "Delinquency and minimal brain dysfunction." J Learn Disabil 3(4): 200-207, April, 1970.

1872 Werner, Emily E.; Honzik, Marjorie P.; Smith, Ruth S. "Prediction of intelligence and achievement at ten years from twenty months pediatric and psychologic examinations." Child Dev 39(4): 1063-75, December, 1968.

1873 Zax, Melvin; Cowen, Emory L.; Rappaport, Julian; et. al. "Follow-up study of children identified early as emotionally disturbed." J Consult Clin Psychol 32(4): 369-74, August, 1968.

1874 Zold, Anthony C., and Speer, David C. "Follow-up study of child guidance clinic patients by means of the Behavior Problem Checklist." J Clin Psychol 27(4): 519-24, October, 1971.

APPENDIX A: NOMENCLATURE

Activity level

Aggressive behavior disorder

Aphasoid syndrome

Association deficit pathology

Attention disorder

Behavior disorder

Brain-damaged

Brain dysfunction

Brain-injured

Cerebral damage

Cerebral dysfunction

Cerebral dys-synchronization
  syndrome

Character impulse disorder

Child behavior disorder

Choreiform syndrome

Clumsy child syndrome

Conceptually handicapped

Developmental dyslexia

Developmental imbalance

Diffuse brain damage

Dyslexia

Educationally handicapped

Emotionally disturbed

Exceptional child

Hyperactive

Hyperexcitability syndrome

Hyperkinesis

Hyperkinetic behavior syndrome

Hyperkinetic impulse disorder

Hyperkinetic syndrome

Hypokinetic syndrome

Interjacent child

Learning disability

Learning disabled

Learning disorder

Learning impaired

Minimal brain damage

Minimal brain dysfunction

Minimal brain injured

Minimal cerebral damage

Minimal cerebral dysfunction

Minimal cerebral injury

Minimal cerebral palsy

Minimal chronic brain syndrome

Minor brain damage

Motor activity

Movement disorder

Nervous

Neurologically handicapped

Neurophrenia

Non-attending behavior

Organic behavior problem

Organic brain disorder

Organic brain damage

Organic brain disease

Organic brain driveness

Organic brain dysfunction

Organic driveness

Organic hyperkinetic syndrome

Overactive

Perceptual cripple

Perceptually handicapped

Performance deviation

Performance disability

Performance handicapped

Primary reading retardation

Problem children

Problem learner

Problem reader

Psychoneurological learning disorder

Slow learner

Special learning disability

Specific learning disability

Specific reading disability

Underachiever

APPENDIX B: DRUGS

Generic Name	Trade Name	Manufacturer	Date
Amitriptyline	Elavil	Merck Sharp & Dohme	1961
Amphetamine	Benzedrine	Smith Kline & French and others	
Carisoprodol	Soma	Wallace	
	Rela	Schering	1959
Chlordiazepoxide	Librium	Roche	1960
Chlorpromazine	Thorazine	Smith Kline & French	1954
Chlorprothixene	Taractan	Roche	
Deanol	Deaner	Riker	1958
Desipramine	Pertofrane	Geigy	
	Norpramin	Lakeside	
Dextroamphetamine	Dexedrine	Smith Kline & French and others	
Diazepam	Valium	Roche	
Diphenhydramine	Benadryl	Parke, Davis	1946
Fluphenazine	Prolixin	Squibb	
	Permitil	White	1959
Haloperidol	Haldol	McNeil	1966
Hydroxyzine	Atarax	Roerig	
	Vistaril	Pfizer	1956
Imipramine	Tofranil	Geigy	1959
Meprobamate	Miltown	Wallace	
	Equanil	Wyeth	1955
Methamphetamine	Methedrine	Burroughs Wellcome	
	Desoxyn	Abbott and others	
Methocarbamol	Robaxin	Robins	1957
Methylphenidate	Ritalin	CIBA	1956
Nortriptyline	Aventyl	Lilly	
Omipramol	Ensidon	Geigy	
Oxazepam	Serax	Wyeth	

Perphenazine	Trilafon	Schering	1957
Pipradol	Meratran	Merrell	1955
Prochlorperazine	Compazine	Smith Kline & French	1956
Promazine	Sparine	Wyeth	1955
Promethazine	Phenergan	Wyeth	1951
Reserpine	Serpasil	CIBA	1953
Thioridazine	Mellaril	Sandoz	1959
Thiothixene	Navane	Roerig	
Trifluoperazine	Stelazine	Smith Kline & French	1959
Triflupromazine	Vesprin	Squibb	1957
Trihexyphenidyl	Artane	Lederle	1949
Tybamate	Solacen	Wallace	

List adapted from: Whitsell, Leon J. "Clinical pharmacology of psycho-tropic drugs with special reference to children." In: Tarnopol, Lester, ed., Learning disorders in children: diagnosis, medication, education. Boston: Little, Brown, 1971. 331-355.

APPENDIX C: LIST OF JOURNAL ABBREVIATIONS

Abbreviation	Title
Acad Ther	Academic Therapy
Acta Paedopsychiatr	Acta Paedopsychiatrica
Acta Psychiatr Neurol Scand	Acta Psychiatrica et Neurologica Scandinavica
Acta Psychiatr Scand	Acta Psychiatrica Scandinavica
Acta Psychiatr Scand (Suppl)	Acta Psychiatrica Scandinavica (Supplement)
Ala J Med Sci	Alabama Journal of Medical Sciences
Am Educ	American Education
Am Fam Physician	American Family Physician
Am J Dis Child	American Journal of Diseases of Children
Am J Hum Genet	American Journal of Human Genetics
Am J Ment Defic	American Journal of Mental Deficiency
Am J Occup Ther	American Journal of Occupational Therapy
Am J Orthopsychiatry	American Journal of Orthopsychiatry
Am J Psychiatry	American Journal of Psychiatry
Am J Psychother	American Journal of Psychotherapy
Am J Public Health	American Journal of Public Health
Am Pract Dig Treat	American Practitioner and Digest of Treatment
Am Psychol	American Psychologist
Am Sch Board J	American School Board Journal
Am Sociol Rev	American Sociological Review
AMA Arch Neurol Psychiatry	AMA Archives of Neurology and Psychiatry
Anim Behav	Animal Behaviour
Ann Allergy	Annals of Allergy
Ann Intern Med	Annals of Internal Medicine
Ann NY Acad Sci	Annals of the New York Academy of Sciences
Annu Rev Psychol	Annual Review of Psychology
Appl Ther	Applied Therapeutics
Arch Dis Child	Archives of Disease in Childhood
Arch Gen Psychiatry	Archives of General Psychiatry
Arch Neurol	Archives of Neurology
Arch Neurol Psychiatry	Archives of Neurology and Psychiatry
Arch Otolaryngol	Archives of Otolaryngology
Arch Pediatr	Archives of Pediatrics
Arch Psychol	Archives of Psychology
Behav Neuropsychiatry	Behavioral Neuropsychiatry
Behav Res Ther	Behaviour Research and Therapy
Behav Ther	Behavior Therapy

Behaviour	Behaviour
Biol Psychiatry	Biological Psychiatry
Br J Clin Pract	British Journal of Clinical Practice
Br J Criminol	British Journal of Criminology
Br J Educ Psychol	British Journal of Educational Psychology
Br J Psychiatry	British Journal of Psychiatry
Br J Psychol	British Journal of Psychology
Br J Radiol	British Journal of Radiology
Br J Soc Clin Psychol	British Journal of Social and Clinical Psychology
Br Med J	British Medical Journal
Bull Los Angeles Neurol Soc	Bulletin of the Los Angeles Neurological Societies
Bull Menninger Clin	Bulletin of the Menninger Clinic
Bull Orton Soc	Bulletin of the Orton Society
Bull WHO	Bulletin of the World Health Organization
Calif Med	California Medicine
Can J Behav Sci	Canadian Journal of Behavioural Science
Can J Public Health	Canadian Journal of Public Health
Can Med Assoc J	Canadian Medical Association Journal
Can Psychiatr Assoc J	Canadian Psychiatric Association Journal
Can Psychol	Canadian Psychologist
Cereb Palsy Bull	Cerebral Palsy Bulletin
Cereb Palsy J	Cerebral Palsy Journal
Cereb Palsy Rev	Cerebral Palsy Review
Chemistry	Chemistry
Chicago Med Sch Q	Chicago Medical School Quarterly
Child Dev	Child Development
Child Educ	Childhood Education
Child House	Children's House
Child Psychiatry Hum Dev	Child Psychiatry and Human Development
Child Welfare	Child Welfare
Children	Children
Claremont Read Conf Yearb	Claremont Reading Conference Yearbook
Clgh House J	Clearing House Journal
Clin Dev Med	Clinics in Developmental Medicine
Clin Pediatr	Clinical Pediatrics
Clin Pharmacol Ther	Clinical Pharmacology and Therapeutics
Clin Proc Child Hosp	Clinical Proceedings of the Children's Hospital
Community Ment Health J	Community Mental Health Journal
Compr Psychiatry	Comprehensive Psychiatry
Cond Reflex	Conditional Reflex: a Pavlovian Journal of Research and Therapy
Confin Neurol	Confinia Neurologica
Consultant	Consultant
Curr Med Dig	Current Medical Digest
Curr Probl Pediatr	Current Problems in Pediatrics
Curr Psychiatr Ther	Current Psychiatric Therapies
Curr Ther Res	Current Therapeutic Research

Current
Del State Med J
Dev Med Child Neurol

Dev Psychol
Dis Nerv Syst
Discoverer
Diss Abstr
Diss Abstr Int
Educ Dig
Educ Leadership
Educ Rep
Educ Technol
Educ Train Ment Retarded

Education
Electroencephalogr Clin
  Neurophysiol
Elem Sch Guid Couns

Elem Sch J
Epilepsia
Except Child
Expectations
Feelings Their Med Significance

Genet Psychol Monogr
GP
Grade Teach
Harv Educ Rev
Hosp Community Psychiatry
Ill Med J
Inequality Educ
Instructor
Int Bobath Alumni Assoc Newsl

Int J Neuropsychiatry

Int J Psychiatry
Int J Soc Psychiatry

Int Psychiatry Clin
Int Rec Med Gen Pract Clin

Int Rev Appl Psychol

Int Surg
IRE Trans Bio-Med Electron

J Abnorm Child Psychol
J Abnorm Psychol
J Abnorm Soc Psychol

J Am Acad Child Psychiatry

Current
Delaware State Medical Journal
Developmental Medicine and Child
  Neurology
Developmental Psychology
Diseases of the Nervous System
Discoverer
Dissertation Abstracts
Dissertation Abstracts International
Education Digest
Educational Leadership
Education Reporter
Educational Technology
Education and Training of the
  Mentally Retarded
Education
Electroencephalography and Clinical
  Neurophysiology
Elementary School Guidance and
  Counseling
Elementary School Journal
Epilepsia
Exceptional Children
Expectations
Feelings and Their Medical Signifi-
  cance
Genetic Psychology Monographs
GP
Grade Teacher
Harvard Education Review
Hospital and Community Psychiatry
Illinois Medical Journal
Inequality in Education
Instructor
International Bobath Alumni Associa-
  tion Newsletter
International Journal of Neuropsy-
  chiatry
International Journal of Psychiatry
International Journal of Social
  Psychiatry
International Psychiatry Clinics
International Record of Medicine and
  General Practice Clinics
International Review of Applied
  Psychology
International Surgery
IRE Transactions on Bio-Medical
  Electronics
Journal of Abnormal Child Psychology
Journal of Abnormal Psychology
Journal of Abnormal and Social
  Psychology
Journal of the American Academy of
  Child Psychiatry

J Am Med Womens Assoc	Journal of the American Medical Women's Association
J Appl Behav Anal	Journal of Applied Behavior Analysis
J Appl Psychol	Journal of Applied Psychology
J Arkansas Med Soc	Journal of the Arkansas Medical Society
J Autism Child Schizophr	Journal of Autism and Childhood Schizophrenia
J Behav Ther Exp Psychiatry	Journal of Behavior Therapy and Experimental Psychiatry
J Child Psychol Psychiatry	Journal of Child Psychology and Psychiatry and Allied Disciplines
J Chronic Dis	Journal of Chronic Diseases
J Clin Child Psychol	Journal of Clinical Child Psychology
J Clin Exp Psychopath Q Rev Psychiatry Neurol	Journal of Clinical and Experimental Psychopathology and Quarterly Review of Psychiatry and Neurology
J Clin Psychol	Journal of Clinical Psychology
J Commun Disord	Journal of Communication Disorders
J Consult Clin Psychol	Journal of Consulting and Clinical Psychology
J Consult Psychol	Journal of Consulting Psychology
J Educ	Journal of Education
J Educ Psychol	Journal of Educational Psychology
J Educ Res	Journal of Educational Research
J Exp Anal Behav	Journal of the Experimental Analysis of Behavior
J Exp Child Psychol	Journal of Experimental Child Psychology
J Exp Psychol	Journal of Experimental Psychology
J Genet Psychol	Journal of Genetic Psychology
J Health Phys Educ Recreat	Journal of Health, Physical Education, and Recreation
J Insur Med	Journal of Insurance Medicine
J Iowa Med Soc	Journal of the Iowa Medical Society
J Learn Disabil	Journal of Learning Disabilities
J Maine Med Assoc	Journal of the Maine Medical Association
J Med Genet	Journal of Medical Genetics
J Med Soc NJ	Journal of the Medical Society of New Jersey
J Ment Sci	Journal of Mental Science
J Natl Med Assoc	Journal of the National Medical Association
J Nerv Ment Dis	Journal of Nervous and Mental Disease
J Neurol Neurosurg Psychiatry	Journal of Neurology, Neurosurgery, and Psychiatry
J Neurol Sci	Journal of the Neurological Sciences
J Neuropsychiatry	Journal of Neuropsychiatry
J Neurosurg Nursing	Journal of Neurosurgical Nursing
J NY Sch Nurse Teach Assoc	Journal of the New York School Nurse Teachers Association
J Obstet Gynaecol Br Commonw	Journal of Obstetrics and Gynaecology of the British Commonwealth
J Obstet Gynaecol Br Emp	Journal of Obstetrics and Gynaecology of the British Empire

J Occup Ther	Journal of Occupational Therapy
J Oper Psychiatry	Journal of Operational Psychiatry
J Pediatr	Journal of Pediatrics
J Pers	Journal of Personality
J Pers Soc Psychol	Journal of Personality and Social Psychology
J Proj Tech	Journal of Projective Techniques
J Psychiatr Res	Journal of Psychiatric Research
J Psychol	Journal of Psychology
J Psychosom Res	Journal of Psychosomatic Research
J Public Health	Journal of Public Health
J Rehabil	Journal of Rehabilitation
J Sch Health	Journal of School Health
J Sch Psychol	Journal of School Psychology
J Spec Educ	Journal of Special Education
J Spec Educ Ment Retarded	Journal of Special Educators of the Mentally Retarded
J Speech Hear Res	Journal of Speech and Hearing Research
J Teach Educ	Journal of Teacher Education
J Urol	Journal of Urology
JAMA	Journal of the American Medical Association
Jap J Child Psychiatry	Japanese Journal of Child Psychiatry
Johns Hopkins Hosp Bull	Johns Hopkins Hospital Bulletin
Johnstone Bull	Johnstone Bulletin
Kansas Stud Educ	Kansas Studies in Education
Ladies Home J	Ladies' Home Journal
Lancet	Lancet
Laryngoscope	Laryngoscope
Logos	Logos
Med Clin North Am	Medical Clinics of North America
Med Insight	Medical Insight
Med J Aust	Medical Journal of Australia
Med Lett Drugs Ther	Medical Letter on Drugs and Therapeutics
Med Times	Medical Times
Med World News	Medical World News
Memphis Mid-South Med J	Memphis and Mid-South Medical Journal
Ment Hyg	Mental Hygiene
Ment Retard	Mental Retardation
Ment Retard Abstr	Mental Retardation Abstracts
Merrill-Palmer Q	Merrill-Palmer Quarterly of Behavior and Development
Mich Educ J	Michigan Education Journal
Mich Med	Michigan Medicine
Midwife Health Visit	Midwife and Health Visitor
Mod Treat	Modern Treatment
Monogr Soc Res Child Dev	Monographs of the Society for Research in Child Development
Multivariate Behav Res	Multivariate Behavioral Research
Music Educ J	Music Educators Journal
Music J	Music Journal
N Engl J Med	New England Journal of Medicine
Nat Bus Educ Q	National Business Education Quarterly
Nat Elem Princ	National Elementary Principal

Nations Sch	Nation's Schools
Nature	Nature (London)
Nebr Med J	Nebraska Medical Journal
Nebr State Med J	Nebraska State Medical Journal
Nerv Child	Nervous Child
Neurol India	Neurology India
Neurology	Neurology
Neuropaediatrie	Neuropaediatrie; Journal of Pediatric Neurobiology, Neurology, and Neurosurgery
New Repub	New Republic
Newsweek	Newsweek
NJ Educ Rev	New Jersey Education Review
Northwest Med	Northwest Medicine
Nurs Mirror Midwives J	Nursing Mirror and Midwives' Journal
Nurs Update	Nursing Update
Nutr Rev	Nutrition Reviews
NY J Med	New York Journal of Medicine
NY Med J	New York Medical Journal
NY State J Med	New York State Journal of Medicine
NZ Med J	New Zealand Medical Journal
Ohio State Med J	Ohio State Medical Journal
Orthomol Psychiatry	Orthomolecular Psychiatry
Pa Med J	Pennsylvania Medical Journal
Pa Psychiatr Q	Pennsylvania Psychiatric Quarterly
Patient Care	Patient Care
Pediatr Clin North Am	Pediatric Clinics of North America
Pediatr News	Pediatric News
Pediatrics	Pediatrics
Percept Mot Skills	Perceptual and Motor Skills
Personnel Guid J	Personnel and Guidance Journal
Pharmacol Rev	Pharmacological Reviews
Phi Delta Kappan	Phi Delta Kappan
Phys Ther	Physical Therapy
Proc R Soc Med	Proceedings of the Royal Society of Medicine
Prof Psychol	Professional Psychology
Prog Neurol Psychiatry	Progress in Neurology and Psychiatry
Provo Papers	Provo Papers
Psychiatr Ann	Psychiatric Annals
Psychiatr Commun	Psychiatric Communications
Psychiatr Forum	Psychiatric Forum
Psychiatr Neurol Neurochir	Psychiatria, Neurologica, Neurochirurgia
Psychiatr Q	Psychiatric Quarterly
Psychiatr Res Rep	Psychiatric Research Reports
Psychiatry	Psychiatry
Psychoanal Study Child	Psychoanalytic Study of the Child
Psychol Bull	Psychological Bulletin
Psychol Med	Psychological Medicine
Psychol Monogr	Psychological Monographs: General and Applied
Psychol Rep	Psychological Reports
Psychol Sch	Psychology in the Schools

Psychopharmacol Bull	Psychopharmacology Bulletin; National Clearinghouse for Mental Health Information
Psychopharmacologia	Psychopharmacologia
Psychophysiology	Psychophysiology
Psychosom Med	Psychosomatic Medicine
Psychosomatics	Psychosomatics
PTA Mag	PTA Magazine
QJ Child Behav	Quarterly Journal of Child Behavior
Read Teach	Reading Teacher
Redbook	Redbook
Rehabil Lit	Rehabilitation Literature
Res Educ	Research in Education
Res J	Research Journal (University of Maryland)
Rev Educ Res	Review of Educational Research
RN	RN; National Magazine for Nurses
S Afr Med J	South African Medical Journal
Saturday Rev	Saturday Review
Sch Appl Learn Theory	School Applications of Learning Theory
Sch Community	School and Community
Sch Couns	School Counselor
Scholastic Teach	Scholastic Teacher Jr/Sr
Sci Am	Scientific American
Sci News	Science News
Sci Teach	Science Teacher
Science	Science
Semin Psychiatry	Seminars in Psychiatry
Smith Coll Stud Social Work	Smith College Studies in Social Work
Sound	Sound
South Med J	Southern Medical Journal
Spastics Q	Spastics Quarterly
Teach Except Child	Teaching Exceptional Children
Tex Med	Texas Medicine
Tex Rep Biol Med	Texas Reports on Biology and Medicine
Time	Time
Times Educ Suppl	Times Educational Supplement
Todays Educ	Today's Education
Todays Health	Today's Health
Train Sch Bull	Training School Bulletin
Trans Am Neurol Assoc	Transactions of the American Neurological Association
Transaction	Trans-action; Social Science and Modern Society
Union Med Can	Union Medicale du Canada
Urban Rev	Urban Review
US News World Rep	U.S. News and World Report
Va Med Mon	Virginia Medical Monthly
Volta Rev	Volta Review
Wash Univ Mag	Washington University Magazine
West J Med	Western Journal of Medicine
West Med	Western Medicine
Wis Med J	Wisconsin Medical Journal
Young Child	Young Children

AUTHOR INDEX

In the list below, the numbers after each name refer to item numbers in the Bibiliography.

A

Abbot, M., 1622
Abbott, P., 1037
Abdou, F. A., 791
Abelson, C., 1273
Abrams, Alfred L., 470
Abrams, J., 1280
Abrams, J. C., 1311, 1593
Achenbach, Thomas M., 241
Ackerman, Peggy T., 577, 651, 652, 1689, 1731, 1780, 1835
Adams, Elizabeth, 303
Adams, Jerry, 1671
Adams, P. A., 349
Adler, Sidney J., 1
Advani, Kan, 1594
Agin, B., 1514
Alabiso, Frank P., 1672, 1673
Albert, K., 1215, 1216
Alderton, H. R., 738, 1038
Alexander, D. F., 931
Alexander, R. H., 1829
Alexander, Theron, 1133
Alexandris, A. R., 1039
Alkire, Armand A., 1790
Allen, Frederick H., 1265
Allen, K. Eileen, 1454, 1455, 1456, 1457, 1458
Allen, Louise, 1368
Allen, Lucile, 1850
Allen, Mary, 1040
Allen, Richard, 1250, 1251
Alley, Gordon R., 269, 1339, 1340
Allmond, Bayard W., Jr., 74, 1351
Altekruse, Michael, 1496
Ambrosino, S. V., 1138
Amin, Mohammed, 1022
Anderson, Camilla M., 2, 3, 304, 361
Anderson, D., 1459
Anderson, David O., 471

Anderson, Kathryn A., 960
Anderson, Lauriel E., 472, 1511
Anderson, Nancy, 1399
Anderson, Robert L., 1448
Anderson, Robert P., 1266, 1312, 1674, 1675
Anderson, Scott, 472
Anderson, William W., 572
Angle, C. R., 431
Annell, A. L., 1217
Annesley, Frederick, 1502
Anthony, E. James, 4, 364
Antolak, S. J., Jr., 409
Anton, Aron H., 1139
Apgar, Virginia, 392
Ardali, Cohit, 981, 1206
Arjundas, G., 416
Armstrong, Marianne, 1574
Arnold, C. R., 1463
Arnold, L. Eugene, 5, 473, 474, 739, 793, 794, 1096, 1097
Aron, Alan M., 6
Aronson, Leonard J., 1267
Arthur, Bettie, 966, 1063
Artuso, A. A., 1367
Asch, Harvey, 1446
Ashby, M. C., 593
Ault, Ruth L., 1723
Avakian, Sonia A., 653
Ayers, A. J., 1722
Aymat, Fernando, 709
Azerrad, J., 426

B

Backus, Joe T., 1781
Backus, Reno, 1649
Badie, Davood, 1051, 1057
Baer, Donald M., 1460, 1461, 1510
Bair, H. V., 985
Bakan, Paul E., 1677

Hellmuth, Jerome, 140, 1363
Helper, Malcolm M., 992, 997
Henke, Lydia B., 1457
Henry, Charles E., 905, 1130
Hentoff, Nat, 882
Herbert, M., 690
Herbertson, Leon M., 588
Herman, W. L., 1512
Herold, W., 985
Herring, Amanda, 1697
Herron, R. E., 1644
Hersh, Marilyn F., 1431
Hertzig, Margaret E., 575, 595, 1806
Hewett, Frank M., 1364, 1365, 1366, 1367, 1754
Hibi, S., 1149
Himelstein, Philip, 207
Hinton, George G., 697, 1180
Hobhouse, E. W. N., 518
Hoch, P., 1215, 1216
Hoddinott, B. A., 1038
Hoffer, A., 1205
Hoffman, M. S., 519
Hoffman, Stanley P., 1157, 1179
Hogg, William F., 520
Hohman, Leslie B., 415, 1147
Holden, R. H., 638
Holroyd, Jean, 691
Holt, Fred D., 1290
Homme, L. E., 1513
Honzik, Marjorie P., 1850, 1872
Hood-Williams, J., 1291
Hooshmand, H., 1244
Hopkins, Kenneth D., 692
Hopson, Buena, 1498
Horenstein, Simon, 1030
Horne, David, 1281
Horowitz, R., 540
Houlihan, Kevin A., 1821
Howell, Mary C., 90
Howell, Rodney R., 417
Huber, Wm. G., 1002
Hudson, B. W., 107
Huessy, Hans R., 277, 278, 1154, 1842
Hughes, James G., 91
Hughes, John R., 596, 597
Hughes, R., 1506
Hunt, Arthur B., 370
Hunt, Brian R., 998
Hunt, J. V., 521
Hunter, H., 999
Hurowitz, Linda, 522
Hurwitz, Irving, 301
Husted, J. R., 1514

Hutt, Corinne, 92, 93, 94, 447, 523, 884, 1645, 1810
Hutt, Sidney J., 92, 93, 94, 447, 523, 610, 1645
Hutton, W. Oran, 1665

I

Ianzito, Benjamin M., 448
Ilem, Priscilla G., 1026
Ingram, T. T. S., 99
Inoff, Gale, 787
Insel, Jonathan, 1112
Ireland, Roderick, 886
Ireton, Harold, 1843
Irwin, Orvis C., 1646
Ishee, B., 1434
Isom, J. B., 499
Ison, M. Gail, 1000
Itil, T. M., 598

J

Jackson, Deloris, 1507
Jackson, P. M., 884
Jacobs, J., 1132
Jacobs, Nora T., 1755
Jacobson, A., 730
Jacquot, W. S., 1368
Jasper, Herbert H., 599, 1114
Jeffrey, W. E., 1723
Jenkins, Richard L., 100, 101, 253, 254, 449, 524, 1610
Johnson, Charles F., 1647, 1648
Johnson, Doris J., 1369
Johnson, John L., 1384
Johnson, K., 102
Johnson, Noel, 1852, 1867
Johnston, Alfred H., 1031
Johnston, Margaret K., 1515
Jolles, Isaac, 1370
Jones, B. E., 1181
Jones, Beverly, 1608
Jones, D., 887
Jones, Mary C., 1756
Jones, Philip R., 1177
Jones, R., 1548, 1549
Jones, Reginald L., 1490
Juliano, Daniel B., 1757
Junkala, John B., 1331

K

Kagan, Jerome, 1758, 1759, 1760, 1761, 1762, 1763, 1844
Kahana, Boaz, 1769

SELECTIVE KEY WORD SUBJECT INDEX

In the list below, the numbers after each word

refer to item numbers in the Bibliography.

A

Ability 660, 712, 1745
Abuse 1199 See also: Drug Abuse
Academic 1145, 1503
Academic Achievement 626, 1339,
  1340, 1354, 1561, 1821, 1836
  See also: Achievement
Academic Success 784, 786, 1438
  See also: Success
Accident-prone 451
Accidental 298, 299, 455, 463, 464,
  466
Accidentally 466
Accidents 462, 1765
Achievement 260, 286, 550, 551,
  626, 702, 779, 785, 929, 1111,
  1143, 1338, 1872 See also:
  Academic Achievement
Acting Out 453, 459, 1294, 1536
Activities 1793
Activity 332, 338, 352, 576, 591,
  612, 1045, 1167, 1174, 1192,
  1273, 1470, 1473, 1704 See also:
  Motor Activity
Activity Level 360, 562, 737, 740,
  830, 1027, 1123, 1160, 1200,
  1480, 1492, (1628-1670)
Actometer 1647
Adaptation 164
Addiction 1120
Adjunctive 1026
Adjustment 738, 807, 1448, 1451,
  1540, 1750, 1814, 1836
Administrators 831
Adolescence 11, 66, 81, 127, 177,
  191, 460, 604, 726, 767
Adolescent 77, 227, 263, 304, 591,
  623, 853, 1211, 1511, 1623, 1840
Adolescents 111, 304, 485, 498,
  598, 602, 711, 739, 750, 791, 813
Adopted 1813

Adoption 1819
Adult 199, 1510, 1859, 1869
  See also: Young Adult
Adults 428, 1201, 1851
Affective 355
Africa 274
Age 279, 430, 593, 758, 777,
  841, 1473, 1576, 1634, 1650,
  1798, 1841, 1843 See also:
  School Age
Ages 653
Aggression 461, 1096, 1479, 1629
Aggressive 1038, 1152, 1258,
  1857
Alcohol 380
Allergic 450, 467, 1249
Allergies 414
Alpha 586, 615, 635, 636
American 296, 1438
Amitriptyline 1206, 1207
Amphetamine 421, 661, 1039,
  1063, (1094-1129), 1247, 1248
  See also: Benzedrine
Amygdalotomy 1254, 1257
Animal 1248
Anorexia Nervosa 811, 1124, 1470
Anoxia 364, 367, 388
Antecedent 593
Antecedents 455, 461, 1738
Antenatal (361-404)
Anticonvulsant 984, 1231
Anticonvulsants 1224, 1244
Antidepressants (1064-1214)
Antisocial 613
Anxiety 211, 1775
Anxious 1737
Apartment 125
Apgar 1866
Aphasia 184
Appetite Pills 938
Appraisal (470-790)
Arithmetic 1355, 1480, 1706

H

Habit 1650
Hahnemann High School Behavior
  Rating Scale 780
Hallucinosis 1182
Haloperidol (1010-1012)
Handbook 62, 1374, 1443, 1608,
  1614, 1618, 1626
Head 379, 434, 442, 445
Head Start 456, 1458, 1789
Health 137, 209, 507, 650, 1474
Hearing 294
Hearings 949, 1442
Heart 1779
Hematologic 1238
Hemophilus 426
Hereditary (330-360)
High School 78, 737
Histidinemia 417
Historical 200, 1357
Histories 519
History 422, 593, 1834
Home 47, 1390, 1575, 1594, 1609,
  1611, 1627, 1820
Hospital 1038
Hospitalized 623, 639
Hostility 211, 307
Hot Dogs 446
Hunt-Minnesota Test 653
Hydrochloride 1230
Hydroxyzine (1013-1016) See
  also: Atarax
Hyperaggressive 85, 1301
Hypercusis 1398
Hyperlexia 1400
Hyperthermia 1124
Hypoactive 1350, 1783
Hypoactives 1641, 1663

I

I. Q. 677
Identification 39, (470-790),
  1873
Illness 333, 593, 1277, 1839,
  1851
Imbecile 1666, 1823, 1824
Imipramine (1153-1159)
Imitation 1476
Immature 894
Improvement 756, 1838
Impulse 251, 1687
Impulsive 459, 1703, 1723, 1733,
  1744, 1758, 1762, 1786, 1795
Impulsivity 577, 1662, (1722-
1789)
Impulsivity-reflectivity (1722-
  1789)
Incentives 1781
Incidence (269-302), 358, 395,
  589
Indexes 614, 742
Indications 519
Indicators 557, 558
Individuality 204, 816
Infancy 66, 120, 325, 385, 391,
  411, 444, 460, 601, 608, 740,
  1639, 1650
Infant 440, 541, 619, 620, 974,
  1843
Infantile 441
Infants 337, 397, 573, 663,
  679, 703, 740, 1197, 1628,
  1646, 1670, 1764, 1845
Infection 423
Influenzae 426
Information processing 1328,
  1763 See also: Processing
Inheritance (330-360)
Inhibition 1635
Inhibitory 1498, 1672, 1673,
  1680
Injuries 394, 455
Injury 370, 442, 445, 492, 593
Ink-blot 715
Inner-city 1559
Inpatients 980
Insomnia 1081
Institutionalized 1166, 1492,
  1665, 1667
Instruction 1417
Instrument 752, 755
Intellectual 402, 660, 684,
  712, 1008, 1151, 1232, 1652,
  1654, 1803, 1841
Intellectually Handicapped 1163,
  1695
Intelligence 331, 575, 626, 663,
  675, 678, 692, 696, 908, 1414,
  1421, 1634, 1709, 1745, 1843,
  1866, 1872
Interdisciplinary 40
International 262
Intersensory 1516
Intervention 476, 644, 835,
  1483, 1777
Interventions 889, 1739
Interview 513, 552, 1140
Involuntary 1256
Isolate 1456
Isolation 1561, 1567

ABOUT THE AUTHOR

Carol Ann Winchell, a graduate of The Ohio State University and Case Western University, is reference librarian at The Ohio State University Libraries. She is presently preparing an annotated update of THE HYPERKINETIC CHILD.